BLACK POPULISM IN THE UNITED STATES

Recent Titles in
Bibliographies and Indexes in Afro-American and African Studies

BLACK POPULISM IN THE UNITED STATES

An Annotated Bibliography

Anthony J. Adam
and
Gerald H. Gaither

Bibliographies and Indexes in Afro-American
and African Studies, Number 45

Westport, Connecticut
London

Library of Congress Cataloging-in-Publication Data

Adam, Anthony J.
   Black populism in the United States : an annotated bibliography / Anthony J. Adam,
Gerald H. Gaither.
      p. cm.—(Bibliographies and indexes in Afro-American and African studies, ISSN
0742–6925 ; no. 45)
   Includes bibliographical references and index.
   ISBN 0–313–32439–5 (alk. paper)
      1. African Americans—Politics and government—Bibliography. 2. African
Americans—History—1877–1964—Bibliography. 3. Populism—United States—Bibliography.
I. Gaither, Gerald H.   II. Title.   III. Series.
Z1361.N4A33 2004
 [E185.6]
016.324′089′96073—dc22   2003062435

British Library Cataloguing in Publication Data is available.

Library of Congress Catalog Card Number: 2003062435
ISBN: 0–313–32439–5
ISSN: 0742–6925

First published in 2004

Praeger Publishers, 88 Post Road West, Westport, CT 06881
An imprint of Greenwood Publishing Group, Inc.
www.praeger.com

Printed in the United States of America

The paper used in this book complies with the
Permanent Paper Standard issued by the National
Information Standards Organization (Z39.48–1984).

10   9   8   7   6   5   4   3   2   1

For family and friends, who supported us through this project

CONTENTS

INTRODUCTION

Who were the Black Populists, and why bother to study them? According to contemporary sources, upwards of 1,200,000 black men and women joined the Colored Farmers' Alliance around 1890, and we find mention of men at People's party conventions and other gatherings until 1900. Without extant membership rosters, however, we can only guess at the actual size of the organization, but recent research has uncovered names of individuals throughout the South and Midwest who participated. The People's party, the political manifestation of Populism, had a love-hate relationship with black membership during the period, and we have endeavored in this bibliography to give some idea of how the political climate radically changed for the worse as the Populists sought to include blacks in their efforts to gain elected office. The political violence that ensued--from the Leflore County Massacre to the Wilmington Riots--coupled with widespread disfranchisement created a charged racial atmosphere that still persists in parts of our nation. However, at its best, the Populist movement proved that biracial coalitions could effect change and create models for the future.

This annotated bibliography on Black Populism covers that period most associated with the rise and fall of the agrarian movement at the close of the nineteenth century. Since no movement can be understood outside its milieu, we have also included select items which relate specifically to black/white relations in the South during that time, with special attention to other attempts at biracial coalitions. All items are in English and with few exceptions published in the United States between 1880-2001. With the notable exception of most master's theses herein, all items have been examined firsthand, in order to correct longstanding citation errors. We also hope that we haven't added any new errors! For the sake of brevity and symmetry, we use "black" rather than "African American" in the annotations throughout, but we keep the original wording in the citations.

This book could not have been written without the help and support of a great number of people across the country, including the staffs of the John B. Coleman Library and Office of Institutional Effectiveness, Research, and Analysis at Prairie View A&M University; the librarians at Rice University's Fondren Library, the University of Texas at Austin's Center for American History, and the Schomburg Collection at New York Public Library; John Bush, for pointing the way to Frank Burkitt; Dr. Charles W. Macune, Jr.; Worth Robert Miller; Gregg Cantrell; Omar Ali; and a special thanks to all our friends, family, and colleagues who listened when we needed to vent.

WORKS CONSULTED

Dethloff, Henry C., and Worth Robert Miller. *A List of References for the History of the Farmers' Alliance and Populist Party*, revised edition. Davis, CA: Agricultural History Center, University of California, 1989.

Edwards, Everett E. *A Bibliography of the History of Agriculture in the United States*. Washington, DC: Government Printing Office, 1930.

Edwards, Helen. *A List of References for the History of Agriculture in the Southern United States, 1865-1900*. Davis, CA: Agricultural History Center, University of California, 1971.

Lucko, Paul M. "Dissertations and Theses Relating to African American Studies in Texas: a selected bibliography, 1904-1990." *Southwestern Historical Quarterly* 96 (April 1993).

Morrison, Denton E., ed. *Farmers' Organizations and Movements: Research Needs and a Bibliography of the United States and Canada (Research Bulletin No. 24)*. East Lansing, MI: Agricultural Experiment Station, Michigan State University, 1970.

Schor, Joel. *A List of References for the History of Black Americans in Agriculture, 1619-1980*. Davis, CA: Agricultural History Center, University of California, 1981.

Wescott, Mary, and Allene Ramage, compilers. *A Checklist of United States Newspapers (and Weeklies Before 1900) in the General Library (Bibliographical Contributions of the Duke University Libraries)*. Durham, NC: Duke University, 1937.

A. MANUSCRIPT COLLECTIONS

A1. Marion Butler Papers, Southern Historical Collection, University of North Carolina at Chapel Hill. A huge, invaluable collection, the Butler papers contain much political correspondence from various Populists throughout the South. The major portion consists of letters from little-known, local, political leaders who injected comments about the grassroots tactics of the Democrats.

A2. Elias Carr Papers, East Carolina Manuscript Collection, East Carolina University, Greenville, North Carolina. Carr was Democratic governor of North Carolina (1893-1997) and president of the North Carolina State Farmers' Alliance and Industrial Union (1889-1892). Most interesting is the correspondence commenting on Polk, Butler, and the role of black laborers in the Alliance.

A3. Colored Farmers' Alliance Charter, Office of Recorder of Deeds, Corporation Division, Instrument #1606, Incorporation Liber #4, Folio 354, Washington, DC. The official incorporation papers for the CFA.

A4. Farmers' State Alliance of South Carolina Records. Clemson University Libraries, Clemson University, Clemson, South Carolina. The collection contains correspondence, printed materials, reports from county alliances and the original minutes that range from its first meeting on 11 July 1888 through 1898.

A5. Farmers' Improvement Society Papers. Texas Collection, Baylor University, Waco. Scattering of items as early as 1902 and proceeding into the 1920s.

A6. Rebecca Latimer Felton Collection, University of Georgia Archives, Athens. Memoranda and personal letters about the 1894 political campaign in Georgia. They were immensely useful for a balanced treatment of the state's political history during this period, especially in the Seventh District.

A7. Marmaduke J. Hawkins Papers, North Carolina State Library and Archives, Raleigh, North Carolina. This small collection contains several prominent examples of the type of political propaganda used during the Populist revolt. Since their circulation was vigorously pushed by Democrats as "inflammatory" material, they were of particular value in assessing the opposition' s psychological attack against Populist racial ideology in the South. The two dominating issues of the "Force Bill" and "Negro domination" are animated by several particulars within the collection. Ostensibly written as propaganda items, their factual merit must be balanced against more objective sources.

A8. Charles W. Macune, "The Farmers' Alliance." Typed manuscript, 1920. The Center for American History, University of Texas at Austin. As described by Lawrence Goodwyn, this fifty-nine page manuscript is "as enigmatic as Macune's own career," raising more questions than it answers. After the creation of the People's party, a move opposed by Macune, he ceased his involvement with the Alliance movement and settled as a Methodist preacher in Texas. Goodwyn notes that Macune never understood how he lost influence in the movement.

A9. Charles W. Macune Papers. Currently in the possession of his great grandson, Dr. Charles W. Macune, Jr., California State University at Northridge. The collection consists primarily of letters, records, photographs, and speeches, in addition to a box of books. A considerable part of the letters running from 1837-1875 is devoted to the correspondence of C. W. Macune's father, the Rev. William Macune, with much of the remainder devoted to correspondence (1900-1940) from Macune's six children to him after he retired from the Farmers' Alliance/Populist movement. The balance of materials, including speeches, personal correspondence, photographs, and records from 1885-1900 contain little on the agrarian movement. Disappointing for black Populist research, but scholars might find the background material useful in a general way.

A10. William J. Northen Papers, Georgia State Archives and Library, Atlanta, Georgia. Northen, although a Democratic governor, was particularly critical about the use of violence against blacks. But as a conservative he accepted the white dictum that "social equality" was highly undesirable to both races. This is a valuable collection for understanding why blacks would vote for a man whose party was very caustic toward blacks. Individuals such as Northen acted as a magnetic force to middle-class black leaders who attempted to adapt to local conditions.

A11. Open Letter Club Correspondence, Tennessee State Library and Archives, Nashville. A small but valuable collection of papers with several interesting pieces debating the "Force Bill" and its possible effects on the South and blacks. After that, the collection is of little value to a study of this nature.

A12. Leonidas L. Polk Collection, Southern Historical Collection, University of North Carolina, Chapel Hill. The Polk papers provided a rich source of information about the Farmers' Alliance movement in the larger context of agrarian reform. The comments of Polk's contemporaries concerning political conditions and the progress of the agrarian movement proved to be of particular value in analyzing the South's slow philosophical shift toward independent political activity. Also, these same references provided an illuminating insight into the ideological struggle taking place in the Southern mind over the "Negro question" and the consequences of a third party.

A13. Terence Vincent Powderly Papers. Available from UMI on 109 reels of microfilm, along with the John William Hayes Papers. Collection contains Powderly's personal papers, correspondence, speeches, etc. from 1864-1937 and spans the entire history of the Knights of Labor, the first major national industrial organization to recruit blacks to membership extensively. The collection also includes newspaper clippings, scrapbooks, photographs, legal files, and reports from local assemblies. An essential collection for studying the early days of biracial industrial organization in both the North and the South.

A14. John B. Rayner Papers. Schomburg Center for Research in Black Culture, New York, NY. Miscellaneous writings, clippings, etc. by and about the black Texas Populist leader. The collection covers the period 1904-1916, when Rayner was variously involved with the foundation of the Conroe Normal and Industrial College near Houston, TX and later with Robert L. Smith's Farmers' Improvement Society. Included are a number of holograph letters and speeches by Rayner on the need for blacks to return to farming and also the importance of Christian-based black education, although his writings on "Political Ingratitude" and why "the Negro vote is no longer a Republican asset in Texas" are also worth noting.

A15. N. T. N. Robinson Letter, Tulane University Library and Archives, Tulane University, New Orleans. Robinson was a United States Marshall in Louisiana's Fifth District. This letter contains his description of the widespread fraud and violence that was occurring during the state elections in April 1892.

A16. Charles A. Roxborough Letter, Special Collections Department, Hill Memorial Library, Louisiana State University, Baton Rouge. A letter of resignation by a black Republican leader from Louisiana. Roxborough includes some interesting reasons for possible black defection from the Republican party. By way of innuendo and nuance, he hints that blacks should support the Democrats. He subsequently joined the Louisiana Populist party and was nominated for the office of state treasurer at the party's first convention in 1892.

A17. Oliver P. Temple Papers, Special Collections Library, James D. Hoskins Library, University of Tennessee, Knoxville. Outside of some interesting mate rial on Southern white Republican attitudes toward blacks, the collection is of little value to Populist studies. The Temple papers are primarily concerned with the political activities of the two major parties. The absence of correspondence concerning the third party in Tennessee is largely indicative of the state's minor role in the Populist revolt.

A18. Benjamin Tillman Papers, South Carolina Department of Archives and History, Columbia, South Carolina. Holdings of Tillman's writings during his tenure as South Carolina governor include letterbooks, correspondence, executive messages, proclamations, etc. Also includes a collection of letters received from numerous individuals.

A19. Thomas E. Watson Papers. Available from LEXISNEXIS Academic & Library Solutions, on 34 reels of microfilm (filmed from the Southern Historical Collection). Unusually disappointing for a collection with its reputation as a source of information on Populist activities. Because of Watson's prominence as a Southern liberal in race relations, it is regrettable that the collection, despite its size, contains so little useful for the period before 1900. "It is a testimony to C. Vann Woodward's thoroughness." Norman Pollack has written, "that he was able to reconstruct so ably Watson's activities in the 1890s, for the papers themselves were of little help." Despite this weakness, however, these papers constitute an indispensable starting point for any study of Southern Populist racial attitudes.

B. NEWSPAPERS

Black-owned and -operated newspapers are indicated by *.

B1. *American Citizen* (Topeka and Kansas City, Kansas). Feb. 23, 1888-Aug. 2, 1907. One of the leading black-owned newspapers in the region.

B2. *Arkansas Economist* (Searcy, Arkansas). Published in Searcy, Arkansas, in the 1880s and 1890s as the official organ of the Farmers' and Laborers' Union of Arkansas, Homer Prince, editor. Merged with *State Wheel-Enterprise*.

B3. *The Banner* (Nashville, Tennessee). 1891-1896. Independent daily covered Alliance and Populist activities in the Nashville vicinity.

B4. *The Caucasian* (Clinton and Raleigh, North Carolina). 1892-1897. Edited by Marion Butler, not as sympathetic to blacks as *The Progressive Farmer*.

B5. *Colored Farmers' Alliance Advocate* (Vaiden, Carroll County, MS). Published in Carroll County until the Leflore County Massacre. An 1894 issue contains the state platform of the Alabama Jeffersonian-Populist party.

B6. *The Enterprise* (Omaha, NE). Aug. 10, 1895-July 3, 1897. Founded by George Franklin, this paper is a prime source for midwest black political news.

B7. *Freeman* (Indianapolis). 1884-1927. Black weekly published by George Knox out of Indianapolis, edited in turn by Louis Howland (1886), Edward E. Cooper (1888-1892), George Knox (1892-1920).

B8. *Gracewood (Georgia) Wool Hat*. Georgia Upcountry Populist paper. Available in the Thomas Watson Papers via LEXIS-NEXIS (**A19**).

B9. *The Helping Hand* (Oakland, Texas). Official organ of the Farmers' Improvement Society of Texas; started in 1897 and claimed a circulation of 4000.

B10. *Kansas State-Ledger* (Topeka, Kansas). July 22, 1892-1906. Weekly African-American newspaper published by F. L. Jeltz out of Topeka, KS which eventually supported the Populist movement at the local and national level.

B11. *Lampasas (TX) People's Journal.* Short-lived (August 1892-January 1893) weekly based in the birthplace of the Populist movement.

B12. *Louisiana Populist* (Natchitoches, Louisiana). 1894-1899. Under the editorship of Hardy Brian, the Populist state secretary, this paper served as the official organ of the Louisiana movement. Brian was particularly vituperative, making hostile comments about Bourbons and blacks alike.

B13. *Midland Express* (Boydton, Virginia). Started in April 1891 and run as a semi-monthly until June 1891, the *Midland Express* was associated with the local Boydton Institute and served briefly as the official organ of the Virginia Colored Farmers' Alliance. In October 1892, the paper ceased publication until March 1893.

B14. *National Economist* (Washington, DC). 1890-1893. The official organ of the Southern Alliance, this weekly quoted extensively from various grassroots Populist papers in a "reform press" section thereby providing a good insight into the diversity of racial attitudes within the region.

B15. *National Labor Tribune.* November 21, 1873-1958. Official paper of the Amalgamated Association of Iron, Steel, and Tin Workers of America. Source of correspondence from Greenback Party organizers around the country. Richard L. Davis, black mine leader in Ohio, had six letters published on interracial unionism in the 1891 editions (available on microfilm through Norman Ross Publishing).

B16. *Opelika State Alliance Banner* (Opelika, Alabama). Cited in William Rogers' "The Negro Alliance in Alabama" (D342) as the state's only black Alliance newspaper, circa 1890.

B17. *Parson's Weekly Blade* (Parsons, Kansas). 1892-1901, editors Simeon O. Clayton (1892-94), J. Monroe Dorsey (1895-99), Charles A. Morris (1899-1901). Primarily supportive of Republicans but finally turned to Populists at end of 1890s. See Cooper (D92) for more information.

B18. *The People's Advocate* (Crawfordville, Georgia). Weekly Populist newspaper, ran 1892-January 1897. Became the Crawfordville Advocate in March 1895. Holmes notes that few issues survive.

B19. *People's Party Advocate* (Ashland, Alabama). April 7, 1893-Nov. 22, 1900. Clay County, Alabama Populist newspaper.

B20. *People's Party Paper* (Atlanta, Georgia). October 1891-1898. The personal organ of Tom Watson, providing an illuminating example of the white Populist liberal ideology toward the black community. Except during political campaigns, however, other states received only superficial commentary on racial and social conditions. See Robert W. Smith, "The People's Party Paper and Georgia's Tom Watson," *Journalism Quarterly* 42 (1965): 110-11 for details.

B21. *People's Weekly Tribune* (Birmingham, Alabama). 1894-1897. With John W. DuBose as editor and Reuben Kolb as business manager, this was easily the most influential Populist newspaper in the state. The Tribune was one of the most hostile Populist newspapers toward blacks--an attitude perhaps prompted by its readership, which seemed less interested in banding together politically with the blacks than did other Southern states.

B22. *The Progressive Farmer* (Raleigh, North Carolina). 1890-1895. Founded by L. L. Polk, president of the Southern Alliance, this weekly is of particular interest for its broad critical evaluation of the South's contributions to the agrarian movement. In the course of its perusal, important data were also gathered due to its wavering between a conservative and conciliatory line toward blacks.

B23. *Public Opinion* (New York, Public Opinion Quarterly Press). 1889-1895. This is a collection of newspaper excerpts arranged topically. The use of these volumes gives a wide geographical and philosophical overview of the Farmers' Alliance and third party movement. Coverage for political events in the Gulf Coast South is particularly good.

B24. **Richmond Planet* (Richmond, Virginia). Weekly, founded in 1883 and published since 1884 by E. A. Randolph; 1885-1890, by John Mitchell, Jr., editor and manager; 1894, by Planet Publishing Co., John Mitchell, Jr., editor. One of the most important black-owned and –operated newspapers in Virginia.

B25. *The Southern Mercury* (Dallas, Texas). 1893-1897. The official organ of Texas Populism, this newspaper was valuable for its regional perspective of the South's political history. Exceedingly important in evaluating the Populists' psychology toward the black voter in the South.

B26. *State Wheel-Enterprise* (Searcy, Arkansas). Official organ of The Grand Agricultural Wheel of the State of Arkansas, published by Louis B. Audigier in the 1880s; merged with *Arkansas Economist*.

B27. **Topeka Times-Observer*. Short-lived (1891-92) black-owned and -operated newspaper.

B28. *Topeka Weekly Call. July 28, 1891-Oct. 29, 1898. Prominent black-owned and -operated Kansas newspaper.

B29. *Washington Bee (Washington, DC). Weekly, founded in 1882, published 1887-1921 by W. Calvin Chase. One of the most important black-owned and – operated weekly newspapers based in the nation's capital.

B30. Weekly Toiler (Nashville, Tennessee). 1888-1892. As the Tennessee Farmers' Alliance organ under the editorship of J. H. McDowell, this paper was almost the sole source of information on the history of the state's Colored Farmers' Alliance and Wheel. Despite the Toiler's official connotation, the Nashville Banner provided a more intricate study of the white Alliance movement during this period.

C. BOOKS

C1. Allen, Emory A., et al. *Labor and Capital: Containing an Account of the Various Organizations of Farmers, Planters, and Mechanics, for Mutual Improvement and Protection Against Monopoly.* Cincinnati, OH: Central Publishing House, 1891. After the usual panagyrics, leaders of each of the major agrarian organizations, including Polk, offer brief essays. The most interesting here, though, might be Colonel Hiram Hawkins' "Achievements of the Grange in the South," which refers repeatedly to a secret "black league."

C2. Allen, Robert L., and Pamela P. Allen *Reluctant Reformers: Racism and Social Reform Movements in the United States.* Washington, DC: Howard University Press, 1974. Allen claims that although white Populists presented blacks with arguments in support of their white brethren, as a matter of self-interest, their was also no implication of political equality. The greater the black presence within Populist leadership, the more misgivings arose about equality.

C3. Allen, Ruth. *Chapters in the History of Organized Labor in Texas (The University of Texas Publication No. 4143).* Austin, TX: University of Texas Press, 1941. Although Allen does not touch on the People's party, she addresses the use of blacks as strikebreakers against the Knights of Labor in the 1880s. Allen also notes the initial attempt in Dallas in 1889 to form a State Federation of Labor; one-fourth of the convention delegates were black, and a black vice-president, T. D. McLeroy, was elected.

C4. Anderson, Eric. *Race and Politics in North Carolina, 1872-1901: the Black Second.* Baton Rouge, LA: Louisiana State University Press, 1981. Anderson details the elections entered into by the Populists and the subsequent collapse of black power in the district. A fine example of research on blacks and populism at the local level.

C5.   Anderson, James D. *The Education of Blacks in the South, 1860-1935.*
Chapel Hill, NC: University of North Carolina Press, 1988. Briefly notes the
era as the second "distinctive campaign for universal education" in the South,
with the Farmers' Alliance and Populist party making "the first substantial gains
in public education since the ex-slaves' campaigns during Reconstruction."

C6.   Aptheker, Herbert, ed. *A Documentary History of the Negro People in the
United States.* New York: Citadel Press, 1951. Still one of the best collections
of primary documents on African-American history. The section on "Populism
and Strikes" is relatively small but includes information on the Florida and Mississippi Colored Farmers' Alliances in 1891, two local groups which have received little modern research.

C7.   Argersinger, Peter H. *The Limits of Agrarian Radicalism: Western Populism and American Politics.* Lawrence, KS: University Press of Kansas, 1995.
Not a new examination of populism, but rather a collection of Argersinger's
scholarly essays published 1969-92, save for an introductory chapter on "The
Political Limits of Western Populism." This is also the only chapter which notes
the presence of blacks as a potential source of votes in Kansas. Although an
excellent collection of his writings, Argersinger here contributes little to the
study of black populism.

C8.   _____. *Populism and Politics: William Alfred Peffer and the People's
Party.* Lexington, KY: University Press of Kentucky, 1974. Peffer's career in
the U.S. Senate coincided exactly with the rise and fall of the Populist movement in the U.S. Argersinger briefly addresses Peffer's views on white supremacy, noting that although the senator felt that "Northern lecturing" would not
help the cause in the South, it was also true that black and white must have equal
protection under the law. Peffer argued that the Kansas Populists made no racial
distinctions and that it would behoove the South to follow their example. Includes a brief report on an interview between Peffer and Josephus Daniels on the
People's party in 1891.

C9.   Arnesen, Eric. *Waterfront Workers of New Orleans: Race, Class, and
Politics, 1863-1923.* New York: Oxford University Press, 1991. The biracial
coalitions formed by New Orleans waterfront workers late in the nineteenth century are fascinating examples of how cooperative class struggles could work
across racial lines. Arnesen briefly touches on the role of the Populists in New
Orleans' politics and how local machine politicians and state Democrats united
in the state disfranchisement campaigns.   A fine study of race and labor, although of minor use for Populist studies.

C10.   Arnett, Alex M. *The Populist Movement in Georgia: a View of the
"Agrarian Crusade" in the Light of Solid-South Politics.* New York: Columbia
University Press, 1922. One of the most-cited monographs on Populism traces

the evolution of the movement from the rise of the Grangers through the collapse of the late 1890s. The "very large element" of corruptible blacks played
"the most conspicuous role in the solemn farce of election day." Arnett is a
lively writer, but he also extensively uses original sources to back his argument
that despite its problems, Populism left a legacy of individual freer play and a
fairer chance for the modern individual--except is he were black. See also **D13**.

C11. Ashby, N. B. *The Riddle of the Sphinx. A discussion of the economic
questions relating to agriculture, land, transportation, money, taxation, and cost
of interchange: a consideration of possible remedies for existing inequalities,
and an outline of the position of agriculture in the industrial world; with a comprehensive history of the leading farm organizations, their constitutions and by-
laws.* Chicago: Mercantile Publishing and Advertising Co., c1890. Reading
through the table of contents--almost every page is a new topic--gives one an
idea of the breadth of Ashby's topics. Detailed examination of taxation, farming, co-operatives, money problems, railways--all of the Populist issues. Chapters 8-12 cover the Alliance, Grange, Farmers' League, and Farmers' Mutual
Benefit Association, with copies of their constitutions and by-laws.

C12. Ayers, Edward L. *The Promise of the New South: Life After Reconstruction.* New York: Oxford University Press, 1992. Ayers takes on a fairly broad
topic: what it meant to live in the South in the post-Reconstruction era. Chapters on urban and rural life, religion, and race relations are all excellent, but the
chapter on "Populism" is of most interest here. Ayers notes that disfranchisement had already begun in some Southern states in one form or another by the
time the People's party began its ascent. Even though white Populists and their
newspapers rarely spoke of interracial cooperation, conservative Democrats
feared an alliance enough to downplay it in their own newspapers and speeches.
Much of the attention here is on Tom Watson's role in the movement.

C13. _____. *Southern Crossing: Life in the South, 1877-1906.* New York:
Oxford University Press, 1995. An abridged version of The Promise of the New
South, this work traces the roots of disfranchisement from the era before the
People's party began its ascent. Of most interest are the chapters on "Alliances"
and "Populism," both of which discuss the relationship of blacks to agrarian
movements.

C14. _____. *Vengeance and Justice: Crime and Punishment in the 19th-
Century American South.* New York: Oxford University Press, 1984. Ayers
asks the basic question: what made the early 1890s the time of the most brutal
mob violence in Southern history? "One obvious answer might be Populism,"
but that is not the sole answer. "Lynching was madness, but with a method."

C15. Bacon, Alice M. *The Negro and the Atlanta Exposition (The Trustees of the John F. Slater Fund Occasional Papers, No. 7)*. Baltimore: Published by the Trustees, 1896. Fascinating contemporary article on blacks and the 1895 Cotton States Exposition in Atlanta. Bacon notes that after a group of black leaders fought against the idea of a separate facilities for the races, the CSE directors offered a building for blacks to "exhibit their progress in the arts of civilization." The lack of the exhibit's complete success of the exhibits must be put down to the failure of many blacks to cooperate with exhibit planners, as a form of protest. Reprints Washington's famous speech and President Cleveland's favorable response.

C16. Bailey, Hugh C. *Liberalism in the New South*. Miami: University of Miami Press, 1969. Populism is seen as one aspect of Southern Progressivism, with "genuine leaders of the white masses" such as Tillman and Hogg rising to power and converting their states to Populist principles. Most useful for its examination of the "liberalism" of many of the notable Southern names of the era, including Cable and Washington.

C17. Baker, Ray Stannard. *Following the Color Line: an Account of Negro Citizenship in the American Democracy*. New York: S. S. McClure, 1904. One of the first monographs of the new century to attempt to view race relations with a degree of impartiality. Most of these chapters were originally articles in either *McClure's Magazine* or *American Magazine*. Despite the expected stereotyping and use of dialect common to the era, even by "liberal" writers, Baker is still useful for his compilation of facts and figures. He also notes that "one of the most significant things I saw in the South--and I saw it everywhere--was the way in which the white people were torn between their feeling of race prejudice and their downright economic need" (p.81). Baker briefly discusses Populism under "The Black Man's Silent Power." This book was also later (1964) reprinted with the subtitled "American Negro Citizenship in the Progressive Era."

C18. Barnes, Donna. *Farmers in Rebellion: The Rise and Fall of the Southern Farmers Alliance and People's Party in Texas*. Austin, TX: University of Texas Press, 1984. More than a simple chronicle of the rise and fall of the SFA and People's party in Texas, Barnes' book examines the movement in terms of the structural strains and mobilization theories of protest movements. Although Barnes examines in detail such aspects of the movement as the Texas Alliance Exchange and Great Jute Boycott, race is rarely mentioned as a variable. Good sociological study of the movement, particularly in the opening chapters.

C19. Barnes, Kenneth C. *Who Killed John Clayton? Political Violence and the Emergence of the New South, 1861-1893*. Durham, NC: Duke University Press, 1998. Notes the impact of secret balloting on voting in the 1892 elections. The new law "appears to have left the white Republican and Wheel-Alliance vote intact but removed almost all of the black vote from the Democratic opposition." Barnes also mentions the Back-to-Africa movement in Conway County.

C20. Barr, Alwyn. *Black Texans: a History of African Americans in Texas, 1528-1995, 2nd ed.* Norman, OK: University of Oklahoma Press, 1996. In his chapter on "Voters and Laborers," Barr discusses the Populist era in Texas politics and the interplay between "Gooseneck Bill" McDonald, Rayner, and Cuney in their struggle for control of black Texas votes. The Populism section has not been updated from the first (1973) edition, however.

C21. ____. *From Reconstruction to Reform: Texas Politics, 1876-1906.* Austin: University of Texas Press, 1971. One of the best books available on Texas politics in the post-Reconstruction era. Barr addresses the People's party at length, noting that the impulse toward the formation of white men's associations or white primaries became statewide when growing Populist strength split the white vote and made it possible for a black minority to swing an election. Also notes People's party links with Farmers' Union, Greenbackers, Socialists, etc.

C22. Barrett, Charles Simon. *The Mission, History, and Times of the Farmers Union.* Nashville, TN: Marshall and Bruce Company, 1909. Everything anyone would want to know about the Farmers' Union, with numerous brief biographies of principal figures and photos. The organization's Constitution is reprinted in full, with Article 1, Section 1 limiting membership to all persons "of sound mind, over the age of sixteen years, a white person or Indian of industrious habits...." Includes short chapter on Alliance and other farm organizations, but no mention of black organizations.

C23. Bartley, Numan V. *The Creation of Modern Georgia.* Athens, GA: University of Georgia Press, 1983. Discusses in particular Watson's flirtation with blacks as potential Populist voters and the problem of the "Negro question," which was what Southern Democrats talked about "when they come back home after one of their big surrenders at a national convention." Watson's decision to support legal and political rights for blacks was a calculated political strategy.

C24. Bauerlein, Mark. *Negrophobia: a Race Riot in Atlanta, 1906.* San Francisco: Encounter Books, 2001. The Atlanta Race Riot of 1906 came in the midst of a state gubernatorial campaign marked by race baiting and the rise of white supremacy. Bauerlein notes the role of the Tom Watson and the People's party in the corrupt campaigns of 1892-96 and the development of Watson's virulent anti-black rhetoric. By 1905, even though Populism had lost its political cohesion and Watson found himself without a party, he remained "a bellwether of labor sentiments and race feeling." An excellent example of the lingering effect of Populism's racial politics.

C25. Beatty, Bess. *A Revolution Gone Backwards: The Black Response to National Politics, 1876-1896*. Westport, CT: Greenwood Press, 1987. Beatty asserts that even though racism plagued the Alliance movement, the CFA and SFA could cooperate on occasion. He also quotes the black Republican press on the Populist movement: "Is it not plain to every colored man that this Alliance intends to plot the oppression of colored farmers?" Good coverage of the relationship between blacks and all the major political parties of the era.

C26. Billings, Dwight B., Jr. *Planters and the Making of a "New South": Class, Politics, and Development in North Carolina, 1865-1900*. Chapel Hill, NC: University of North Carolina Press, 1979. Contradicting the standard theory that it was "new men" that owned the the majority of early mills in postbellum North Carolina, Billings demonstrate that the traditional planter class and agrarians were the chief owners, thereby extending their reach from farm to village. Although the Populist revolt threatened the power structure, the white Populist leaders wree members of the lowest rung of this class and were unwilling to significantly alter the agrarian social structure. Billings cites the Cotton Pickers' Strike and its white Populist opponents as an example of this split in the class structure which prevented further advance of a biracial Populist agenda.

C27. Blair, Lewis H. *A Southern Prophecy: The Prosperity of the South Dependent Upon the Elevation of the Negro*. Edited with an introduction by C. Vann Woodward. Boston: Little, Brown, 1964. Blair's 1889 monograph argues that paternalism and noblesse oblige toward Southern blacks was not the answer to the South's continuing economic problems. Instead, blacks must have complete and free access to all public settings, including hotels and places of public entertainment, on an equal basis as whites. Treatment of blacks and whites as equal citizens would bring "peace, happiness, prosperity to all." Complete subordination or half-measures would only keep the South from prosperity.

C28. Blake, Nelson Morehouse. *William Mahone of Virginia, Soldier and Political Insurgent*. Richmond, VA: Garrett and Massie, 1935. Somewhat dated but still useful biography of the leader of Virginia's Readjuster movement in the years prior to the rise of Populism. Blake notes that Mahone "never once entertained the thought of 'social equality' between the races, nor did he lead the negro to believe that such was the case." Mahone "interested himself in the negro vote because he needed the cooperation" of blacks and liberal whites to secure his reform programs.

C29. Blocker, Jack S., Jr. *Retreat from Reform: the Prohibition Movement in the United States, 1890-1913*. Westport, CT: Greenwood Press, 1976. Paralleling the rise of Populism as a political power, and occasionally employing the same rhetoric and leadership (e.g., James B. Weaver, Ignatius Donnelly), was the Prohibition movement of the 1880s and 1890s. Blocker makes no mention of Rayner, who played a leading role in the Texas campaign, but his chapter on "The Magnet of Populism" is worth examining for his discussion of the attraction of blacks to a third party. The Prohibitionists, after much discussion with the Populists, sought their own path of reform after abandoning the Republican model as unsatisfactory, with strong anti-lynching and suffrage planks in their party's platform of 1892.

C30. Blood, Fred G., ed. *Hand Book and History of the National Farmers' Alliance and Industrial Union.* Washington, DC: [n.p.], 1893. This seventy-one page guide to the Alliance features photos and biographies of some of the organization's luminaries, including H. L. Loucks, H. C. Demming, Marion Butler, and Mann Page, among others. Also featured are detailed histories of the Wheel and Alliance, reports on the national meetings in Meridian, St. Louis, Ocala, Indianapolis, and Memphis, and reports from state chapters. Of note is the report of the 1888 Meridian meeting, which states that "the most serious question, and the one that very nearly prevented any consolidation taking place, was the admission of colored men into the organization. This question was finally settled by leaving it optional with each state, and providing that no colored delegates should be sent to the National meetings."

C31. Bond, Bradley G. *Political Culture in the Nineteenth-Century South: Mississippi, 1830-1900.* Baton Rouge, LA: Louisiana State University Press, 1995. Little has been written on Populism in Mississippi. Frank Burkitt lead the Populist assault on the Democratic rulers, fusing with the white wing of the Republican party. Democrats courted black voters to halt the fusion efforts, with the death of Mississippi Populism soon following.

C32. Bond, Horace Mann. *Negro Education in Alabama: A Study in Cotton and Steel.* Washington, DC: The Associated Publishers, Inc., 1939. Briefly notes the changes in educational funding and policy in Alabama during the Populist insurgency. Bond also discusses the "Colored Convention" held in Montgomery in 1890 intended 'to discuss subjects which would benefit the Negro race in Alabama." Useful primarily for its liberal use of quotations from Alabama state government documents. Bond repeats his contentions, with data on other Deep South states, in his *The Education of the Negro in the American Social Order* (Prentice-Hall, 1934).

C33. Bonner, James C. *Georgia's Last Frontier: the Development of Carroll County.* Athens, GA: University of Georgia Press, 1971. Of most interest for this study is Bonner's chapter "Postwar Political Developments," which touches on the effects of the various agrarians movements—Grangers, the Alliance, etc.—which reflect the urban-rural schism of the Carroll County. Part of the problem arose as a result of the "fence laws," which required citizens to post fences at their own expense or pay fines for roaming livestock. Bonner traces the effect of this law and the growing class consciousness of the region's small farmers on the development particularly of the Populist movement, which threatened white conservative Democratic control with radical and black voters. Excellent examination of black influence at the local political level.

C34. Bracey, John H., Jr., August Meier, and Elliott Rudwick, ed. *Black Nationalism in America*. Indianapolis, IN: Bobbs-Merrill Company, 1970. An excellent collection of primary documents on the history of black nationalism in America. Of most interest for this study are Alexander Crummell's 1882 sermon on race and power, Bishop Henry M. Turner's "Back to Africa" appeals, T. Thomas Fortune's writings in the *Proceedings of the Afro-American League National Convention of 1900*, writings of Du Bois and Washington, and an excerpt from the *1879 Proceedings of the Colored Laborers' and Business Men's Industrial Convention*.

C35. Brewer, J. Mason. *Negro Legislators of Texas and Their Descendents, 2nd ed.* Austin, TX: Jenkins Publishing Company, 1935. One of the first books to seriously examine the role of blacks in the Texas political process. Discusses the role of the "Lily Whites" in the disfranchisement process and briefly touches on the legislative career of Robert Lloyd Smith, who served in the Twenty-Fourth Legislature.

C36. Brewton,. William W. *The Life of Thomas E. Watson*. Atlanta: The Author, 1926. Early self-published biography of Watson occasionally paints an entirely different picture of events in the Georgia Populist's life. Case in point: the story of the mob attacking Doyle (here simply "a negro preacher") has Watson "compelled" to protect him in his back yard. A mob gathered, and Watson assembled his friends. The "old guard," some sixty farmers, rushed the twenty miles to Watson's home and stayed until the mob disapated. Brewton downplays Watson's racism, although he devotes considerable space to his anti-Catholicism.

C37. Brooks, Robert Preston. *The Agrarian Revolution in Georgia, 1865-1912 (Bulletin of the University of Wisconsin, No. 639, History Series Vol. 3, No. 3)*. Madison, WI: University of Wisconsin Press, 1914. Often cited as "The Agrarian Revolt" in the literature, Brooks' dissertation makes no mention of the Alliance, Greenbackers, or any other farmers' movement, black or white. Almost every page is filled with often outlandish generalizations concerning Georgia blacks, although Brooks' statistics might be useful.

C38. Brotz, Howard, ed. *Negro Social and Political Thought, 1850-1920: Representative Texts*. New York: Basic Books, 1966. Although the number of writers here is limited, Brotz presents a range of opinion by these select few. Of most interest for Populist studies would be Booker T. Washington articles on black education, the rejoinders of W. E. B. Du Bois, and the early writings of Marcus Garvey. The material is posted with little commentary, other than the introduction, but Brotz serves as a handy single-volume of black social thought of the era.

C39.   Brown, William Garrott. *The Lower South in American History*. New York: Macmillan, 1902. Reprint of essays originally appearing in the Atlantic Monthly. Most interesting is the final essay, "Shifting the White Man's Burden," which addresses disfranchisement. "The main thing is not what to do for the negro, but what to do for the white man living among negroes." Discontent was not alone adequate to bring about a change in the Southern political system; it needed to be reinforced by the discontent of "the less thoughtful but far larger class" that drifted to Tillman and Kolb.

C40.   Bruce, Philip Alexander. *The Plantation Negro as a Freeman: Observation on His Character, Condition, and Prospects in Virginia*. New York: G.P. Putnam's sons, 1889. "Not only can the negro successfully compete with the white man, and drive him from the field, but he is also able to expel the immigrant competitor who does not shrink at all from working in his company and at the same tasks." Generally positive consideration of black agricultural workers. Concludes with remarks on the suffrage: "the triumph of any faction composed of a small minority of white voters and a large majority of the blacks cannot be lasting . . . ." Partial disfranchisement would appear inevitable and essential.

C41.   Brundage, W. Fitzhugh. *Lynching in the New South: Virginia and Georgia, 1880-1930*. Urbana, IL: University of Illinois Press, 1993. By promising to take strong action against lynching, Georgia Populists and Democrats hoped to sway black voters. Populists officially passed a resolution denouncing the "evil practice of lawless persons taking the law into their own hands," and the Democrats passed a similar resolution. Governor Northen also campaigned vigorously against the practice.

C42.   Bryan, Ferald J. *Henry Grady or Tom Watson? The Rhetorical Struggle for the New South, 1880-1890*. Macon, GA: Mercer University Press, 1994. Bryan examines the metaphorical style of two of the most significant Southern orators of the 1880s, Watson and Brady, to shed light on how they attempted to impart "a new symbolic vision of the South" in their listeners' minds. Significant for understanding the power of persuasion in building both the Populist and New South movements. Includes key speeches by both men.

C43.   Bryan, J. E. *The Farmers' Alliance: Its Origin, Progress and Purposes*. Fayetteville, AR: [n.p.], 1891. Bryan was the Arkansas state Alliance lecturer when he wrote his book, which includes original sub-alliance charters, brief membership lists, and statistics. Good information also on the Knights of Labor and the FMBA. "The Alliance is not a political party--it cannot be a political party. To become such would destroy its chief characteristic."

C44. Bryant, Girard Thompson. *The Colored Brother: a History of the Negro and the Populist Movement.* Kansas City, MO: Maple Woods Community College Press, 1981. Written apparently as a class assignment, Bryant's study of blacks in the Populist movement is well-worth examining, particularly for its attention to factual detail. Extensive use of contemporary newspaper articles suggests a more activist role for blacks than better-known critics offer. Very useful for its information on black populism in Texas.

C45. Buck, Solon Justus. *The Agrarian Crusade: a Chronicle of the Farmer in Politics.* New Haven, CT: Yale University Press, 1921. This pocketsized volume is still one of earliest and best overviews of the entire agrarian movement, from the inception of the Grange through the Greenback Party, Farmers' Alliance and launch of the People's party. Buck notes almost in passing the exclusion of blacks from the Farmers' Alliance and the existence of the Colored Farmers' Alliance, but not much else is mentioned of that group. Most useful for its broad sweep, including notes on the campaigns in the Pacific Northwest and California, but does not add much unique material to the corpus.

C46. _____. *The Granger Movement: a Study of Agricultural Organization and Its Political, Economic, and Social Manifestations, 1870-1880.* Cambridge, MA: Harvard University Press, 1913. Although dated, Buck's examination of the rise and fall of the Patrons of Husbandry serves as useful background for understanding the beginnings of the Populist movement. In a footnote, Buck notes that blacks were not allowed to join the Grange, although the head of the Missouri State Grange wanted to organize separate granges for them. However, Buck finds no evidence that blacks were admitted to membership anywhere in the country. He does, however, note that the CFA delegates attended the Ocala conference and that the group became part of the national movement.

C47. Bundy, William Oliver. *Life of William Madison McDonald, Ph.D.* Fort Worth, TX: Bunker Printing and Book Co., 1925. William Madison "Gooseneck Bill" McDonald was one of the more influential black Texas Republican leaders who lived well into the 20th C. Of most interest in this testimonial to his life and work is Chapter IX, "Political Career," which spans his entry into local politics in 1890 through his election to the Republican Party Convention from 1892-1924. McDonald opposed the Populists throughout his political career, often speaking at rallies against them. Bundy reprints one of his anti-Populist speeches of 1 October 1896 in full, in which McDonald states that "every enemy that this government has had and that my race has had for the last twenty-five years is a Populist or one who is strongly thinking of joining that party."

C48. Burnham, Walter Dean. *Critical Elections and the Mainsprings of American Politics.* New York: Norton, 1970. Burnham is one of the leading proponents of the election of 1896, which saw the collapse of Populism, as one of the critical junctures in U.S. electoral history. The most important section here is

Chapter 4, "The Movement Toward Depoliticization: the 'System of 1896' and the American Electorate." The manipulation of voting requirements for blacks was one of the most significant "reforms" of the period, and some critics see disfranchisement as a "progressive" move aimed at restoring good government and order to the electoral process.

C49. Cable, George Washington. *The Negro Question.* New York: Scribners, 1890. Collection of Cable's excellent essays from the 1880s, including "The Freedman's Case in Equity," "The Silent South," "The Negro Question," "What Shall the Negro Do?" and "What the Negro Must Learn." Essential documents for understanding Southern white liberal thought during the birth of Populism.

C50. _____. *The Silent South, together with The Freedman's Case in Equity and The Convict Lease System.* New York: Scribners, 1889. Basic essays by the Southern social reform writer. The Patterson Smith reprint edition (1969) also includes Arlin Turner's essay, "George W. Cable as Social Reformer."

C51. _____. *The Southern Struggle for Pure Government.* Boston: Press of Samuel Usher, 1890. Reprint of speech delivered by Cable before the Massachusetts Club (Boston). Points to the failure of the New South movement in providing educational and other kinds of aid to Southern blacks. Cable addresses many of the proposed "solutions" to the Negro Problem, including deportation, formation of a separate black state or region, and the institution of the Australian ballot. Available online at Library of Congress' "American Memory" Project, http://memory.loc.gov/.

C52. Cantrell, Gregg. *Kenneth and John B. Rayner and the Limits of Southern Dissent.* Urbana, IL: University of Illinois Press, 1993. Biography of the black Southern reformers, with particular attention paid to the role of Rayner in the Populist and other reform movements in Texas. Essential for understanding the role of blacks in the party in that state. A shorter, revised version of this work was published as *Feeding the Wolf: John B. Rayner and the Politics of Race, 1850-1918* (Wheeling, IL: Harlan Davidson, 2001).

C53. Carstensen, Vernon R., ed. *Farmer Discontent, 1865-1900.* New York: John Wiley and Sons, 1974. Reprints a few basic documents of the Populist movement, including the Ocala demands, Lloyd's "The Populists at St. Louis," (**D251**) and Tracy's "Rise and Doom of the Populist Party" (**D409**).

C54. Casdorph, Paul. *A History of the Republican Party in Texas, 1865-1965.* Austin, TX: Pemberton Press, 1965. The one great benefit of this volume is its severe chronological arrangement: each year is a separate section, and it's very easy to trace events. Unfortunately, although the Populist and fusion efforts snake through the narrative, there is no mention of the movement or party in the index, and typos abound. Most useful for its detailed discussion of black Republican Party officials and candidates, including Cuney and McDonald.

C55. Cash, Wilbur J. *The Mind of the South*. New York: Knopf, 1941. One of the truly great and well-written works of United States history and cultural studies, *The Mind of the South* examines the mindset of the Southerner through history, in terms of individualism, violence, pride of region, traditionalism, and deeply-rooted racial prejudice. The white Southerner had the chance during the Populist era to unite with black voters and truly reform the South, but "when he had reached the impasse we have seen, the common white of the South did in overwhelming tide abandon his advance upon class consciousness and relapse into his ancient focus." By the time of Populism's collapse, the aristocratic Southerner had vanished from the Southern political scene, with the new landscape dominated by and devoted to the interests of industrialists and planters who wished to retain the region's conservative bent.

C56. Cecelski, David S. and Timothy B. Tyson, ed., *Democracy Betrayed: the Wilmington Race Riot of 1898 and Its Legacy*. Chapel Hill, NC: University of North Carolina Press, 1998. Collection of twelve essays on various aspects of the Wilmington Race Riot of 1898. Of particular interest are articles by Cecelski, "Abraham H. Galloway;" Kantrowitz, "The Two Faces of Domination in North Carolina, 1800-1898;" Laura Edwards on the riot and historical memories of political conflict; and LeeAnn White on Rebecca Latimer Felton and the gender politics of racial violence.

C57. Cell, John W. *The Highest Stage of White Supremacy: The Origins of Segregation in South Africa and the American South*. Cambridge: Cambridge University Press, 1982.   In his comparative study of the growth of white supremacy in South Africa and the American South, Cell discusses at length the Woodward Thesis and its critics, in addition to the problems of black Populists. Cell praises Kousser's re-evaluation of Woodward, particularly his use of statistical evidence, and notes that agrarian distress may only account in part for the racial violence of the period.

C58. Chamberlain, Henry Richardson. *The Farmers' Alliance. What It Aims to Accomplish*. New York: The Minerva Publishing Co., 1892. Chamberlain, a writer for the New York Sun, offers an excellent outsider's view on the workings of the Alliance and its prime movers. He reports CFA membership at almost 1,200,000 members, mostly in the South, and notes the success of the Alliance in electing candidates to state offices. The detailed report on the Ocala convention and short chapter on the CFA are not to be missed. Chamberlain claims Humphrey told him at the Ocala meeting that "From the inception of the Alliance movement among the negroes they have been in favor of a new political party." But Humphrey claims also to be non-political, until the formation of a third party.

C59. Clanton, Gene. *Congressional Populism and the Crisis of the 1890s.*
Lawrence, KS: University Press of Kansas, 1998. The best book for understanding the success and failures of the numerous Populist congressmen, including Peffer and Watson. William Vincent Allen presented to Congress a petition
signed by 3200 blacks protesting widespread violation of their civil rights.
Marion Butler, in turn, fought to defeat legislation designed to further disfranchise state blacks. See also **C159**.

C60. _____. *Populism: the Humane Preference in America, 1890-1900.* Boston: Twayne, 1991. Excellent general overview with good illustrations of the
movement. Clanton notes that no Populist elected to Congress during the period
employed racist language against blacks, and that Watson "courageously appealed for justice for the eight million oppressed black citizens" as part of a
congressional eulogy. Also notes claims that blacks wanted a third party.

C61. Clark, John B. *Populism in Alabama, 1874-1896.* Auburn, AL: Auburn
Printing Company, 1927. Still one of the best books on Alabama Populism,
covering in detail all aspects of the movement. Populism failed for a number of
reasons, including the amelioration of economic ills and the rift caused by con-
tending parties and factions fighting for the black vote. Populism is Alabama
was political rather than economic and "more than one politician" feathered his
nest by manipulating the black vote.

C62. Cobb, James C. *The Most Southern Place on Earth: The Mississippi
Delta and the Roots of Southern Identity.* New York: Oxford University Press,
1992. Brief reference to CFA and Leflore County Massacre. Local officials
noted the incident and the threat of a black population explosion; a push for
white supremacy was the response. Some interesting discussion on the limited
success of fusion politics in the 1880s at the town and county levels.

C63. Cohen, William. *At Freedom's Edge: Black Mobility and the Southern
White Quest for Racial Control, 1861-1915.* Baton Rouge, LA: Louisiana State
University Press, 1991. Brief mention of Populism as a factor in Southern race
relations. The culture of Southern life was such that there never was a real
chance of success in forming biracial coalitions.

C64. Coleman, Kenneth, ed. *A History of Georgia, 2nd ed.* Athens, GA: University of Georgia Press, 1991. Devotes a chapter to Populism and Progressivism, noting the general failure of the "Farmers' Legislature" of 1890. "Some
insight can be gained into the relation between white Populists and black voters
by observing Tom Watson's 1892 congressional campaign. Watson asked
blacks to vote for him on the basis of common interest." Blacks also knew,
however, that the Populists harbored in their ranks many poor white farmers
who despised their presence in the party.

C65. Colored Farmers' National Alliance and Co-operative Union. *Constitution of the Colored Farmers' National Alliance and Co-operative Union of the United States*. Houston, TX: J. J. Pastoriza, [n.d.]. The constitution of the CFA, published separately from that of the National Alliance. Outlines in ten articles the structure, attendance policies, officers, and other important organizational matters.   In terms of membership, Article II, Section 2 states that "No Alliance shall be organized with less than six nor more than twenty male members; nor within less than three miles of the nearest Alliance, except that they may be nearer together by obtaining the consent of the nearest Alliance, or where a river or county lines is between them."

C66. Colored Farmers' National Alliance and Co-operative Union. *Ritual of the Colored Farmers' National Alliance and Co-operative Union of the United States*. Houston, TX: Culmore Bros., [n.d.]. The official manual of ritual for the CFA describes how to "open the Alliance," the various elected and appointed positions (including doorkeeper, who keeps the door secure from strangers), and the Alliance Funeral Service. Essential for understanding not only the Alliance's ties to other secret societies but the importance of the group social aspect. Cited by Gerteis (**E72**).

C67. Cooper, John Milton, Jr. *Walter Hines Page: the Southerner as American, 1855-1918*. Chapel Hill, NC: University of North Carolina Press, 1977. As one of the most influential Southern editors of the period and mentor to Josephus Daniels, Page's writings should be studied as those of a Southern intellectual commenting on "the Negro Problem." Writing in *The Forum*, *The Atlantic*, and other important publications of the era, Page viewed the rise of Southern "Populist" demagogues such as Tillman and Watson with alarm. However, Page rarely addressed the problem of disfranchisement and loss of black civil rights, although he admired Booker T. Washington.

C68. Cooper, William J. *The Conservative Regime: South Carolina, 1877-1890 (Johns Hopkins University Studies in Historical and Political Science, Series LXVI, No. 1)*. Baltimore: Johns Hopkins University Press, 1968. Cooper addresses the "challenge of Tillmanism" at length, although he notes that "the Negro played no significant part" in the 1890 gubernatorial campaign. The CFA endorsed Tillman but made no public campaign for him.

C69. Copeland, Vincent. *Southern Populism and Black Labor*. New York: World View Publishers, 1975. Marxist critique compares the Populism of the 1970s to the 1890s version, particularly as it relates to black workers. The "old populism," was a "big social movement of the masses themselves against the corporate monopolies." Copeland tends to view the average white Southern Populist as more racially liberal than he perhaps was but also notes the critical distinction between black farm tenants and black farm laborers and how that difference fits into the contemporary class struggle.

C70. Corbin, David Alan. *Life, Work, and Rebellion in the Coal Fields: The Southern West Virginia Miners, 1880-1922.* Urbana, IL: University of Illinois Press, 1981. Excellent study of race relations in the mining regions of Southern West Virginia in part during the Populist era. Black and white miners worked together and joined biracial unions, occasionally with blacks in leadership positions. Particularly interesting here, however, are Corbin's comments on class and race. He notes that although both races respected black teachers and preachers, neither profession could serve in leadership positions because they could not address themselves to the miners' economic needs. Middle-class blacks and black miners were also mistrustful of each other, primarily for economic reasons. Blacks also gained a degree of success on the political front, winning a number of state and local offices.

C71. Cotner, Robert C., ed. *Addresses and State Papers of James Stephen Hogg.* Austin, TX: University of Texas Press, 1951. One of the standard collections of the speeches and official papers of the liberal Democratic Texas governor who championed black civil rights and drew a significant number of black votes away from the Populists. Essential for original documents from the period, along with Raines' standard collection of Hogg's works (**C239**).

C72. _____. *James Stephen Hogg: A Biography.* Austin, TX: University of Texas Press, 1959. The standard biography of the progressive Democratic governor of Texas during the Populist era. Hogg regularly lambasted Populist economic proposals as ruinous, but he simultaneously was a strong outspoken opponent of lynching and racial injustice. Essential for understanding why Populism never took hold of state blacks.

C73. Coulter, E. Merton. *Georgia: A Short History.* Chapel Hill, NC: University of North Carolina Press, 1947. Often colorful account of the Alliance and Populist movements in Georgia. Coulter notes that in the 1892 elections "Negro voters were bought and sold like merchandise and herded around the polls like so many cattle." Two years later, "the Negro vote was so corrupted as to make an unbearable stench to all honest men in both parties."

C74. Cox, Thomas C. *Blacks in Topeka, Kansas, 1865-1915: a Social History.* Baton Rouge, LA: Louisiana State University Press, 1982. Considering the emigration movement under "Pap" Singleton and others into Kansas, it is not surprising that state blacks were forced to address the Populist issue in the early 1890s. The Kansas Alliance admitted blacks as members, with the permission of Leonidas L. Polk. Black Topeka Populists endorsed the Populist stance on labor problems and viewed askance the coalition between Republicans and the money interests. A black Topeka minister, Benjamin Foster, was the Alliance candidate for state auditor in 1890. One of the supreme drawing cards of Populism for black Topekans appears to be the party's strong endorsement of black political participation. A rich source of state information.

C75. Cresswell, Stephen. *Multiparty Politics in Mississippi, 1877-1902.* Jackson, MS: University Press of Mississippi, 1995. The best book available on the workings of the Greenback and People's parties in Mississippi. Cresswell traces the history of these opposition parties, describing their beliefs and what they accomplished in the state. As in other states, Mississippi blacks voted Republican. Cresswell also points out that, contrary to Hyman's research (**C162**), the Greenbackers and Populists flourished throughout the state, although in different counties. Additionally, although Greenbackers supported black voting rights and consequently got black votes, Mississippi Populists generally neglected blacks, and no black Populist leaders emerged. As in other states, leaders and members tended to move from one party to another.

C76. Crow, Jeffrey J., and Robert F. Durden. *Maverick Republican in the Old North State: A Political Biography of Daniel L. Russell.* Baton Rouge, LA: Louisiana State University Press, 1977. Excellent biography of North Carolina's governor during the Populist years. Conservative black leaders distrusted the Populists and opposed fusion in 1896, although other blacks saw fusion as a means of achieving black political rights.

C77. _____, Paul D. Escott, and Flora J. Hatley. *A History of African Americans in North Carolina.* Raleigh, NC: Division of Archives and History, North Carolina Department of Cultural Resources, 1992. Of most interest for populism researchers in this excellent overview of North Carolina black history is Escott's Chapter 6, "Progress and Repression." The cooperation between white Populists and black Republicans "was revolutionizing state politics" and laying waste to Democratic control. Escott does not add anything new to the debate, but the photos and cartoon reprints from period newspapers bring a new dimension to understanding the period.

C78. Culp, Daniel Wallace. *Twentieth Century Negro Literature, or a Cyclopedia of Thought.* Naperville, IL: J. L. Nichols and Co., 1902. Contains brief biographical sketch and photo of George Washington Murray, South Carolina congressman. Murray was at the center of one of the bitterest campaigns in the state's history which underscored the weaknesses of the Populist movement in the region. Culp also reprints Murray's "What Should Be the Negro's Attitude in Politics?" (**D294**).

C79. Cuney-Hare, Maud. *Norris Wright Cuney: A Tribune of the Black People.* New York: G.K. Hall, 1995. Norris Wright Cuney (1846-98) long served as a Republican leader in Texas and was influential in not only dispensing federal patronage (as collector of customs) but also helping to organize black long-shoremen in the port city of Galveston. Tera W. Hunter's "Introduction" to this edition (originally issued in 1913) suggests that Cuney's opposition to Populism and the Kansas Exodus resulted from his city roots and focus on urban rather than rural issues. As a Republican leader in southeast Texas, however, Cuney found the Populists too far removed from capitalism for his comfort, although late in his political career he understood the logic of fusion politics. His daughter's biography remains the primary source of information on the life of this major mover and shaker in Southern and national politics.

C80. Cutler, James Elbert. *Lynch Law: an Investigation into the History of Lynching in the United States*. New York: Longmans, Green, and Co., 1905. One of the earliest investigations into lynching, with numerous single-page charts and graphs for statistical representation. Primarily a straightforward factual account, with minimal commentary.

C81. Dailey, Jane. *Before Jim Crow: the Politics of Race in Postemancipation Virginia*. Chapel Hill, NC: University of North Carolina Press, 2000. Dailey focuses on the Readjuster movement in Virginia's history, which was the most successful biracial political coalition of the post-Reconstruction era. Opponents to the movement used divisive racial rhetoric--the "Negro Domination" theme, for example--to convince poor whites to remain loyal to the mainstream Democratic Party.

C82. Daniels, Josephus. *Editor in Politics*. Chapel Hill, NC: University of North Carolina Press, 1941. The second volume of the autobiography of one of North Carolina's leading anti-Populists. As an insider's account of state politics during that period, from his position as a newspaper editor, Daniels' opinions are always worth noting, although with an obvious grain of salt. Daniels notes that when Jim Young, the black edtor of the Gazette, was nominated along with a number of other blacks for the legislature, "some of the Populists gagged at this, and many of them quietly did not support the candidates, but forty thousand or more North Carolinians had crossed the Rubicon."

C83. _____. *Tar Heel Editor*. Chapel Hill, NC: University of North Carolina Press, 1939. The first part of Daniels' autobiography (followed by *Editor in Politics*, above), takes the reader from his early years in North Carolina through his career as editor of the *Raleigh State Chronicle*, later absorbed by the *News and Observer*, and the *North Carolinian*. As editor of one of the state's most powerful newspapers, Daniels had an excellent and often vituperative view of North Carolina politics during the rise and fall of the Populist movement. Daniels devotes considerable attention to the Knights of Labor, the campaigns of 1888 and 1892, and the relationships of Leonidas L. Polk and Zebulon Vance to the Farmers' Alliance. Includes some interesting commentary on the role of blacks in the People's party and other campaigns.

C84. Davidson, Chandler. *Race and Class in Texas Politics*. Princeton, NJ: Princeton University Press, 1990. Briefly notes the role of the Populists and the Democratic campaign against them. Blacks shifted between Republicans and third-party candidates in gubernatorial elections between 1880 and 1896, with large majorities voting for Greenback, Alliance, and Populist candidates. Texas Populists had a better race record than their colleagues in other Southern states.

C85. Davis, Harold E. *Henry Grady's New South: Atlanta, A Brave and Beautiful City*. Tuscaloosa, AL: University of Alabama Press, 1990. Davis argues that Grady's heart "belonged not to the whole South, but to Atlanta, proclaimed at the height of his powers as his 'first and only love'." With that understood, Davis seeks to define what the New South movement really meant to Grady and how that belief affected Georgia agrarian blacks and the Alliance. Of especial interest here is Davis' account of three black "conventions of protest" in 1883, 1888, and 1889.

C86. DeCanio, Stephen J. *Agriculture in the Postbellum South: The Economics of Production and Supply*. Cambridge, MA: M.I.T. Press, 1974. Data-driven economic study of postbellum Southern agricultural economics, with attention paid to inequalities in black and white farm issues. DeCanio argues that although social and political gains were great for Southern blacks following the Civil War, the defeat of various land reform proposals was important in allowing a continued unequal distribution of wealth and income, and this inequality impeded the movement of poor whites and blacks toward full social and political equality. The Alliance and Populist movements are briefly mentioned.

C87. Degler, Carl N. *The Other South: Southern Dissenters in the Nineteenth Century*. New York: Harper and Row, 1974. One greatest interest here is Chapter 10, "The Last Great Dissent," which focuses on the rise and fall of Populism in the South within the tradition of dissent. Degler addresses the issue of blacks within the Populist movement at length, noting that although both Populists and Democrats softened their rhetoric when necessary to get black support, Democrats also responded with violence. However, the "willingness of some white Southerners to work with blacks in the political arena" was a timid attempt at biracial cooperation.

C88. _____. *Out of Our Past: the Forces That Shaped Modern America*. New York: Harper and Row, 1959. Degler notes that the "new and radical demands" of the People's party platforms constituted a turning point in the history of the modern American political process. The "Farmers' Revolt," as Degler puts it, brought the balance down on the side of increased restrictions against blacks. Farmers believed that black votes were used against them by conservative and business elements they were fighting. Removing blacks from the political arena would allow whites of different classes to fight out their differences without the racial equation coming into the picture.

C89. Democratic Party (North Carolina) State Executive Committee. *Comments by the State Democratic Committee on the Hand Book Issued by the Peoples Party State Executive Committee. A Discussion of the Contents of This Book, Showing That It Is Not Issued in the Interest of the Populist Party. It Does Not Contain Any Platform of the Populist Party, Nor Does It Discuss or Advocate Any of Its Well-Known Principles.* Raleigh, NC: [n.p.], c1898. The title is pretty much self-explanatory. The Democrats go to great lengths to note how they are the "white man's party," despite the claims of the Populists. Fascinating contemporary document pits Democrats against Populists and Republicans for white supremacy. Available online at the Documenting the American South project, http://docsouth.unc.edu/nc/comments/comments.html

C90. De Santis, Vincent P. *Republicans Face the Southern Question: The New Departure Years, 1877-1897.* Baltimore: Johns Hopkins University Press, 1959. Of most interest here is the final chapter, "Fusion Again," which discusses in detail the efforts of Republicans to work with Populists on defeating Southern Democrats. Notes that "while most Negroes continued to vote Republican they disliked fusion, and a number of them openly denounced" links with the Populists.

C91. Donnelly, Ignatius. *Doctor Huguet: A Novel.* Chicago: F.J. Schulte & Co., 1891. Donnelly's tale of what happens when a white Southern doctor miraculously switches bodies with a black criminal for a short period serves as a good exposition of the Populist leader's views of race relationships. Some of Tom Watson's own statements from this period can be traced to this novel.

C92. Du Bois, W. E. B. *Economic Co-operation Among Negro Americans.* Atlanta: Atlanta University Press, 1907. Available online at "Documenting the American South," http://docsouth.unc.edu/church/dubois07/menu.html. This continuation of the 1898 Atlanta University study (**C93**) serves as a good follow-up to the post-Populist era. Du Bois and his team again study a number of black self-help organizations, including churches, secret and beneficial societies, and co-operative businesses, in great detail. As with the preceding document, there is no specific mention of the effects of the Populist/agrarian revolt.

C93. _____. *Some Efforts of American Negroes for Their Own Social Betterment.* Atlanta: Atlanta University Press, 1898. Available online at the Documenting the American South project, http://docsouth.unc.edu/church/ duboisau/dubois.html. A broad study conducted in a number of Southern cities to determine to what extent blacks, especially those in the South, were participating in self-help ventures. Du Bois' team focused on the work of churches, secret societies, beneficial and insurance societies, and co-operative business enterprises. Although there is no mention of agriculture per se, the report remains an excellent source of financial and membership data on these self-help groups.

C94. Durden, Robert F. *The Climax of Populism: the Election of 1896*. Lexington, KY: University of Kentucky Press, 1965. Most of the attention here is on the national Populist campaign with William Jennings Bryan, but Durden notes the role of blacks in the North Carolina campaign.

C95. Dyson, Lowell K. *Farmers' Organizations*. Westport, CT: Greenwood Press, 1986. Volume 10 of the *Greenwood Encyclopedia of American Institutions* includes a generous short essay on the CFA (under "Colored Farmers' National Alliance and Cooperative"). Dyson underscores the difficulty of pinpointing with any accuracy membership numbers, but even more interesting is his acknowledgement that, at least until 1986, no one had found the papers or spoken with the relatives of Humphrey, Shuffer, or other CFA leaders, and "no one seems to have thought of going to isolated Houston county for research." An extremely useful volume for understanding the CFA in relation to other agrarian movements before and after.

C96. Edmonds, Helen. *The Negro and Fusion Politics in North Carolina, 1894-1901*. Chapel Hill, NC: University of North Carolina Press, 1951. One of the first monographs to focus on the role of blacks in the fusion politics of the Populists and Republicans. Edmonds examined county records and provides breakdowns on population, literacy, and some election records. According to the Democrats, black voters had elected into office "unscrupulous, office-hunting exploiters." Black voters at the time felt that they were right in the light of their historical past and psychological fears, but they committed political suicide by supporting only one political party.

C97. Edwards, William J. *Twenty-Five Years in the Black Belt*. Boston: Cornhill Co., 1918. Autobiography of a black educator who spent much of his life in the Deep South, first at Tuskegee and later at the Snow Hill School. Edwards worked with a number of black self-help organizations, including the Negro Farmers Conference, the Workers Conference, and the Black-Belt Improvement Society during the heyday of Populism.

C98. Escott, Paul D. *Many Excellent People: Power and Privilege in North Carolina, 1850-1900*. Chapel Hill, NC: University of North Carolina Press, 1985. Escott's final chapter addresses the rise and fall of Populism as it related to the entrenched power structure in North Carolina. A combination of fraud, segregation, and disfranchisement would eviscerate the coalition of poorer whites and blacks and insure that established interests would not be threatened in the future. Good full page photos of many of the leading state figures of the era, including Butler, Russell, Simmons, and Daniels.

C99. Factor, Robert L. *The Black Response to America: Men, Ideals, and Organization from Frederick Douglass to the NAACP*. Reading, MA: Addison-Wesley, 1970. Foster places black populism in the context of black leaders and others searching for secular approaches to dealing with new problems, including industrialization. The author focuses primarily on Alabama and the effect of the Sayre Law on disfranchisement, although his comments on Booker T. Washington's silence toward Populism--and his possible surreptitious support, as evidenced by the Populist success in his own county--are provocative.

C100. Faulkner, Harold U. *Politics, Reform, and Expansion, 1890-1900.* New York: Harper and Brothers, 1959. Popular history of the era places the Populist movement in relation to imperialism and expansion. The movement disintegrated in part because of feuding factions, but also in the South because of the influx of black voters.

C101. Felton, Rebecca Latimer. *My Memoirs of Georgia Politics.* Atlanta: The Index Printing Company, 1911. Written and published by the wife of Congressman William H. Felton "after she had reached her 75th birthday," this account is a goldmine of insider's information for the Alliance and Populist eras. The pages on election fraud, with charges and countercharges, are particularly amusing at times. Rebecca Felton would go on to become U.S. Senator from Georgia and herself convert from racial liberalism (for the time) to near rabid racism (on occasion).

C102. Fine, Nathan. *Labor and Farmer Parties in the United States, 1828-1928.* New York: Rand School of Social Science, 1928. Includes chapter on "Grangers, Greenbackers, and Populists." Quite useful for its wealth of statistical information, including a delegate count for the twenty-seven different organizations attending the 1892 St. Louis convention (the National Farmers' Alliance lead with 246 delegates, followed by the CFA with 97 and Knights of Labor with 82).

C103. Fink, Leon. *Workingman's Democracy: The Knights of Labor and American Politics.* Urbana, IL: University of Illinois Press, 1983. Discusses black politics in Richmond, Virginia and Kansas City during the rise of Populism. Fink argues that by the time the Populists arrived, "Kansas City politics offered little room for ideas that were not couched in terms of immediate interest, power, and position." Black politics assumed a "no-holds-barred quality." Quotes J. W. Voorhees, a local black shoe manufacturer, who had reportedly been "catered to" by the Populists but left when he found no "boodle" there.

C104. Fite, Gilbert C. *Cotton Fields No More: Southern Agriculture, 1865-1980.* Lexington, KY: University Press of Kentucky, 1984. Brief history of the Southern Farmers' Alliance, which collapsed in part because of the heavy burden of racism that kept whites and blacks from working together. Fite notes the organization in 1902 of the first local of the Farmers' Educational and Cooperative Union of America, near Dallas, Texas. As blacks were excluded from this group also, they formed their own Negro Farmers' and Laborers Educational Cooperative Union of America in 1908.

C105. Fitzgerald, Michael W. *The Union League Movement in the Deep South: Politics and Agricultural Change During Reconstruction*. Baton Rouge, LA: Louisiana State University Press, 1989. As the first Radical Republican organization in the South, the Union League was instrumental in attempting to organize freedmen into a political force. The League held public meetings and urged black attendance, but some were turned off by the secrecy of the group.

C106. Flynn, Charles L., Jr. *White Land, Black Labor: Caste and Class in Late Nineteenth-Century Georgia*. Baton Rouge, LA: Louisiana State University Press, 1983. Alliancemen "frequently repeated to each other the conventional New South wisdom that blamed black labor for many of the South's troubles." Although the Alliance Legislature created farmer institutes in 1889 to improve agricultural training, blacks were not supposed to attend.

C107. Flynt, Wayne. *Poor But Proud: Alabama's Poor Whites*. Tuscaloosa, AL: University of Alabama Press, 1989. One of the best recent scholarly studies of the Southern "poor white" community. Flynt analyzes a number of different groups, including farmers, miners, and timber workers, and suggests that earlier theories that white tenant farmers did not vote in the Populist era cannot be supported by empirical evidence. Although on occasion biracialism could be made to work in Alabama, "separate black and white Alliances made sure that venerated racial traditions remained intact."

C108. Foner, Philip S. *American Socialism and Black Americans: From the Age of Jackson to World War II*. Westport, CT: Greenwood Press, 1977. Arguably the best detailed overview of the relationship between blacks and left-of-center organizations, including Christian Socialists, Fabians, the Socialist Labor Party. Foner notes the influence of T. Thomas Fortune's Black and White (**C112**) on the concept among members of the Colored Farmers' Alliance that "land is not property; can never be made property... the land belongs to the sovereign people."

C109. _____, ed. *History of the Labor Movement in the United States. Volume II: From the Founding of the American Federation of Labor to the Emergence of American Imperialism*. New York: International Publishers, 1955. Standard history of the labor movement in the U.S., in four volumes, number two of which focuses on the Knights of Labor, Populism, the People's party, and the AFL, among other organizations. Foner even devotes a brief section to "Negro Officers" of the Knights and another on "Jim Crow Unionism and White Workers." Excellent for a basic understanding of the relationships between the various elements interested in the fate of the black laborer.

C110. _____. *Organized Labor and the Black Worker, 1619-198*1. New York: International Publishers, 1982. One of the best overviews of organized labor and the black worker in the U.S. Foner devotes one chapter to the Knights of Labor and two to the AFL, in addition to studies of the Railroad Brotherhoods and IWW. One organization not covered (or even mentioned) in many other studies of black workers, but addressed at length by Foner, is the Colored National Labor Union, active before the end of Reconstruction in the South.

C111. _____, and Ronald L. Lewis, ed. *The Black Worker: a Documentary History from Colonial Times to the Present*. Philadelphia: Temple University Press, 1978. Essential collection of original documents on black workers in the U.S. Of most interest for this study is volume 3, *The Black Worker During the Era of the Knights of Labor*, although volume 4, which covers the AFL's relationship with blacks, is also interesting and potentially valuable. Volume 3 selections include correspondence relating to the black worker from the Powderly papers, the 1886-89 Knights convention, the 1887 sugar strike, the 1891 cotton pickers' strike, and thirty-two documents specifically on the CFA. Select documents are also available in their one-volume *Black Workers* (Temple University Press, 1989).

C112. Fortune, T. Thomas. *Black and White: Land, Labor, and Capital in the South*. New York: Fords, Howard, and Hulbert, 1884. Foner (**C108**) argues that Fortune influenced "to no small extent" the view among some blacks that "land is not property." Land monopoly is the great problem, particularly in the South. The essential Southern conflict pits rich against poor, landed against landless, rather than black against white. Southern workers, regardless of race, had a common goal and destiny, and it is natural that they should "take sides with the labor forces in their fight for a juster distribution of the results of labor."

C113. Frazier, E. Franklin. *The Negro in the United States*. New York: Macmillan, 1949. Classic study by the great African-American historian. No specific mention of the CFA, but good coverage of numerous secret societies and fraternal organizations in the post-bellum years, including the Grand United Order of True Reformers, a black Virginia self-help organization which established its own bank and ran assorted businesses. Short section on "Mutual Aid Societies and Fraternal Organizations Among Rural Negroes."

C114. Frazier, Thomas R., ed. *Afro-American History Primary Sources*. New York: Harcourt, Brace and World, 1970. Includes excerpt from a rare document, "Report of the Committee on Grievances at the State Convention of Colored Men of Texas," from the *Proceedings of the State Convention of Colored Men of Texas, Held at the City of Austin, July 10-12, 1883* (Houston, 1883). The Committee urge fair and equal treatment of all citizens, regardless of race, but is willing to accept "separate but equal" status if necessary. Pre-Populist example of black Texas activism at the grassroots level.

C115. Fredman, L. E. *The Australian Ballot: The Story of an American Reform*. East Lansing, MI: Michigan State University Press, 1968. The best work available on the Australian Ballot, a major electoral reform issue in the U.S. during the Populist era. The Northern Farmers' Alliance adopted a plank supporting use of the ballot at the St. Louis convention, although the reform was ultimately used to disfranchise blacks throughout the South.

C116. Fredrickson, George M. *The Arrogance of Race: Historical Perspectives on Slavery, Racism, and Social Inequality*. Middletown, CT: Wesleyan University Press, 1988. Collection of essays on slavery, Reconstruction, and white supremacy. Of most interest to this study are "C. Vann Woodward and Southern History," "The Historiography of Postemancipation Southern Race Relations," "Some Recent Views of the Postemancipation South," and "The Triumph of Radical Racism: Joel Williamson's The Crucible of Race." The author follows the tradition of Woodward, believing that a dominant elitist class responded to the threat of lower class white movements, including Populism, by drawing the color line more sharply.

C117. _____. *The Black Image in the White Mind: The Debate on Afro-American Character and Destiny, 1817-1914*. New York: Harper and Row, 1971. One of the best studies available on the wide range of white thought and attitude toward blacks, particularly in the South. Of most interest will be Frederickson's chapters on "The New South," Social Darwinism and "the vanishing negro," and Southern Negrophobia at the turn of the century. The author note in passing that the agrarian-Populist revolt of the 1890s led briefly to a competition for black voters, which was disastrous for the side that most openly courted them because of the subsequent white backlash. See also **D109**.

C118. _____. *Black Liberation: a Comparative History of Black Ideologies in the United States and South Africa*. New York: Oxford University Press, 1995. Comparative study of black reaction to white supremacy with a focus on the ideologies and ideologists in the black freedom struggle. Mention is made of disfranchisement around the time of the Force Bill, but Frederickson does not address the People's party or any of the farmers' movements of the era. Of greatest interest here is chapter four, "'Africa for the Africans': Pan-Africanism and Black Populism, 1918-1930," in which the author discusses Marcus Garvey's United Negro Improvement Association (UNIA) as a black Populist group opposed not only to white rule but the claims of educated or "advanced" black elites—Du Bois' "talented tenth," for example—to represent black communities and direct the main movements of protest and resistance. A black populism would obviously have to involve racial consciousness, but it would also have to be constructed in opposition to more parochial loyalties. The collapse of UNIA came in part because of the paradoxical fact of its being a Populist mass movement with a charismatic leader with authoritarian tendencies.

C119. Friedman, Lawrence J. *The White Savage: Racial Fantasies in the Post-bellum South.* Englewood Cliffs, NJ: Prentice-Hall, 1970. Friedman addresses the Populist relationship with Southern blacks in his chapter on "From Politics to Purity: The Crusade of the Powerless." Woodward was mistaken in his belief that Watson made a "sincere and genuine plea" for biracial cooperation, failing to note that Watson's rhetoric was often blandly phrased yet linked to racist qualifications.

C120. Fuller, Henry C. *"A Texas Sheriff."* Nacogdoches, TX: Baker Printing Co., 1931. Colorful biography of Texas sheriff A. J. Spradley, repeatedly reelected on the Populist ticket in Nacogdoches County, TX and serving as sheriff a total of thirty years. Spradley, according to Fuller, joined the Populists when he felt the two major parties were ignoring the interests of the common people. When the Republicans and Democrats adopted many of the Populist platforms, he rejoined the Democrats. Spradley was famous for his impartiality towards both races and was popular among black and white voters alike.

C121. Fuller, Thomas O. *Twenty Years in Public Life, 1890-1910: North Carolina-Tennessee.* Nashville, TN: National Baptist Publishing Board, 1910. Memoirs of black state senator Fuller, from North Carolina's Eleventh District. Seated in 1899, Fuller describes campaigning in the state, the Wilmington Riot, and the Democrats' use of "Negro Domination" as a rallying cry for white supremacy against the Populists. Includes Fuller's 1898 speech to his black constituents, in which he argues that, because of the 13th, 14th, and 15th Amendments, "the color of your skin can never become a legal barrier to the exercise of the right of franchise." Ironically, Fuller also reprints his "Protest Against the Passage of the Proposed Election Law" from the North Carolina Senate Journal.

C122. Gaither, Gerald H. *Blacks and the Populist Revolt: Ballots and Bigotry in the 'New South'.* University, AL: University of Alabama Press, 1977. Gaither examines the rise and fall of the Farmers' Alliance and Populist movements throughout Texas, Louisiana, Alabama, Georgia, Virginia, and the Carolinas. One of the major stumbling blocks to Populist success was the difference in class interests between landless blacks and small landholding white farmers. He also stresses the importance of Tom Watson's concept that "self interest always rules" in the formation of the Populist mindset.

C123. Garlock, Jonathan, ed. *Guide to the Local Assemblies of the Knights of Labor.* Westport, CT: Greenwood Press, 1982. An impressive work, essential for understanding the workings and organization of the twelve thousand local assemblies of the Knights of Labor founded between 1869 and 1896. Whenever possible, Garlock provides information on a member's race and occupation.

C124. Gaston, Paul. *The New South Creed: A Study in Southern Mythmaking.* New York: Knopf, 1970. The best overall analysis of Grady's "New South Creed" and its effect of the transformation of the South into a more industrial, urbanized region. Populism was a potentially "erosive force" for the New South beliefs, but instead the agrarian revolt "proved to be crucial in assuring their longevity." The Jim Crow system seemed a natural addition to the growing movement toward disfranchisement and segregation, all of which in turn gave reassuring guarantees of the safety of those standards celebrated by the New South myth. See also **D432**.

C125. George, Milton. *The Industrial Struggle: A History of the Farmers Alliance Movement and Its Work From Its Incipient Stages in 1879 to the Culmination of perfect National Organization, Oct. 14, 1880.* Chicago: The Western Rural, 1893. Brief mention in the chapter on "Organization" that "the colored people of Texas and Arkansas caught the reform spirit and were asking for charters from the National Secretary and were receiving the same, which created some dissatisfaction among the leaders in Texas. . . ," as noted in Macune's report to the National Alliance convention of fall 1889. Macune wrote "that while Milton George was deserving of much credit for the work he had done for the Alliance movement, he was granting charters to colored Alliances and was running the work of the organization loosely . . . ."

C126. Gilbert, Charlene, and Quinn Eli. *Homecoming: the Story of African-American Farmers.* Boston: Beacon Press, 2000. Rather misleading account of the rise and fall of the CFA. Gilbert and Eli claim the organization was started in 1889 by Rev. J. W. Carter, and it "continued to thrive into the twentieth century." As the CFA "blossomed," members were occasionally made welcome at the meetings of the National Farmers Alliance, "although such occasions were rare and usually marked by strife."

C127. Gilmore, Glenda Elizabeth. *Gender and Jim Crow: Women and the Politics of White Supremacy in North Carolina, 1896-1920.* Chapel Hill, NC: University of North Carolina Press, 1996. Lively history of the role of North Carolina women during the Populist era unfortunately says next to nothing about the relationship of women to the movement. Gilmore notes the Populist victory for blacks in the 1894 election and the final disfranchisement campaigns. She does note the "few strategies" that blacks took to fight loss of suffrage.

C128. Goldman, Robert M. *"A Free ballot and a Fair Count": the Department of Justice and the Enforcement of Voting Rights in the South, 1877-1893.* New York: Garland, 1990. Goldman, commenting on Woodward, argues that Southern black disfranchisement after 1877 was neither immediate nor inevitable. Between 1877 and 1893, the federal Department of Justice attempted to enforce voting rights throughout the region, with varying degrees of success. One basic problem was that enforcement of national policy was in the hands of an agency that was local in character, with little centralized control. However, the Populist revolt postponed and sometimes hastened the disfranchisement movement.

C129. Goodwyn, Lawrence. *Democratic Promise: the Populist Moment in America.* New York: Oxford University Press, 1976. One of the central works on the agrarian revolt in the U.S. Goodwyn argues that the Alliance was more than just a party or ethos—it was "a new way of looking at things." The racial question is dealt with in Chapter Ten, "The Populist Approach to Black America," in addition to other scattered references throughout the volume. Goodwyn stresses the difficulty of studying this aspect of the movement, including the lack of extant original black resources. Populists were thwarted by three mutually supportive political factors: a continuation of the culture of white supremacy, the use of the "Negro domination" theme by Democrats, and the use of violence to maintain Democratic hegemony. Includes brief sketches of R. H. Hayes, Melvin Wade, and H. J. Jennings, all movement activists in Texas.

C130. _____. *The Populist Moment: A Short History of the Agrarian Revolt in America.* New York: Oxford University Press, 1978. An abridged version of Goodwyn's Democratic Promise (**C129**).

C131. Gordon, Fon Louise. *Caste and Class: The Black Experience in Arkansas, 1880-1920.* Athens, GA: University of Georgia Press, 1995. Gordon addresses the issue of the separate racial philosophies of black landowners and landless black workers particularly in response to the Cotton Pickers' Strike of 1891 and other radical activities of the CFA. The majority of black working-class Arkansans and the majority of those working in agriculture did not prosper behind the color line. Brief study overall, but helpful for understanding the racial caste system during the era.

C132. Grady, Henry W. *The Complete Speeches and Orations of Henry W. Grady.* Ed. Edwin Dubois Shurter. Austin, TX: Southwest Publ. Co., 1910. The standard collection of Grady's speeches, particularly on the "New South." For an earlier collection and appreciation by a fellow Southerner, see also Joel Chandler Harris, ed., *Life of Henry W. Grady* (**C149**).

C133. _____. *The New South: Writings and Speeches of Henry Grady.* Savannah, GA: The Beehive Press, 1971. Reprints a number of speeches and articles by Grady, including "The New South," "The South and Her Problems," "The Solid South," "The Farmer and the Cities," "The Race Problem in the South," and his New York Ledger articles of 1889. Introduction by Mills Lane.

C134. Grady, John Howard. *Grady's Great Speech at Dallas, October 27th, 1888, on the Future of the Two Races.* New Orleans, LA: Hopkins Printing Office, 1889. Reprint of Henry Grady's famous 1888 Texas State Fair speech in which he calls for the white race to remain united against the danger of splitting its vote and losing control in the South.   Whites must remain in power because they are the dominant race everywhere, as ordained by God. But the Republican Party seeks to use Southern blacks in an effort to destroy the natural order of things. See **D57** for an analysis of this speech.

C135. Grant, Donald L. *The Way It Was In the South: the Black Experience in Georgia*. New York: Carol Publishing Group, 1993. Grant discusses the developing relationship between blacks and the Populist movement in Georgia, noting the twenty-four delegates to the 1894 state convention but also the radically changed attitudes of Watson and Rebecca Felton. Grant suggests that a combination of white fear of black domination and a return to prosperity in the late 1890s contributed to Populism's collapse.

C136. Grantham, Dewey W. *Hoke Smith and the Politics of the New South*. Baton Rouge, LA: Louisiana State University Press, 1958. As a leading Georgia Democrat during the Populist years, Hoke Smith won praise from both white and black leaders for his stand on the issues and ability to muster the vote for his party. Grantham notes the moderate position Smith took in the 1890s towards blacks, urging education and the right to vote (although he opposed the Force Bill). However, as Tom Watson's power within Georgia increased, Smith knew that he needed his support if he were to obtain the governorship and thus did a turnaround on disfranchisement. An essential book for understanding Georgia politics during the 1890s.

C137. _____. *Southern Progressivism: The Reconciliation of Progress and Tradition*. Knoxville, TN: University of Tennessee Press, 1983. Although Grantham focuses here on the Progressive rather than Populist movement, his work is still important for research in agrarian studies for its comparison of the two movements and its special attention to "black progressivism." Robert Lloyd Smith's Farmers' Improvement Agricultural College in Texas, the Colored Farmers' Union, and the Snow Hill Institute in Alabama are mentioned as attempts at black self-help at the local level.

C138. Graves, John William. *Town and Country: Race Relations in an Urban-Rural Context, Arkansas, 1865-1905*. Fayetteville, AR: University of Arkansas Press, 1990. Briefly mentions the Cotton Pickers' Strike of 1891 and the CFA as active in the state. When the "political farmers" of the Wheel and Alliance moved from self-help and protest into politics, they took their racial attitudes with them. As early as May 1888, the Union Labor Party allowed black Knights of Labor members into their convention, but after Republicans and Unionists threatened the Democratic hold on the state, racial tensions grew. Also quotes sources claiming "eleven black men" in attendance at the state Populist convention of June 1892.

C139. Greer, Thomas H. *American Social Reform Movements: Their Pattern Since 1865*. New York: Prentice-Hall, 1949. General history of reform movements in the U.S., including the Greenback and Populist parties. Greer addresses the race issue briefly, noting that the Farmers' Alliance was open to women but closed to blacks, and that the proposed membership of blacks to a national organization was a significant point of contention between the Northern and Southern Alliances.

C140. Grob, Gerald N. *Workers and Utopia: A Study of Ideological Conflict in the American Labor Movement, 1865-1900*. Evanston, IL: Northwestern University Press, 1961. Grob attempts to assess from a historical standpoint the development of the ideology of organized labor as an integral part of American society. The Alliance, AFL, and Knights are considered, the latter at some length, and Grob additionally examines the relationship between these organizations, each other, and black labor.

C141. Hackney, Sheldon, ed. *Populism: the Critical Issues*. Boston: Little, Brown, 1971. Reprints Abramowitz' "The Negro in the Populist Movement" (**D4**) and Saunders' "Southern Populists and the Negro" (**D356**) among other essays by Durden, Woodward, Hofstadter, and other scholars of the movement.

C142. _____. *Populism to Progressivism in Alabama*. Princeton, NJ: Princeton University Press, 1969. One of the best works on Populism in Alabama. Hackney considers the relationship between the Populist movement and blacks at length, including the disfranchisement issues. Ultimately the Populists were neither revolutionaries nor reformists; they repeatedly showed a propensity to vote against reforms to which they were pledged. The Populists, after their final defeats, were not essentially interested in protecting black suffrage, which left the field open to Democrats to amend the state constitution.

C143. Hahn, Steven. *The Roots of Southern Populism: Yeoman Farmers and the Transformation of the Georgia Upcountry, 1850-1890*. New Haven, CT: Yale University Press, 1982. Drawing on a considerable number of primary sources, Hahn devotes only a small portion of his excellent volume to the effects of the Populist movement in the region. Georgia's Upcountry communities saw the benefits inherent in biracial coalition politics as argued by Tom Watson and other Populist leaders. By 1896, the region had sent twenty-four delegates (about one-third of the total) to the state legislature. The People's Party of Jackson County is noted as opening meetings to both races, welcoming black delegates to their county conventions, and inviting a black speaker from Atlanta. Although local black leaders in the region viewed the Party with skepticism, local papers claimed that blacks voted the Populist line. Hahn notes the "enduring racism" of many white Populists, however, which undermined any success black Populists hoped to achieve. See also **C159, D207**.

C144. Hair, William Ivy. *Bourbonism and Agrarian Protest: Louisiana Politics, 1877-1900*. Baton Rouge, LA: Louisiana State University Press, 1969. One of the more useful studies of agrarian politics in Louisiana. Hair discusses the relationship between the Louisiana Farmers' Union and the state's blacks, noting that some of the more liberal members of the group urged basic rights for everyone "regardless of race, color, or previous condition of servitude." The first CFA lodge in the state was reported in Grant Parish in October 1889, and most black Alliancemen were found in the cotton parishes along the Red River and St. Landry Parish. Hair also comments that the membership total given for the Louisiana locals is probably actually much lower.

C145. Haller, John S., Jr. *Outcasts from Evolution: Scientific Attitudes of Racial Inferiority, 1859-1900*. Urbana, IL: University of Illinois Press, 1971. Good analysis of the "scientific" basis for judging blacks naturally inferior used by many Southern writers of the period in their arguments for disfranchisement, etc. Although Populism is not mentioned per se, Haller's overview will help those unfamiliar with this aspect of late nineteenth century thought gain a clearer understanding of the background for a variety Southern progressive and reformist thinking.

C146. Hamilton, Green Polonius. *Beacon Lights of the Race*. Memphis, TN: E. H. Clarke and Brother, 1911. Contains biographical sketch of Dr. Joseph Hercules Barabin, one of the leading black professional men in the Progressive Movement in Arkansas following the collapse of the Populist party. Cited in some resources as a supporter of Roosevelt's Bull Moose Party, although he spent his youth and early adulthood at Gilbert Academy in Baldwin, Louisiana. The 1915 edition of *Who's Who of the Colored Race* has additional information on Barabin, with an excellent photo in the *National Cyclopedia of the Colored Race* (1919).

C147. Hamilton, Joseph G. de R. *North Carolina Since 1860*. Chicago: University of Chicago Press, 1919. Notes the rise of the Farmers' Alliance and Populist movements in North Carolina and their effects upon state government. The Republican-Populist fusion campaign gained significant ground in the early to mid-1890s, electing a number of black and white officials to local and statewide office. However, the state Democratic Party rebounded in 1896 after a white supremacy campaign used the threat of "Negro domination" to scare poor white voters.

C148. Harlan, Louis R. *Booker T. Washington: The Making of a Black Leader, 1865-1901*. New York: Oxford University Press, 1972. Harlan agrees with the opinion of Abramowitz and others that Washington was not "chosen" the leader of his race by fellow blacks, but rather his acclaim by whites who favored his accomodationist leanings at the time of the Atlanta Exposition address thrust him into prominence. Washington, although arguably the most prominent figure

for black rural and industrial improvement, was promoted by whites to counter-
balance the more radical ideas of the Populists and other movements seeking to
improve conditions for black Southerners. Indeed, the CFA and other groups
not affiliated with Washington's plans seem to have been ignored by him.

C149. Harris, Joel Chandler. *Life of Henry W. Grady, including his Writings
and Speeches.* New York: Cassell Publishing Company, 1890. Memorial volume to Henry Grady, spokesman for the New South. Includes some of Grady's
essential speeches, including that before the Merchants' Association in Boston
in 1889, a lengthy biographical sketch by Harris, and editorial tributes from the
national and Georgia press. See also Shurter's collection (**C132**).

C150. Hart, Roger L. *Redeemers, Bourbons, and Populists: Tennessee, 1870-
1896.* Baton Rouge, LA: Louisiana State University Press, 1975. Blacks did not
play a large role in the Populist movement in Tennessee, with only one black
member attending the 1892 state convention. Hart claims that many blacks
voted for state Populist candidates, however, but these were through fusion ballots handed them by white Republican leader. Populist candidate John P. Buchanan even sided with the Democrats in opposing the Force Bill. Generally,
Tennessee Populists and Democrats thought alike on race matters. Tennessee
Alliance spokesmen never varied from the Southern norm on racial issues, despite some friendly statements on black organizational attempts which appeared
in the *Weekly Toiler*. An essential book for understanding the movement with
this state.

C151. Hayden, Harry. *The Story of the Wilmington Rebellion.* Wilmington,
NC: [n.p.], 1936. Pamphlet, apparently self-published, claiming to be "the first
authentic account of the Wilmington Revolution of 1898, which resulted in the
elimination of the Negro as a political factor in Wilmington and North Carolina
and which led to the disfranchisement of the race throughout the South through
the instrumentality of the 'Grandfather Clause'." Extremely detailed, but places
the blame squarely on the shoulders of Wilmington's blacks.

C152. Haynes, Frederick Emory. *James Baird Weaver.* Iowa City, IA: The
State Historical Society of Iowa, 1919. Early and somwhat hagiographic account of Weaver's life. Haynes considers Weaver to be the first real progressive, always interested in "social and industrial justice." His 1892 campaign trip
through the South was met with "rowdyism and disorder," in part because of the
"race problem." Haynes notes that in the South "the majority of the white people were with the Populist."

C153. _____. *Third Party Movements Since the Civil War; with Special Reference to Iowa: a Study in Social Politics.* Iowa City, IA: The State Historical
Society of Iowa, 1916. Interesting and detailed account of the major agrarian
movements of the era, especially the Greenbackers and Populists. Haynes notes

the merger at Ocala between the Southern Alliance, CFA, and the Farmers' Mutual Benefit Association and the January 1891 meeting in Washington between the CFA, Knights of Labor, the Farmers' Union, Farmers' Alliance, and the Citizen's Alliance.

C154. Hicks, John D. *The Populist Revolt: a History of the Farmers' Alliance and the People's Party*. Lincoln, NE: University of Nebraska Press, 1931. The first great scholarly study of the Alliance and Populist movements. Hicks claims that the Populists "deliberately set out to obtain for the new party all the negro votes they could get," spreading their "third-party propaganda" through the Colored Farmers' Alliance, "always a mere adjunct of the Southern Alliance." Hicks seems to argue that black Populist election victories in North Carolina were not necessarily a good thing: "there seemed to be nothing else for the white Populists to do but to return to their former allegiance until the menace of the negro voter could be removed." He also notes that blacks, "attracted by the ritual as well as by the possible economic benefits of the order . . . flocked to the colored Alliance in prodigious numbers."

C155. Hine, Darlene Clark. *Black Victory: The Rise and Fall of the White Primary in Texas*. Millwood, NJ: KTO Press, 1979. Hine traces the rise of the white primary in Texas to the post-Civil War era, when white men exaggerated the threat of black political ascendency yet often refused to vote. Cuney is cited as one black Republican who refused to jump on the Populist bandwagon, although the party simultaneously was moving in a "lily white" direction. Hogg, the reform Democrat candidate for governor, successfully appealed to the black vote, although the Populists made a good showing. Once the Populist threat was weathered, both major parties worked to remove the franchise from black voters.

C156. Hofstadter, Richard. *The Age of Reform: From Bryan to F. D. R.* New York: Knopf, 1955. One of the seminal works on the Populist and Progressive eras, although there is precious little mention of the status of blacks here. Hofstadter views Populism as part of a trend stretching from the Age of Jackson well into modern times, and that it had a strong influence on the Democratic Party from 1896. With the onslaught of industrialism, farmers grew more important as a "special interest." According to Hofstadter, the Populist movement was not "foolish and destructive" but rather had an ambiguous character.

C157. Holland, Lynwood M. *The Direct Primary in Georgia (Illinois Studies in the Social Sciences 30, No. 4)*. Urbana, IL: University of Illinois Press, 1949. Holland notes that the rising power of the black vote much influenced legislative action, in that the Democrats feared the fusion of Republicans with Populists and the use of blacks as the deciding element. Watson is quoted as stating that prior to 1904 it had been unnecessary to use the word "white" as a restrictive label in primary legislation, in that blacks had essentially been "white primaried" for several years.

C158. Holmes, William F. *The White Chief. James Kimble Vardaman*. Baton Rouge, LA: Louisiana State University Press, 1970. Mississippi Senator James K. Vardaman was an odd mixture of rabid racist and radical progressive, supporting black disfranchisement and women's suffrage and opposing whitecapping simultaneously. As a young Democratic party official, however, he toured Mississippi during the 1892 congressional races, attacking Populist candidate Frank Burkitt as an opponent of white supremacy.

C159. _____, ed. *American Populism: Problems in American Civilization*. Lexington, KY: University Press of Kentucky, 1994. Excellent collection of articles by some of today's movement scholars, including Cantrell and Barton's "Texas Populists and the Failure of Biracial Politics" (**D73**), Clanton's "Congressional Populism" (**C59**), and Hahn's "The Transformation of the Countryside" (**C143**).

C160. Howard, Perry H. *Political Tendencies in Louisiana, 1812-1952*. Revised and expanded ed. Baton Rouge, LA: Louisiana State University Press, 1971. Good overview of the "Bourbon Ascendency," including the revolt of the farmers, the Populist-Republican fusion of 1896, and "the great disfranchisement of 1898." Very useful for its breakdown by parish of black/white voting strength by party.

C161. Hunt, Robert Lee. *A History of Farmer Movements in the Southwest, 1873-1925*. [n.p.]: [n.p.], c1935. Hunt focuses primarily on Texas, with coverage of the Grange, Farmers' Alliance, Texas Farmers' Union, and the Farm-Labor Union of America, with emphasis on their political activities. Extremely detailed, but completely omits any mention of black agrarian movements.

C162. Hyman, Michael R. *The Anti-Redeemers: Hill Country Political Dissenters in the Lower South from Redemption to Populism*. Baton Rouge, LA: Louisiana State University Press, 1990. In his excellent study on Southern social and political tensions following Reconstruction, Hyman argues that political dissent in that period did not simply foreshadow the more intense discontent expressed by the Populists, but that the issues rather were redefined because of the political controversies. His chapter on "Race and Politics" is especially illuminating, as Hyman outlines the attempts by Democrat "Redeemers" and anti-Redeemers to use black voters to maintain power. See Cresswell (**C75**) for a quite different picture of Populist power in the state.

C163. Jones, Stanley L. *The Presidential Election of 1896*. Madison, WI: University of Wisconsin Press, 1964. Complete coverage of the 1896 presidential campaign, with particularly attention paid to the Populists. Jones notes the battles between Watson and Butler, as the latter urged maintenance of a middle-of-the-road strategy in an attempt to build a strong fusion campaign. Southern Democrats stood united under the "white supremacy" banner. Populists in some states refused to vote, in protest of various concerns, and blacks had already been disfranchised in a number of states.

C164. Kantrowitz, Stephen. *Ben Tillman and the Reconstruction of White Supremacy*. Chapel Hill, NC: University of North Carolina Press, 2000. Essential for understanding South Carolina politics in the Populist era. Tillman's career "helps explain how white men came to be their own worst enemies—or at least to elect them." Although conservatives accused Tillman of being a Populist, he was nothing like Watson, Polk, Kolb, and other contemporaries in their attempts to form biracial reform coalitions. Whites who supported black political causes were "white negroes" and came under special attack by Tillman.

C165. Katz, William Loren. *Eyewitness: A Living Documentary of the African American Contribution to American History*. Revised and Updated Edition. New York: Simon and Schuster, 1995. Excellent collection of original documents, photos, and commentary on the broad spectrum of African-American history. A short section on the Populists notes the presence of black delegates at the conventions and the speeches of the Rev. H. S. Doyle for Tom Watson. North Carolina Congressman George Henry White's career is highlighted.

C166. Kazin, Michael. *The Populist Persuasion: an American History*. Revised edition. New York: Basic Books, 1998. Excellent history of the Populist movements in U.S. history, from the earliest days to the contemporary scene. Kazin examines the People's party as just one nineteenth century movement, arguing that the Populists were caught in a bind with attempting to attract white Southern Democrat voters without neglecting black voters. The Southern Populist thus appealed to blacks on matters of shared economic concern while assuring whites that "nothing resembling a biracial order was being contemplated."

C167. Kelsey, Carl. *The Negro Farmer*. Chicago: Jennings and Pye, 1903. Originally presented as his dissertation at the University of Pennsylvania, Kelsey's work is a treasurehouse of information on the state of the black farmer in the Deep South in the years up to the turn of the century. His state and regional maps showing population distribution by race are especially useful. Excellent source of statistics on agrarian conditions.

C168. Kenzer, Robert C. *Enterprising Southerners: Black Economic Success in North Carolina, 1865-1915*. Charlottesville, VA: University Press of Virginia, 1997. During the height of the Populist movement, North Carolina blacks were finding a degree of economic success through their own individual initiative and the establishment of business cooperatives. Kenzer examines both the black business community and the rural landscape, finding that land acquisition continued to grow slowly but steadily in the years after Emancipation. Whether disfranchisement adversely affected black economic prospects is a complex question, however, as it is possible that blacks might have fared even better financially if they had not lost their political influence.

C169. Kerr-Ritchie, Jeffrey R. *Freedpeople in the Tobacco South: Virginia, 1860-1900*. Chapel Hill, NC: University of North Carolina Press, 1999. Addresses the work of the Virginia Colored Farmers' Alliance, noting that Humphrey spoke at the first meeting in Richmond in August 1890. That fall, the VCFA claimed 5,000 members, with a hub in Norfolk. At the second annual meeting in August 1891, members unanimously elected black state legislator William H. Warwick as state superintendent. Most rank-and-file members were farmers or tenants, he argues, and the CFA in southside Virginia was an expression of freedpeople's self-determinationist agrarian protest linked to older movements, including the Readjusters, rather than "a weathervane pointing to possibly better race relations."

C170. Kirby, Jack Temple. *Darkness at the Dawning: Race and Reform in the Progressive South*. Philadelphia: J. B. Lippincott, 1972. Kirby studies the period from about 1890 to the end of World War I to trace the rise of "progressivism" in all its aspects. Addressing the question of race and reform in the South, Kirby argues that "progress" for Southern whites in education and prohibition would also mean disfranchisement and segregation for blacks. But numerous instances of black self-help operations, from Robert Lloyd Smith's schools to the black-owned "social settlement" in Calhoun, Alabama.

C171. Kirk, J. Allen. *A Statement of Facts Concerning the Bloody Riot in Wilmington, N.C.* Wilmington, NC: [n.p.], November 10, 1898. The Reverend Kirk was the black pastor of the Central Baptist Church in Wilmington and one of the leaders of the community at the time of the riot. His sixteen-page pamphlet describes the events leading up to the massacre and decries the violence of the white mob. Kirk also reprints some of the circulars of the day, including one signed by Marion Butler urging blacks to vote and then return home immediately. Available online at the Documenting the American South project, http://docsouth.unc.edu/nc/kirk/menu.html

C172. Kirwan, Albert D. *Revolt of the Rednecks: Mississippi Politics, 1876-1925*. Lexington, KY: University of Kentucky Press, 1951. Kirwan states that the People's party was comprised mostly of small farmers but also a surprising number of large landowners, who united in common cause against "the crushing oppression of capitalist finance and industrialism." Frank L. Burkitt, editor of the *Chickasaw Messenger*, was the leader of the Mississippi Populists. Democrats, as elsewhere, warned that a Populist victory would mean black supremacy, a counterblast so successful that Kirwan suggests the Populists might have swept the state in the early 1890s if it weren't for "the presence of the Negro."

C173. Kousser, J. Morgan. *The Shaping of Southern Politics: Suffrage Restriction and the Establishment of the One-Party South, 1880-1910.* New Haven, CT: Yale University Press, 1974. One of the seminal works on disfranchisement and the Populist movement. Using the ecological regression technique to examine election returns, Kousser argues that V. O. Key's thesis on Southern suffrage restriction needs to be abandoned. An essential resource (replete with tables) for examining a variety of potential issues, including the effect of the poll tax on black voting patterns and the impact of other election laws on both underclass white and black voters.

C174. Kramer, Dale. *The Wild Jackasses: the American Farmer in* Revolt. New York: Hastings House, 1956. Probably the most enjoyable read of all the various books on Populism. Kramer's breezy style captures the celebrities and episodes of the movement wonderfully, with just enough detail to keep scholars happy. He addresses the problem of the CFA and relationship between voting black agrarians and the white Populist leadership, noting the violence that plagued the Southern campaigns, especially those of Tom Watson.

C175. Leiman, Melvin M. *Political Economy of Racism.* Boulder, CO: Pluto Press, 1993. Briefly mentions the effect of the Populist movement on stemming the counterrevolution in the South. Leiman suggests that "important elements of class solidarity partly overrode racial factors." The farmer-labor alliance of poor whites and blacks along class lines was, "in fact, the backbone of Southern Populism." The Populists were eventually defeated by "external power"—the rise of industrialism in a traditionally agricultural system.

C176. Letwin, Daniel L. *The Challenge of Interracial Unionism: Alabama Coal Miners, 1878-1921.* Chapel Hill, NC: University of North Carolina Press, 1998. Interracial populism can be traced in northern Alabama to the fusion Greenback-Labor Party of the 1870s, which typically had members of both races as members in the small mining towns and spoke out openly on racial issues and against the convict lease system as used in the mines, while often aligning themselves with farm issues. These early experiences of interracial cooperation paved the way for later Populist movements throughout the region. By the mid-1880s, however, the Greenback-Labor Party had faded and was replaced by the Knights of Labor, a biracial labor union which often allied itself politically with the Agricultural Wheel, Farmers' Alliance, and other rural Populist groups. These groups ultimately crystallized in 1887 as the Alabama Union Labor Party and the People's party of 1892, but none of these groups would effectively supplant the power of the Bourbon Democrats and coalfield owners.

C177. Lewinson, Paul. *Race, Class, and Party: a History of Negro Suffrage and White Politics in the South*. New York: Oxford University Press, 1932. The agrarian revolt was one in a series of movements by the underclass to gain some political power. The elections of the 1890s throughout the South were rife with fraud and violence from both the power elite and the agrarians, with blacks courted and threatened from all sides through a voter intimidation campaign. Of especial interest are Lewinson's appendices, which although not covering the period in question do present an excellent statistical and legal overview of Populist's Southern legacy for black voters.

C178. Lewis, David Levering. *W. E. B. Du Bois: Biography of a Race, 1868-1919*. New York: Henry Holt, 1993. Lewis' excellent biography of the first forty years of Du Bois' life touches on the development of his economic beliefs during his graduate studies, which coincided with the rise of the Populist and other reform movements. By the 1896 presidential election, which he considered one of the most important in the history of the Republic, he began to seriously doubt the laissez-faire economic theories of his mentor, Frank Taussig, and recognize that the Populists were "a third party movement of deep significance." Although Du Bois agreed to an extent with Booker T. Washinton's political approach to race relations, he was dismayed by its cultural dimensions.

C179. Lewis, Ronald L. *Black Coal Miners in America: Race, Class, and Community Conflict, 1780-1980*. Lexington, KY: University Press of Kentucky, 1987. Excellent general study of black coal miners in the U.S., with particular attention to Alabama and Appalachia. Lewis claims that during the 1908 miners' strike, only "the reform farmers of the district, those who had experience in cooperating with labor during the Populist insurgency against the Bourbons, and organized labor in Birmingham demonstrated any sympathy for the miners' cause." The black middle class also invariably supported the companies against the unions.

C180. Litwack, Leon F. *Trouble in Mind: Black Southerners in the Age of Jim Crow*. New York: Knopf, 1998. Passing references to blacks and the Populist party. Orators made their appeal to blacks with talk of bridging racial differences and animosities for the sake of fixing common economic problems. "But such moments proved fleeting, the promise was rarely fulfilled, and whites dictated the terms and the degree of black participation."

C181. Logan, Frenise A. *The Negro in North Carolina, 1876-1894*. Chapel Hill, NC: University of North Carolina Press, 1964. Surprisingly little here on Populism or the CFA, although Logan devotes a chapter each to "The Black Second" congressional district, "Organizations for Economic Betterment," and the early union movement, including the Knights of Labor.

C182. Logan, Rayford W. *The Betrayal of the Negro from Rutherford B. Hayes to Woodrow Wilson.* New Enlarged ed. New York: Da Capo Press, 1997. The Populists did well in the Congressional and state elections of 1894, particularly in the South, where a black-dominated Republican Party fused with them against the conservative business-supported Democrats. By the 1896 election, however, the fear of "Negro domination" drove white supporters away from blacks, with the Republicans also offering next to no support. "The return to prosperity left Southern Negroes worse off, politically, than they had been before."

C183. _____. *The Negro in American Life and Thought: the Nadir, 1877-1901.* New York: The Dial Press, 1954. Many of the Populist victories in the South were "curiously" attributable to fusion politics involving black Republicans and Populists. Thus, in addition to the class struggle of the 1896 election there loomed the spectre of a revival of black electoral participation in the South. The result was a rise in Southern demagogery that in some instances won for poor whites the power previously exercised by the Bourbons elite.

C184. Lynch, John Roy. *Reminiscences of an Active Life: The Autobiography of John Roy Lynch.* Ed. John Hope Franklin. Chicago: University of Chicago Press, 1970. One-time black congressman from Mississippi, John Roy Lynch reached prominence not only as a politician but as a successful plantation owner in Mississippi in the 1890s. He devotes one chapter of his autobiography to the politics of disfranchisement in Mississippi but also discusses the turnabout in political and social thinking of Kansas Senator John J. Ingalls, who attempted to win support for re-election from the Populist legislators of that state.

C185. Manning, Joseph Columbus. *The Fadeout of Populism, Presenting, in connection, the Political combat between the Pot and the Kettle.* New York: T. A. Hebbons, Publisher, 1928. One of the few books written by someone central to the Populist movement to critically examine what went wrong. Manning, one of the most racially liberal of all Populist spokespersons, understood that as long as the ruling Democratic elite continued to raise the race issue in elections, the common farmer and laborer would never unite. The Republicans and Populists must also be faulted for not supporting black civil (especially electoral) rights consistently throughout the South. Excellent source for firsthand information on role of blacks in the People's party.

C186. _____. *From Five to Twenty-Five: His Early Life as Recalled by Joseph Columbus Manning* . New York: T.A. Hebbons Company, 1929. Manning's autobiography is important for understanding how his racial tolerance developed in the Deep South of the post-Reconstruction era. This volume takes Manning's career from his days as a traveling bookseller in Texas during the rise of the Farmers' Alliance through the heyday of Populism in Alabama.

C187. _____. *Letting the South Alone: Class Government That Defrauds White and Blacks* (n.p., 1903). Fifteen page pamphlet mentioned by Rogers and Shofner (**D346**) continues Manning's central argument that it is the governments of the Southern states which are keeping the elite class in power and using the race issue as a red herring for keeping the agrarian class from gaining control.

C188. Marshall, Ray, and Lamond Godwin. *Cooperatives and Rural Poverty in the South*. Baltimore: Johns Hopkins Press, 1971. Brief but useful monograph of black "poor people's" cooperative in the rural South. The authors note the beginnings of the cooperative movement with the Farmers' Alliance and its connections with the CFA. The cooperatives established by the Alliance and other groups were short-lived, however, and eventually failed.

C189. Martin, Roscoe C. *The People's Party in Texas: A Study in Third Party Politics (University of Texas Bulletin No. 3308)*. Austin, TX: University of Texas Press, 1933. The standard general history of the People's Party in the state of Texas. John B. Rayner is mentioned repeatedly as a major black Populist whose efforts, though valiant, were often in vain. The two biggest problems facing Populist success with Texas blacks were white unity against Republicans and blacks in counties with large black populations, and "the simple truth was that the negro vote was purchaseable." A number of charts and graphs outline the rise and fall of Populist voting strength among specific populations, including blacks and immigrants.

C190. McKenna, George. *American Populism*. New York: Putnam, 1974. Reprints excerpts from "The People's Party Platform of 1892," Weaver's *A Call to Action* (1892), and Lloyd's *Wealth Against Commonwealth* (1894), with brief commentary.

C191. McKinney, Gordon B. *Southern Mountain Republicans, 1865-1900: Politics and the Appalachian Community*. Chapel Hill, NC: University of North Carolina Press, 1978. Focuses on the regions including North Carolina, Virginia, West Virginia, and Tennessee. After Reconstruction, black leaders demanded a more prominent part in Republican Party politics, including nomination for public office. The rise of the Populists forced Appalachian Democrats to re-examine their election laws, and consequently they forced through a variety of measures which reduced the black vote in the region.

C192. McLaurin, Melton Alonza. *The Knights of Labor in the South*. Westport, CT: Greenwood Press, 1978. Excellent study of the labor movement in the South, with one chapter devoted exclusively to the Knights of Labor and Southern blacks. McLaurin suggests that the racial views of the national and regional Knights leaders were far advanced over those of the rank and file membership, and the difference was in part the cause for the collapse of the movement in the region.

C193. _____. *Paternalism and Protest: Southern Cotton Mill Workers and Organized Labor, 1875-1905.* Westport, CT: Greenwood Press, 1971. Although McLaurin focuses on the souther cotton mill industry during the period, he also addresses at length the relationship between black Southern labor, the Knights of Labor's efforts to organize black workers, and the Farmers' Alliance's platforms on industrial workers. The efforts of black workers to enter the mills, and white threats against the move, are intertwined.

C194. McMath, Robert C., Jr. *American Populism: a Social History, 1877-1898.* New York: Farrar, Straus, and Giroux, 1993. As one of the modern authorities on the Populist movement, McMath is not only an excellent, extremely readable starting point for all researchers but also ideal for understanding the role of blacks in the movement. McMath's is probably the best summation of the true Populist milieu in the South: ". . . for a brief moment the People's Party, made up of various strands from the region's social fabric, included threads of a quarter-century-old biracial tradition and a new and fragile multi-hued skein, but it also included older and uglier strands woven tightly into the life of the region and the nation."

C195. _____. *Populist Vanguard: a History of the Southern Farmers' Alliance.* Chapel Hill: University of North Carolina Press, 1975. One of the best modern treatments of all aspects of the Southern Farmers' Alliance. McMath notes the origins of the CFA and efforts to align black and white voters, with little success. Black Alliancemen mistrusted their white counterparts, fearing that the Southern Alliance would focus on the needs of white farmers and leave blacks worse off than before. Includes an interesting chart comparing Alliance and Grange membership by state.

C196. McMillan, Malcolm Cook. *Constitutional Development in Alabama, 1798-1901: a Study in Politics, the Negro, and Sectionalism (James Sprunt Studies in History and Political Science, Volume 37).* Chapel Hill, NC: University of North Carolina Press, 1955. Detailed study of the constitutional suffrage debates in Alabama, particularly in the post-Reconstruction era. McMillan notes that voters in the Black Belt generally voted against Populist candidates, and that it was the massive fraud during these elections that triggered the move toward removal of the franchise. Excellent source for statistics on pre- and post-Populist black political activity in the state.

C197. Meier, August. *Negro Thought in America, 1880-1915: Racial Ideologies in the Age of Booker T. Washington.* Ann Arbor, MI: University of Michigan Press, 1966. Extremely useful study of protest and black accommodationist thought in the late nineteenth century, with an emphasis on the contrary beliefs of Washington and Du Bois. The CFA is mentioned as part of the movement towards economic solidarity among the laboring classes rather than within the races. Meier also notes the influence of the writings of Henry George on a small group of black intellectuals, including T. Thomas Fortune, D. A. Stryker, and T. McCants Stewart. However, Fortune also by decades end veered away from the radicalism of the Farmers' Alliance and into a more mainstream economic approach.

C198. _____, and Elliot Rudwick. *From Plantation to Ghetto: an Interpretive History of American Negroes*. New York: Hill and Wang, 1966. Mentions the CFA as part of the agrarian protest movement of the 1890s which coincided with the wave of disfranchisement legislation. The authors raise a number of provocative questions concerning the CFA: under what circumstances did blacks join and to what extent was participation encouraged (or demanded) by white employers who were Southern Alliance members? Why did the CFA collapse so quickly after the aborted Cotton Pickers' Strike? To what extent did members share in a conscious feeling of class solidarity against the Redeemers and the capitalists? How were Alliancemen and Populists lead so easily into virulent anti-black sentiment?

C199. *Memorial Record of Alabama, volume 2*. Madison, WI: Brant and Fuller, 1893. Includes brief biographical sketch of Augustus Parker Longshore, Shelby County, Alabama attorney and state legislator who was a strong and vocal supporter of full black participation in the state's Populist movement. One of the few sources of information on him.

C200. Miller, Edward A., Jr. *Gullah Statesman: Robert Smalls from Slavery to Congress, 1839-1915*. Columbia, SC: University of South Carolina Press, 1995. Miller suggests that the story of black South Carolina congressman Robert Smalls could have been titled "The Rise and Fall of the Republican Party in South Carolina." With Tillman virtually eliminating the Populists from consideration in that state, Smalls and others fought for black civil rights and against disfranchisement by forming an independent coalition, to little avail.

C201. Miller, Worth Robert. *Oklahoma Populism: A History of the People's Party in the Oklahoma Territory*. Norman, OK: University of Oklahoma Press, 1987. The best study of populism in the Oklahoma Territory. In the 1894 elections, the Populists nominated black legislator Green I. Currin for a House seat and also supported black Independent Republican C. H. Tandy for a House seat. The Populists failed to carry areas where blacks were most numerous. Miller lists party choice by race for each election.

C202. Mitchell, Theodore R. *Political Education in the Southern Farmers' Alliance, 1887-1900*. Madison, WI: University of Wisconsin Press, 1987. Alliance leaders understood the importance of education for politicizing the agrarian class; education was the key to equalization of wealth and improvement of the farmers' status overall. The Colored Farmers' Alliance took education seriously, perhaps more seriously than their white counterparts wanted, claims Mitchell. The interests of the two groups were occasionally in opposition, as can be witnessed by the abortive Cotton Pickers' Strike of 1891. However, the Alliance left a legacy of support for public schooling for both races that was picked up by later Progressives.

C203. Moneyhon, Carl H. *Arkansas and the New South, 1874-1929*. Fayetteville, AR: University of Arkansas Press, 1997. Brief but useful resource for understanding the rise of rural black protest in Arkansas in the 1890s. Moneyhon notes the economic conditions which increased black farm tenancy and also pushed more white farms into tenancy arrangements. The 1891 Cotton Pickers' Strike is cited as one "fairly typical" example of the violence against rural blacks which pervaded the state, along with the rise of the Klan. The 1892 election also proved to be a turning point, with the overall black turnout reduced for the first time since enfranchisement.

C204. Moore, Albert Burton. *History of Alabama*. Tuscaloosa, AL: Alabama Book Store, 1951. Revised edition of his History of Alabama and Her People (1927) addresses at length the "Turbulent Nineties." Notes the powerful opposition to Kolb campaign by many of the state's newspapers, who used the threat of black domination to sway opinion. Despite the tenor of the campaign, it became apparent that people were interested in discussing "the live issues of the day" rather than the old shibboleths of "Reconstruction, Negro rule, and carpetbagism." The chapter on "Radicalism Versus Bourbonism" covers electoral reform in light of Populism.

C205. Morgan, W. Scott. *History of the Wheel and Alliance and the Impending Revolution*. Fort Scott, KS: J. H. Rice and Sons, 1889; rpt. New York, 1967. Highly detailed account of the Agricultural Wheel and Farmers' Alliance, with reprints of convention rules, by-laws, officers, organizational reports from individual state Wheels, etc. Also features a useful section on "portraits and biographies of prominent Wheelers." Notes that provisions were made to "organize the colored farmers into separate Wheels." Book 1 is of most interest, Book 2 focusing on fiscal problems and their remedies.

C206. Morris, Ollie. *Negro Progress Since Slavery*. Dallas, TX: [n.p.], 1940. Contains brief biographical sketch, with photo, of William M. "Gooseneck Bill" McDonald, black Texas anti-Populist leader. "For some 20 years Wm. M. McDonald conducted the colored Republican Party in Texas . . . ."

C207. Morrison, Joseph L. *Josephus Daniels Says...: An Editor's Political Odyssey from Bryan to Wilson to F.D.R., 1894-1913*. Chapel Hill, NC: University of North Carolina Press, 1962. Solid study of Daniels, one of the most influential opinion makers in North Carolina during the Populist era. Morrison covers at length the "Political Battles of the Nineties," noting that during the white supremacy campaign of the era, "the hapless Populists could not surmount the handicap of their irresolute stand on the Negro issue."

C208. Murphy, Edgar Gardner. *The Basis of Ascendancy.* New York: Longmans, Green, 1909. In one of the more popular works of Southern Liberalism in the immediate post-Populist era, Murphy argues for better understanding between the races, but assumed that as whites were the dominant race, they should exhibit a paternalist attitude towards the other races. However, Murphy denied universal manhood suffrage and the possibility of social equality for Southern blacks. His work was praised by Washington (*Independent*, 11/25/09) as giving both races the chance to share in the building of a New South.

C209. _____. *Problems of the Present South.* New York: Longmans, Green, 1904. Murphy was an Alabama clergyman whose main focus was the evils of child labor exploitation. He also believed, however, that the elimination of class distinctions within the races was essential for progress. On the other hand, although blacks deserved political rights, it wasn't beneficial for the races to unite in common cause. Division on racial grounds was preferable to class division. Like Cable, Murphy felt black education was essential, but he also believed that unfortunately most blacks were fit only for field work or unskilled labor.

C210. National Association for the Advancement of Colored People. *Thirty Years of Lynching in the United States, 1889-1910.* New York: NAACP, 1919; rpt. Arno Press, 1969. The NAACP's Anti-Lynching Committee surveyed the period and listed 3,224 persons, including approximately 2500 blacks, as having been lynched. One of the earliest studies of the phenomenon to cover the entire United States, and essential for basic statistics.

C211. National Farmers Alliance and Industrial Union. *Proceedings of the Annual Session of the Supreme Council of the National Farmers Alliance and Industrial Union, at Ocala, Florida, December 2-8, 1890.* Washington, DC: The National Economist Pub. Co., 1891. Reprints the "Communication from the Colored Farmers Alliance," recognizing the NFAIU's "fraternal greeting" and pledging "fullest co-operation and confederation in all essential things." One of the few mentions of the CFA to appear in a NFAIU document.

C212. National Farmers Alliance and Industrial Union. *Proceedings of the National Farmers' Alliance and Industrial Union, and the Colored Farmers' National Alliance and Co-operative Union, Representing 3,000,000 Farmers, at Ocala, Florida, December 2d and 8th, 1890 in reference to the Paddock Pure Food Bill and the Conger Lard Bill* (n.p., n.d.). The title is self-explanatory on this collection, which includes the "Memorial Adopted by the Colored Farmers'

National Alliance and Co-Operative Union, in convention assembled at Ocala, Florida" (the petition to the U.S. Senate and House against the Conger Bill) and two letters from CFA President J. S. Jackson on the bill posted in the *Congressional Record*, 6 December 1890. This last is the source for the "two million of colored farmers" membership figure.

C213. Nixon, Raymond B. *Henry W. Grady: Spokesman of the New South*. New York: Knopf, 1943. Standard biography of the Atlanta editor and spokesman for the New South movement. Notes the problems relating to Senator Felton, the Independent leader, in the election of 1882 and the threat of "Africanizing" the South through a combination of black voters and disaffected Democrats.

C214. Noblin, Stuart. *Leonidas LaFayette Polk: Agrarian Crusader*. Chapel Hill, NC: University of North Carolina Press, 1949. Standard biography of the agrarian leader. According to Noblin, Polk believed, at least at the end of Reconstruction, that there must be an impartial protection of the laws for blacks, if they were to learn that Southern whites were not their enemy. He praised the "Negro exodus" from the South, believing that exiting blacks would be replaced by white settlers. Noblin comments that the "exodusters" also condemned the Farmers' Alliance as "an oppressive institution to the colored laborer."

C215. Nordin, D. Sven. *Rich Harvest: A History of the Grange, 1867-1900*. Jackson, MS: University Press of Mississippi, 1974. Excellent history of the Grange mentions that "Negroes were the largest excluded group" from membership. The National Grange "generally ignored the problem of discrimination and refused to censure subordinate and state chapters which barred minorities on racial grounds." Southern Grangers as a result organized an allied black group, the "Council of Laborers."

C216. Northen, W. J. *The Negro at the South. Address by W. J. Northen (Ex-Governor of Georgia) Before the Congregational Club, Boston, Mass., May 22, 1899*. Atlanta: The Franklin Printing and Publishing Co., 1899. Reprinted in John David Smith, ed., *Disfranchisement Proposals and the Ku Klux Klan, volume nine: Solutions to the "Negro Problem," part one*. New York: Garland Pub., 1993. A former slaveholder and ex-governor of Georgia, Northen speaks of the absolute loyalty of Southern slaves who only developed a sense of self-interest during the Reconstruction Era. Blacks "vote against the white man, regardless of what he may have done to protect and advance them. They have been so instructed to use their ballot." Northen further decries that the Southern black is "a Republican, an Independent, or a what-not, just so he may oppose and fight against anything he believes the white man wants." On the problem of lynching, Northen cites his record as governor in opposing mob law, but he also blames the Northern press for its incendiary and malicious coverage of the problem in the South. If left alone, the South will solve its own problems.

C217. Nugent, Catharine, ed. *Life Work of Thomas L. Nugent*. Chicago: Laird and Lee, 1896. Loving collection of tributes and sketches, along with speeches and public communications, collected by Nugent's wife. As Populist candidate for Governor of Texas in 1892, Nugent played a leading role in that party's statewide efforts. References to blacks are scattered throughout, which may in part illuminate Nugent's character. One anecdote in particular has him state that former slaves "ought to have been paid at least enough to start them in life."

C218. Ogden, Frederic D. *The Poll Tax in the South*. Tuscaloosa, AL: University of Alabama Press, 1958. Ogden lays the blame squarely at the feet of the Populists: "The rise of the Populist party is another important reason why the Southern movement for legalized disfranchisement occurred at this time." With blacks as the balance of power between Southern Democrats and Populists, nothing prevented either party from soliciting their votes through illegal means. The poll tax became one means used throughout the region, to varying degrees, to keep blacks and some whites away from the polls.

C219. Olsen, Otto H. *The Carpetbagger's Crusade: A Life of Albion Winegar Tourgee*. Baltimore: Johns Hopkins Press, 1965. As one of the South's most outspoken racial liberals, Tourgee's opinions were reprinted throughout the country, in both the black and white press. Although there is little here on Populism, Tourgee's repeated calls during the period for biracial cooperation and black activism must be noted. He did not counsel a policy of black violence against whites to gain civil and political rights, but he foresaw that violence might occur and urged black self-defense. Tourgee was also strongly opposed to any accommodationism and caution on the part of black leaders.

C220. _____, ed. *The Negro Question: From Slavery to Caste, 1863-1910*. New York: Pitman Publishing Corporation, 1971. Excellent collection of reprint articles by many of the major figures of the day, including Cable's "Freedman's Case in Equity," Tourgee's "Our Semi-Citizens," Blair's speech on his education bill, Watson's "The Negro Question in the South," Washington's "The Case of the Negro," and Du Bois' "Of Mr. Booker T. Washington and Others."

C221. Otken, Charles H. *The Ills of the South; or, Related Causes Hostile to the General Prosperity of the Southern People*. New York: G. P. Putnam and Sons, 1894. An interesting contemporary survey of "the ills of the South" with special attention to the black agrarian population. Otken draws on statistics to prove his contention that, although a few blacks have show significant progress, the grand majority are on a downward slope. Black farm owners and laborers are rarely productive, based on 1876 figures. The solution, according to Otken, is African colonization and separation of the races.

C222. Painter, Nell Irvin. *Exodusters: Black Migration to Kansas After Reconstruction*. New York: Knopf, 1977. The best single book on the Exoduster movement of the late 1870s, when large numbers of blacks migrated from the Deep South to Kansas.   Useful for understanding the relative strength of Kansas blacks during the Populist era.

C223. Palmer, Bruce. *"Man Over Money": the Southern Populist Critique of American Capitalism.* Chapel Hill, NC: University of North Carolina Press, 1980. Chapter Five, "Blacks as a White Problem," is particularly important, as Palmer argues that the Populists were neither color blind nor typical Southern racists. Instead, their racial attitudes were basically indistiguishable from those of the average white Southerner, although some such as Tom Watson stand out as moving against the tide and offering limited improvement to blacks which could not be classed as merely expedient.

C224. Peffer, William A. *Populism: Its Rise and Fall.* Edited and with an introduction by Peter H. Argersinger. Lawrence, KS: University Press of Kansas, 1992. Peffer, a racial liberal, claims that the Farmers' Alliance granted permission "to colored people to form alliances of their own and a few were organized; they conferred with their white brethren, but they had no influence, and it was not intended that they should have." Argersinger's introduction and notes are illuminating and informative.

C225.   Penn, Irvine Garland.   *The Afro-American Press, and Its Editors.* Springfield, MA: Wiley and Co., 1891. Includes a brief biography and photo of C. H. J. Taylor, editor of *The American Citizen, The Public Educator,* and *The World,* Minister Resident and Consul General to the Republic of Liberia, and Populist candidate for the Kansas state legislature in 1892.

C226. _____. *Souvenir and Official Program: The Negro Young Peoples' Christian and Educational Congress.* Washington, DC: [n.p.], 1906. Includes a brief biographical sketch and photograph of the Rev. H. Sebastian Doyle (also listed as Henry S. Doyle in some sources), Georgia black Populist leader.

C227. Perman, Michael. *The Road to Redemption: Southern Politics, 1869-1879.* Chapel Hill, NC: University of North Carolina Press, 1984. Perman argues that Reconstruction, rather than being "a discrete event cut out of the normal flow of the region's political development," was an episode in Southern political history and must be treated not as an outside force that came and went, but as a step along the way. The author examines Reconstruction not in terms of how it failed, but instead on how it worked. Third party movements, including the Grange, and their relations to the growing black political constituency are also discussed.

C228. _____. *Struggle for Mastery: Disfranchisement in the South, 1888-1908.* Chapel Hill, NC: University of North Carolina Press, 2001. The Populist movement was but one factor in the growth of Southern disfranchisement in the

1890s. As the region's farmers assumed a political form as the People's party, the challenge to Democratic control of the South became a real threat. However, Perman argues that the "pressure for disfranchisement arose from the existence of an African American constituency that could never be won over by the Democrats but would always be available to a rival party, whether Republican, Populist, or independent." It is wrong to claim that loss of voting rights throughout the South was a direct result of blacks joining the Populist ranks, although locally the argument could be made.

C229. Phelan, Craig. *Grand Master Workman: Terence Powderly and the Knights of Labor.* Westport, CT: Greenwood Press, 2000. Phelan argues that Powderly, "the first American working-class hero of national stature," possessed the makings of a great leader. Powderly was also a strong advocate for the rights of black workers, although in the South he favored the politically expedient move of forming separate black and white locals.

C230. Pitre, Merline. *Through Many Dangers, Toils and Snares: Black Leadership in Texas, 1870-1890.* 2nd ed. Austin, TX: Eakin Press, 1997. This excellent study of black Texas legislators in the post-Reconstruction era is an essential resource for Populist studies in that state. Of particular interest are Alexander Asberry, who served in the 1889 session, and Robert L. Smith, who served in both the 1895 and 1897 legislatures. Chapter Seven, "Fusion or Fission," covers the Greenback and Populist years in detail, especially the roles of Norris Wright Cuney and John Rayner.

C231. Pollack, Norman, ed. *The Populist Mind.* New York: Bobbs-Merrill Company, 1967. Excellent, inexpensive collection of primary documents on the movement, with a number specifically addressing blacks and Populism. The collection features a number of speeches and writings by Tom Watson, including his "The Negro Question in the South" (**D425**) and "The Cause of Both," excerpts from the *Wool Hat* and *People's Weekly Tribune*, and selections from Donnelly's novels.

C232. Powderly, Terence V. *Thirty Years of Labor, 1859 to 1889. In which the history of the attempts to form organizations of workingmen for the discussion of political, social, and economic questions is traced.* Columbus, OH: Excelsior Publishing House, 1889. Readers should note Terence Powderly's account of the Knights' October 1886 convention in Richmond, Virginia, at which a black New York City representative agreed to introduce Powderly at the podium. Powderly claims that "the sole object in selecting a colored man to introduce me was to encourage and help to uplift his race from a bondage worse than which held him in chains twenty-five years ago--viz., mental slavery." Powderly also states, however, that he has "no wish to interfere with the social relations which exist between the races of the South," but he recognizes that both races must be educated. Although political equality must not be trampled on, social equality was another thing altogether.

C233. Prather, H. Leon. *We Have Taken a City: Wilmington Racial Massacre and Coup of 1898*. Rutherford, NJ: Fairleigh Dickinson University Press, 1984. Useful study of the Wilmington Massacre of 1898, which sealed the fate of Populism and black suffrage in North Carolina until the modern era. Prather examines city council records, local newspapers, and other primary sources to argue that the state white supremacy campaign manipulated by the Democrats succeeded in removing from office a duly-elected body of officials.

C234. Price, H. D. *The Negro and Southern Politics: a Chapter of Florida History*. New York: New York University Press, 1957. Even with a significant black population in the 1890s, there has been little research done on the Populist movement in Florida. Price notes that the combined poll tax and multiple-ballot-box law resulted in a "spectacular drop" in total votes starting in 1892, most of it attributable to the loss of black voters. A large increase in the Democratic vote count is also at least partially attributable to state Populist activity.

C235. *The Proposed Suffrage Amendment. The Platform and Resolutions of the People's Party*. Sixteen page pamphlet published by the People's Party of North Carolina, c1900, on the suffrage amendment submitted to the 1899 state legislature. "The People's Party is and has always been more distinctly than any other party in North Carolina a white man's party, and is more anxious than any other party to solve the race problem . . . ." Also calls for the disqualification from elected office "All negroes and all persons of negro descent to the third generation inclusive."   Available online at the Documenting the American South project, http://docsouth.unc.edu/nc/politics.html

C236. Quarles, Benjamin. *The Negro in the Making of America*. 3rd ed. New York: Macmillan, 1987. Short section on Populism in what is still one of the best general histories of Black America available. Quarles argues that more than any other factor, Populism disfranshised Southern blacks. Although agrarian leaders such as Tom Watson courted black voters, the cry of "black domination" rose again, with the business and planter communities attempting to sway white and even black voters into their camps. Quarles also briefly discusses other early national black organizations, including the National Negro Labor Union and the National Labor Convention of Colored Men, although neither was "Populist" per se.

C237. Rabinowitz, Howard N. *The First New South, 1865-1920*. Arlington Heights, IL: Harlan Davidson, 1992. Rabinowitz suggests that Southern blacks had three strategies for survival when faced with ever-present racial hostility: leave the U.S. altogether, as suggested by Delaney and others; internal colonization, along the lines of 'Pap' Singleton; and remaining but trying to change the system, joining such groups as the Knights of Labor or the Populists.

C238. Rachleff, Peter J. *Black Labor in the South: Richmond, Virginia, 1865-1890*. Philadelphia: Temple University Press, 1984. Fine study of the black worker as it relates to one of the South's oldest cities. Rachleff defines the rise and fall of the reform movement, from its earliest days following the Civil War through the foundation of the Colored National Labor Union, the Readjuster movement, the entrance of the Knights of Labor into local politics, and the Virginia Colored Farmers' Alliance. Rachleff also highlights a wide variety of secret societies, both religious and secular.

C239. Raines, C. W., ed. *Speeches and State Papers of James Stephen Hogg, ex-Governor of Texas, with a Sketch of His Life*. Austin, TX: The State Printing Company, 1905. Collection of the writings of Texas progressive Democratic governor James Stephen Hogg. No index or table of contents, but worth sifting through for his speeches and writings attacking the Populist stance on black rights in the state. See also Cotner (**C71**) for standard collection of Hogg's speeches.

C240. Range, Willard. *A Century of Georgia Agriculture, 1850-1950*. Athens, GA: University of Georgia Press, 1954. Range devotes a chapter to the "Agrarian Revolt" of the post-Reconstruction years, starting with the Grange through the rise and fall of the Populist movement. Although the CFA was little heard from, eight black sub-Alliances were known to exist in Screven County, Georgia alone. The Populist Party gave rise to some hope, but it faded in part due to the mistrust of white farmers aligning with blacks.

C241. Raper, Arthur F. *Tenants of the Almighty*. New York: Macmillan, 1943. This fascinating sociological study of Greene County, Georgia, offers a brief vignette of a speech Tom Watson gave in Greensboro in 1894. Watson appealed to blacks in the crowd "'to investigate as best they might public questions'. He suggested that they vote with the Democrats or with the Republicans if they wished, but to be sure to vote with the Populists if they found they were right. In any event, the Negroes' votes ought to be counted, Watson said. He stated that he did want the Negro vote, and he was going to get it, if he could do so by honorable means."

C242. Redkey, Edwin S. *Black Exodus: Black Nationalist and Back-to-Africa Movements, 1890-1910*. New Haven, CT: Yale University Press, 1969. As the Populist movement failed to achieve its hoped-for successes throughout the South and blacks became more disillusioned with that and other local movements, a number of Back-to-Africa movements took shape. Redkey examines in particular the American Colonization Society and the International Migration Society.

C243. Reynolds, George M. *Machine Politics in New Orleans, 1877-1926.*
New York: Columbia University Press, 1936. The division between Louisiana's white voters which had been growing since the end of the Civil War was
greatly accentuated by the Populist movement. When the Populists fused with
the Republicans, blacks were brought back into the political arena, as laws designed to disfranchise them were temporarily swept aside to gain their votes.
Reynolds also notes that the reason black disfranchisement succeeded while
efforts to destroy machine politics in New Orleans failed is because there was a
desire on the part of all factions to eliminate the black voter.

C244. Rice, Lawrence D. *The Negro in Texas, 1874-1900.* Baton Rouge, LA:
Louisiana State University Press, 1971. Good overview of blacks in the agrarian
movement in Texas, from the founding of the CFA through the fall of Populism.
Rice devotes an entire chapter to "Black Populism," noting that as early as 1888
the Alliance had nominated a slate of candidates in Colorado County that included blacks for county clerk and public weigher. The pattern found in that
county of forming biracial party structures with equal numbers of blacks and
whites "seems to have been the general plan followed in most counties."

C245. Richardson, Heather Cox. *The Death of Reconstruction: Race, Labor,
and Politics in the Post-Civil War North, 1865-1901.* Cambridge, MA: Harvard
University Press, 2001. Brief mention of black involvement in the Southern
Populist movement. 1892 election rhetoric confirmed that some "disaffected
black workers who rejected the core American value of working for success
sought to change the nature of American government." The fact that some black
Southerners had joined the Populist movement "cemented the conviction" that
they wanted an activist government operating on behalf of "the people."

C246. Riley, Jerome R. *The Philosophy of Negro Suffrage.* Hartford, CT:
Jerome R. Riley, 1897. One of the most accommodationist works anyone is
likely to come across. Riley, a northern black medical doctor and president of
the John M. Palmer Democratic Club of the District of Columbia, argues that
Southern blacks should accept second class status. Southern disfranchisement is
the fault of ignorant local blacks, and especially black leaders who have lead
them astray. Riley also takes to task Ida B. Wells and other anti-lynching cru-
saders for their "un-called for" criticisms, which will only stir up racial antago-
nisms. He does, however, strongly support the Atlanta Exposition. Cited by
Calista (**D66**).

C247. Rippy, J. Fred, ed. *F. M. Simmons, Statesman of the New South: Mem-
oirs and Addresses.* Durham, NC: Duke University Press, 1936. Furnifold M.
Simmons was one of the most powerful voices in North Carolina during the
Populist era. Rippy reprints two of Simmons' campaign speeches of the era, "To
the People of North Carolina" (6 October 1892) and "To the Voters of North
Carolina" (3 November 1898), in which he warns against third-party coalitions

and the rise of black political power in the state. His latter speeches are also worth examining, especially an address from 1928 that notes the rise and fall of the agrarian movement in North Carolina.

C248. Robinson, Cedric J. *Black Movements in America*. New York: Rout- ledge, 1997. Briefly considers black agrarians and populism as part of the con- tinuum of black resistance movements in the U.S. from the early days to the present. Robinson sometime has his facts askew (e.g., the Farmers' Alliance "sprung up" in the western part of Texas) and claims that the mission of the Al- liance was compromised by racism and "muted by the ambitions of powerful pro-farmer dissidents," including Polk, Watson, and Kolb (mispelled "Kolk" in the text). The CFA finally succumbed to the forces that undermined the Farm- ers' Alliance and People's party, including racism and the failure of the organi- zations to protect the black franchise.

C249. Rochester, Anna. *The Populist Movement in the United States. The Rise, Growth, and Decline of the People's Party--a Social and Economic Interpreta- tion.* New York: International Publishers, 1943. Marxist interpretation of Populism, written during the height of World War II in support of the laborers and farmers who "won our victory in the war for independence." Includes a short chapter on "Southern Populists and the Negroes," in which Rochester ar- gues that the Populists only had two choices: either try to win the black vote or work to eliminate it altogether. Everywhere but South Carolina the Populists chose the first route. However, white Southern Populists "seem to have had little understanding of racial discrimination as essentially a crime against the democratic principles which they professed."

C250. Rogers, William Warren. *The One-Gallused Rebellion: Agrarianism in Alabama, 1865-1896*. Baton Rouge, LA: Louisiana State University Press, 1970. One of the most cited monographs in contemporary Populism studies. Rogers claims agrarians and their allies tried to include blacks in the Populist movement, and although black voters were courted "for reasons obviously po- litical, sincere efforts to effect permanent benefits for Negroes were significant features of the agrarian revolt." He further agrees which Abramowitz that the collapse of the Populist movement meant "political oblivion" for Southern blacks, and supports other theorists who believe the black presence in the Peo- ple's party prevented the Populists from expressing "the true extent of the farmer's dissatisfaction with the Democratic Party."

C251. _____, and Robert David Ward. *Labor Revolt in Alabama: the Great Strike of 1894*. University, AL: University of Alabama Press, 1965. The story of the coal miners' strike in Alabama in 1894, which coincided with the rise and fall of Kolb's gubernatorial campaign. The black vote was of prime considera- tion to all parties, considering the factionalized race. As mine owners hired black scab laborers to keep the mines open, strikers resorted to violence against them, which was in turn "presented as evidence of the anti-Negro sentiment of the Jeffersonians."

C252. _____, Robert David Ward, Leah Rawls Atkins, and Wayne Flint. *Alabama: the History of a Deep South State*. Tuscaloosa, AL: University of Alabama Press, 1994. Of most interest for the current study are the central chapters written by Rogers and Ward, especially Chapter 18, "New Winds and Old Voices," and Chapter 19, "The Defeat of Reform." In the "strange amalgam" of farmers, miners, federal officeholders, and blacks, it was understood by both fusionists and their opponents that blacks were a crucial force. The problems of voter fraud in the Black Belt are recounted. The Populists wanted political power but did not seek cataclysmic change, especially in race matters.

C253. Roper, John Herbert. *C. Vann Woodward, Southerner*. Athens, GA: University of Georgia Press, 1987. Excellent "extended essay" of the Southern historian as he struggles to understand his section of the country, as seen through the development of his "authorial activism." Roper examines each of his major works chronologically, with a good deal of attention paid to *The Strange Career of Jim Crow, Origins of the New South, Reunion and Reaction*, and the critics of those works.

C254. Rosenstone, Steven J., Roy L. Behr, and Edward H. Lazarus. *Third Parties in America: Citizen Response to Major Party Failure*. 2nd ed., revised and expanded. Princeton, NJ: Princeton University Press, 1996. In the South, the Farmers' Alliance tried to co-opt the Democratic Party machinery, which would prevent blacks from coming to power from a fractured white vote. Essentially an overview history of the People's Party, Rosenstone is primarily useful here as a quick guide for placing populism in context with other political movements affecting blacks for prior to and following the 1890s.

C255. Rozwenc, Edwin C., and John C. Malton, ed. *Myth and Reality in the Populist Revolt*. Boston: D. C. Heath and Company, 1967. Collection of basic texts of the Populist movement by a variety of writers, including Donnelly, Mary Lease, White's "What's the Matter with Kansas?" etc. Also includes the preamble and proposals from the Omaha Platform and two "attacks on the platform from contemporary newspapers.

C256. Saloutos, Theodore. *Farmer Movements in the South, 1865-1933 University of California Publications in History, Volume 64)*. Berkeley, CA: University of California Press, 1960. The activities of the various agrarian reform movements of the South are a history of trial and error compounded by inexperienced leadership, a lack of foresight, and lack of funding. Saloutos notes the early difficulties of trying to organize workers not long out of slavery, and the organizational talents of the Cooperative Workers of America in South Carolina are discussed. Saloutos remains a major post-Hicks resource for all aspects of the movement, particularly for his liberal usage of statistics from the *Western Rural and American Stockman* newspaper.

C257. ____, ed. *Populism: Reaction or Reform?* New York: Holt, Rinehart and Winston, 1968. Brief collection of essays by a variety of scholars of Populism, including Woodward, "The Populist Heritage and the Individual"; Martin, "The Texas Experience"; Abramowitz, "The Negro and the Populist Movement"; Walter T.K. Nugent, "The Tolerant Populists"; and Saloutos, "The Professors and the Populists."

C258. Sanders, Elizabeth. *Roots of Reform: Farmers, Workers, and the American State, 1877-1917.* Chicago: University of Chicago Press, 1999. Notes the existence of the CFA as an "inevitable" offshoot of the Farmers' Alliance, due in part to Southern racist sentiment, divergent party attachments, and "blacks' considerable skepticism of white farmers." Sanders also argues that it was the political activists of the Alliance who reached out to black farmers and adopted the grievances of the Knights of Labor. See also **D223**.

C259. Schurz, Carl. *The New South.* New York: The American News Company, 1885. Pamphlet recounts Schurz' thoughts on the New South after his extensive travels in that part of the country. Schurz argues that "the employer class" will control Southern black votes until the voter is sufficiently educated and independent to think and act for himself. Significant document outlines the problems that would lead to the Populist revolt.

C260. Schwartz, Michael. *Radical Protest and Social Structure: The Southern Farmers' Alliance and Cotton Tenancy, 1880-1890.* New York: Academic Press, 1976. Schwartz argues that the Southern Farmers' Alliance's protests against the tenant farming system can best be studied within the framework of movement theory. The year 1890 was in many ways a turning point in Southern history, not only because it marked the zenith of the SFA but also the beginning of racial hatred to an unprecedented degree. Simultaneously, the traditional landlord-industrialist conflicts of the previous decades all but disappeared, and blacks were virtually excluded from the growing industrialization of the region.

C261. Scull, William Ellis, ed. *Great Leaders and National Issues of 1896. Containing the Lives of the Republican and Democratic Candidates for President and Vice-President, Biographical Sketches of the Leading Men of All Parties, the Story of Famous Campaigns of the Past, History of Political Parties, Lives of Our Former Presidents, Together with a full Presentation of the Live Questions of the Day, including the Tariff, Gold and Silver, Cuba, Armenia, Venezuela, Monroe Doctrine, etc.* [n.p.]: Non-Partisan Bureau of Political Information, 1896. Includes chapters on "The National Convention of the People's Party," "The Platform of the People's Party," and "Thomas Edward Watson." Good details on convention mayhem.

C262. Shadgett, Olive Hall. *The Republican Party in Georgia: From Recon-struction Through 1900*. Athens, GA: University of Georgia Press, 1964. Dis-cusses fusion efforts between Georgia Republicans and Populists. In the 1892 gubernatorial campaign, Governor Northen had the approval of many blacks because of his support for black education and his anti-lynching stand. The Populists welcomed blacks, especially Alliancemen, to their rallies, but the Buck circular threw the campaign into discord.

C263. Shannon, Fred A. *American Farmers' Movements*. Princeton, NJ: D. Van Nostrand, 1957. Short account of the agrarian movements of the period, including the Alliance and Populists. Shannon notes how Watson "fairly grov-eled before the black man to gain his support" and how Southern Democrats simultaneously used huge blocks of black voters to maintain the status quo. Shannon also reprints a number of original documents particularly related to the various conventions.

C264. _____. *The Farmers' Last Frontier: Agriculture, 1860-1900*. New York: Farrar and Rinehart, 1945. Popular account of agricultural in the latter half of the nineteenth century, with attention to the "agrarian uprising" and "farmers' cooperative movements." Shannon briefly notes that "both Democrats and Populists sought colored support."

C265. Shapiro, Herbert. *White Violence and Black Response: From Recon-struction to Montgomery*. Amherst, MA: University of Massachusetts Press, 1988. Briefly notes that the agrarian struggles of the 1890s were accompanied by widespread violence, with racists employing terror tactics to retain power for the privileged few. Shapiro quotes the *Houston Daily News* claim in 1896 that 25,000 Texas blacks supported the People's party, but that such groups as the White Man's Union sprung up to destroy the biracial Populist coalition.

C266. Shapiro, Karin A. *A New South Rebellion: The Battle Against Convict Labor in the Tennessee Coalfields, 1871-1896*. Chapel Hill, NC: University of North Carolina Press, 1998. Alliance and Populist activity in Tennessee has been overshadowed by struggles in the Deep South, but Shapiro resurrects some important debates over the use of the convict lease system in that state during the rise of Populism. With the growth of unionism in the region, rebellion broke out amongst both black and white miners on wage issues. The Nashville Ameri-can even noted that the Briceville, TN miners' revolts of 1892 were prompting the state Colored Farmers' Alliance to contemplate militant action. An excellent work on the racial interweavings of the Knights of Labor, the Alliance, and state politics as relates to a single issue.

C267. Shaw, Barton C. *The Wool-Hat Boys: Georgia's Populist Party*. Baton Rouge, LA: Louisiana State University Press, 1984. The term "wool-hat boys" refers to the rural farmers of Georgia who often found themselves politically and economically in opposition to the ruling class in Atlanta—the "silk hat" crowd. The wool-hatters helped create the Georgia Populist Party in 1892, a faction of the larger Populist movement. Georgian Populism differs significantly from that of the rest of the South, in that it thrived in areas with a significant black lower and middle class and few new settlers, whereas traditionally the movement found its greatest support in areas with few blacks and many new settlers. Additionally, Georgian Populism usually triumphed where the Farmers' Alliance commanded only moderate support, and it failed where the Alliance was strong and had established co-operatives. Shaw contends that blacks gave populism little support, contrary to the opinion of Woodward. Of particular interest is Chapter V, "The Populists After Dark," which focuses on race relations within the Georgia movement.

C268. Sheldon, William DuBose. *Populism in the Old Dominion: Virginia Farm Politics, 1885-1900*. Princeton, NJ: Princeton University Press, 1935. Sheldon immediately discounts the role of the CFA in Virginia as an "aspect of minor significance." Membership allegedly stood at 5,000 members in fall 1890, with strength centered around Norfolk, although two years later party leaders spoke of a membership of 20,000 in forty-two counties. Sheldon also claims that Virginia blacks were "carefully regimented by Mahone, and such a potentially political organization was not encouraged by his party lieutenants, the colored preachers."

C269. Simkins, Francis Butler. *Pitchfork Ben Tillman: South Carolinian*. Baton Rouge, LA: Louisiana State University Press, 1944. Still one of the most comprehensive biographies of the South Carolina political boss. Tillman had such a strong hold over the state by the early 1890s that "he tied the hands of the Farmers' Alliance directors who were toying with Populism and prevented South Carolinians from voting for the Populist candidate," arguing that it was "simply infamous" for a true Tillmanite to violate pledges to the Democratic Party. Simkins also attributes South Carolina's low lynching rate with Tillman's strong law and order stance.

C270. _____. *The Tillman Movement in South Carolina*. Durham, SC: Duke University Press, 1926. Simkins argues that "it is hard to believe" that disfranchisement in South Carolina "has had a vital effect upon the political status of the Negro," since blacks were kept from the polls both before and after the new constitutional provisions.

C271. Skaggs, William H. *The Southern Oligarchy: An Appeal in Behalf of the Silent Masses of Our Country Against the Despotic Rule of the Few*. New York: The Devin-Adair Company, 1924. Skaggs, an Alabamian, writes "an authoritative and candid survey of the corrupt practices and criminal lawlessness of a provincial Oligarchy. . . ." The Populist movement gave Southerners their first chance since the Civil War to organize and fight the elite. Skaggs argues that during the period "there were very few Negroes whom the leaders of the Oligarchy could buy at any price." Occasionally powerful class diatribe against the Southern elite with a strong appeal for racial cooperation.

C272. Smith, J. Clay, Jr., ed. *Rebels in Law: Voices in History of Black Women Lawyers.* Ann Arbor, MI: University of Michigan Press, 1998. Includes a reprint of an interview given to the *Topeka Daily Capital* on September 15, 1897 by Lutie A. Lytle, the former Topeka Populist who went on to become the first African-American woman to teach law in the United States. Smith notes that this interview records "the earliest known recorded words by a black woman lawyer." When asked about her politics, Lytle declined to commit to any party. Smith also includes a picture of Lytle from her teaching days.

C273. Sosna, Morton. *In Search of the Silent South: Southern Liberals and the Race Issue.* New York: Columbia University Press, 1977. Places the Populists and late nineteenth century Southern liberals in the context of a long Southern tradition. The third party struggles of the period added a new dimension of class alliance along racial lines to Southern liberalism, which Cable, Atticus G. Haygood, and others had not addressed. Even after the collapse of the Populist movement and the rise of the "Dixie Demagogue," biracial alliances continued.

C274. Spero, Sterling D., and Abram L. Harris. *The Black Worker: The Negro and the Labor Movement.* New York: Columbia University Press, 1931. Good early analysis of the relationship between black workers and the labor movement. Probably most useful for its numerous statistical charts, including black membership in national and international unions by trade. Reprints a letter from Powderly to *Public Opinion* (October-April 1886-87) on racial social equality.

C275. *State Executive Committee of the People's Party of North Carolina. People's Party Hand-Book of Facts. Campaign of 1898.* Raleigh, NC: Capital Printing Company, 1898. Guidebook for party members and others interested in the details of the party's campaign. Much of the material concerns Populist responses to Democratic accusations of "negro domination" and election fraud. Quite a bit of statistical data throughout, particularly on voting by county. Available online at the Documenting the American South project, http://docsouth.unc.edu/nc/politics.html

C276. Steelman, Lala Carr. *The North Carolina Farmers' Alliance: a Political History, 1887-1893 (East Carolina University Publications in History, Volume 6).* Greenville, NC: East Carolina University Publications, 1985. The best overall history of the Alliance in North Carolina covers the period from its inception to the birth of the People's party in 1893. The Alliance sought to convert blacks to the Democratic Party, and the CFA was particularly active in the "Black Second" district. Steelman does not devote much attention to black organizational efforts.

C277. Stiller, Richard. *Queen of Populists: the Story of Mary Elizabeth Lease.* New York: T.Y. Crowell, 1970. Breezy biography of Populist orator and suffragette Lease makes passing references to black Kansas Populist Benjamin Foster and his creation of the Negro Populist League. Notes Stiller, "What pleased black Kansans most was the fact that the Populists did not hesitate to run black men for office. And when the People's Party won they appointed black men to state and local jobs." Also mentions the violent Georgia elections of the early 1890s.

C278. Talmadge, John E. *Rebecca Latimer Felton: Nine Stormy Decades.* Athens, GA: University of Georgia Press, 1960. Biography of the Georgia woman who was at the center of it all, first as the wife of Congressman William H. Felton and later as a U.S. Senator in her own right. When her husband got caught up in Populist fervor, about all his wife could do for his campaign "was to keep him from collapsing." Her speeches, particularly her 1897 speech which equated blacks with wild beasts and called for lynching for a "proven" black rapist, illustrates in part the dualist mindset of some Southern reformers and progressives.

C279. Taylor, Charles H. J. *Whites and Blacks, or The Question Settled.* Atlanta: James P. Harrison and Co., 1889. One of the true clarion calls for black self-help in the late nineteenth century, written by editor and politician Taylor. The author called for blacks, especially in the South, to vote for their own self-interest, rather than the interest of a particular party or issue on the bidding of whites. Blacks must become self-reliant, he argued, and stop sending up "baby appeals as though they were never to grow to manhood . . . ."

C280. Thornbrough, Emma Lou. *T. Thomas Fortune: Militant Journalist.* Chicago: University of Chicago Press, 1972. Biography of the late nineteenth century black journalist who supported many black grassroots and other self-help organizations of the time. His great work, *Black and White* (1884), focuses on the combined issues of class and race in the South. Fortune argued that the issues were the same for both white and black farmers of the South, and that to unite in common cause was necessary for economic advancement.

C281. Thorpe, Earl E. *The Mind of the Negro: An Intellectual History of Afro-Americans.* Baton Rouge, LA: Ortlieb Press, 1961. Brief mention of the CFA as part of the agrarian movement of the late nineteenth century. The political fusion efforts between poor Southern blacks and whites resulted in "considerable democratic legislation in the South before it was destroyed. . . ." One of the main causes for the collapse of the biracial coalition was the immaturity of Southern poor white economic and social thought needed to effect a genuine and lasting alliance.

C282. Tindall, George Brown. *The Disruption of the Solid South (Mercer University Lamar Memorial Lectures, No. 14)*. Athens, GA: University of Georgia Press, 1972. Tindall, in this slim volume, points to the presidential campaign of Benjamin Harrison as a chance to coordinate Republican and Populist groups, but the Southern strategy failed, partly because of a growing doctrine of racial distinctions. The threat of Populism compelled the Democrats to tighten their control over the ballot, leading to disfranchisement.

C283. _____, ed. *A Populist Reader: Selections from the Works of American Populist Leaders*. New York: Harper Torchbooks, 1966. Good collection of works by leading Populists of the era, including N. B. Ashby on railroads, Peffer on farm mortgages, Weaver's "call to action," and Watson's "The Negro Question in the South" **(D425)**. Also includes the Subtreasury Plan, Ocala and Omaha Platforms, St. Louis Demands, and Lloyd's "The Populists at St. Louis" **(D251)**.

C284. _____. *South Carolina Negroes, 1877-1900*. Columbia, SC: University of South Carolina Press, 1952. Excellent study of black South Carolinians during the Populist era. Tindall notes the career of George Washington Murray, who was "closely associated with the Colored Farmers' Alliance." Also notes the spread of the CFA throughout the state during 1888-1889 "without molestation and with neutral and occasionally sympathetic reaction from the white farmers" who had joined the Southern Farmers' Alliance.

C285. Tolnay, Stewart Emory, and E. M. Beck. *A Festival of Violence: an Analysis of Southern Lynchings, 1882-1930*. Urbana, IL: University of Illinois Press, 1995. One of the seminal modern studies on lynching in the South during the Populist era. The authors specifically address the theoretical relationship between black lynching and Populism, using the presidential election of 1892 as a vehicle for testing the validity of the hypothesis. They find that although there appears to be some correlation between Republican/Populist strength and the intensity of lynchings within countries, the direction of association is opposite of that predicted by the political threat model. Counties with strong Republican or Populist localss actually offered greater protection from lynching to blacks.

C286. *Twenty-two Years' Work of Hampton Normal and Agricultural Institute*. Hampton, VA: Hampton School Press, c1891. Contains brief autobiographical sketch of alumnae George A. Gwaltney, Isle of Wight County (Virginia) delegate to the Virginia CFA convention, and brief item on Frank B. Ivy, a member of the VCFA board of directors.

C287. Unger, Irwin. *Populism: Nostalgic or Progressive?* Chicago: Rand McNally, 1964. Brief (sixty page) collection of writings on the Populist movement by a variety of contemporary and modern essayists, including Hicks, Hofstadter, Peffer, N. B. Ashby, and Donnelly.

C288. Union League Club of New York City. *Report of the Committee on political reform of the Union league club of the city of New York, dated April 9th, 1903.* New York: Union League Club, 1903. Report on suffrage restriction in the South, noted by Caffey, "Suffrage Limitations at the South" (**D65**).

C289. Uya, Okon Edet. *From Slavery to Public Service: Robert Smalls, 1839-1915.* New York: Oxford University Press, 1971. Brief discussion of black former South Carolina congressman Robert Smalls' roll in the anti-disfranchisement campaigns in that state in the early 1890s. Smalls eventually supported the Conservative-Independent coalition in opposition to Tillman.

C290. Van Noppen, Ina W., ed. *The South: A Documentary History.* Princeton, NJ: Van Nostrand, 1958. Most significant here is the "Farmers' Revolt," which includes brief excerpts from some of the basic documents of the period.

C291. Walton, Hanes, Jr. *Black Political Parties: an Historical and Political Analysis.* New York: Free Press, 1972. As Walton demonstrates, coalition politics are nothing new to black political life. Black third party involvement in the South started with the Populist party, which blacks saw as at least a temporary solution to some of their problems. But Walton also notes that the Populist threat lead in part to disfranchisement, despite some benefits (such as the creation of educational institutions) which came of it. Walton is most useful here for getting a historic sense of the modern black political struggle's lineage.

C292. _____. *Black Politics: a Theoretical and Structural Analysis.* New York: J. B. Lippincott, 1972. The Populists are one example of black third party involvement since the Civil War. Walton notes the problems at the St. Louis convention, and that blacks turned out in large numbers to hear candidate Weaver speak. Walton also names a few black Populists, including Roxborough, the Reverend I. P. Langlay from Arkansas, and Kansan Benjamin Foster.

C293. _____. *Black Republicans: the Politics of the Black and Tans.* Metuchen, NJ: Scarecrow Press, 1975. Walton's is one of the first monographs to systematically address the issue of the "Blacks and Tans" Republican biracial coalitions which arose in opposition to the Lily-White movements of the major political parties at the turn of the century. The author addresses the issue within each Southern state, noting especially when the groups were forced to react to the Populist challenge.

C294. Wardlaw, Ralph. *Negro Suffrage in Georgia, 1867-1930 (Phelps-Stokes Fellowship Studies, Number 11)* (Bulletin of the University of Georgia Volume 33, September 1932). The influence of the Populist party was perceptible but "evanescent," being finally swallowed up by the Democratic Party. "The fear of negro domination in politics, through the exercise of voting rights, was the main reason for this re-unification."

C295. Washington, Booker T., et al. *A New Negro for a New Century: an Accurate and Up-to-date Record of the Upward Struggles of the Negro Race.* Chicago, IL: American Publishing House, c1900. Contains photo of Kansas black Populist and future lawyer Lutie A. Lytle, one of the few black women identified in Populist studies.

C296. Watson, Thomas E. *The Life and Speeches of Thomas E. Watson*, 2nd ed. Thomson, GA: Jeffersonian Publishing Company, 1911. Excellent primary source for Watsoniana, as he details his experiences with the Alliance and People's party in a 1908 autobiographical sketch. Watson mentions the Doyle episode, and that sixty men armed with Winchesters came to their aid. Reprints significant speeches and articles about Watson, including J. T. Graves' "Sam Jones and Tom Watson" (*Atlanta Georgian*), W. Wellman's "Tom Watson" (*Review of Reviews*, 1904), the 1892 Sandersville debate between Watson and J. C. C. Black; the 4 July 1893 Douglasville speech (in which he negates social equality but supports political equality with blacks); and his 1904 speeches in Nashville and Newton (NC), which call for white supremacy.

C297. _____. *The People's Party Campaign Book. Not a Revolt; It Is a Revolution.* Washington, DC: National Watchman Publishing Co, 1892; rpt. Richard E. Rubinstein and Dan C. McCurry, ed., Ayer Publishing, 1975. A central document for all Populist research, reprinted in part in Pollack's *The Populist Mind* (**C231**). As this is a campaign book and meant to be used for outlining essential creeds, the prose is often bare and Watson's arguments simplistic.

C298. Weaver, James B. *A Call to Action. An Interpretation of the Great Uprising, Its Sources and Causes.* Des Moines, IA: Iowa Printing Co., 1892. A central document by one of the movement's prime figures. Weaver comments on many national issues, ranging from disposal of public lands to the Pinkertons, but race is not mentioned. See also **C283**.

C299. Webb, Samuel L. *Two-Party Politics in the One-Party South: Alabama's Hill Country, 1874-1920.* Tuscaloosa, AL: University of Alabama Press, 1997. Despite the title, Webb focuses on the three-party politics of Alabama's Hill Country, involving Republicans, Democrats, and at times the Populists. Shelby County Democrats claimed Populists were "Negro sympathizers," although that was only partially true. Joseph Manning, for example, recommended the Alabama state committee send a black delegate to the Populist convention in Omaha, and though another delegate feared that would label the party as "Negro lovers," Manning prevailed. Webb also highlights the role of Adolphus Parker Longshore, who continually (along with Manning) supported black involvement in the movement and urged blacks to vote for Populist candidates.

C300. Wetherington, Mark V. *The New South Comes to Wiregrass Georgia, 1860-1910.* Knoxville, TN: University of Tennessee Press, 1994. The Farmers'

Alliance and Populist party failed to attract much support in Georgia's piney woods region, partly because of Tom Watson's anti-lynching stand and his calls for unity between black and white Alliancemen. Wetherington stresses that the area was a developing frontier section where traditional social customs were strained by industrialization, and racial violence was on the rise.

C301. Williams, David A. *Bricks Without Straw: a Comprehensive History of African Americans in Texas*. Austin, TX: Eakin Press, 1997. Not as scholarly as one one like or hope, but a good overview of the Texas African American experience in the late nineteenth century. Williams profiles some of the major players important to the Populist revolt, including "Gooseneck Bill" McDonald and Norris Wright Cuney, although John B. Rayner is completely absent from these pages.

C302. Williams, T. Harry. *Romance and Realism in Southern Politics*. Baton Rouge, LA: Louisiana State University Press, 1966. Reprint of Williams' Eugenia Dorothy Blount Lamar Memorial Lectures from 1960, of which Lecture Three, "The Politics of Populism and Progressivism," is the most relevant for this study. Williams argues that Woodward's analysis of the relationship between post-bellum politics and economics is not completely correct. The politics of the ruling Southern elite was not quite of the romantic type Woodward believes, considering the active political role blacks had throughout the region until the collapse of Populism. "The Populist leaders were undoubtedly sincere in their professions for racial cooperation," he continues. But they were never able to surmount the racial antagonism held by the region's farmers.

C303. Winkler, Ernest William, ed. *Platforms of Political Parties in Texas (Bulletin of the University of Texas, No. 53)*. Austin, TX: University of Texas, 1916. Reprints every known platform of Texas political parties from 1845 through 1916. Populist platforms are available for 1891-1908. Also includes minority reports, lists of officers and electors, and nominees for state offices.

C304. Wood, Philip J. *Southern Capitalism: the Political Economy of North Carolina, 1880-1980*. Durham, NC: Duke University Press, 1986. The class struggle in North Carolina was reflected in the formation of a number of organizations, including the Farmers' Association, Farmers' Alliance, Knights of Labor, and Colored Farmers' Alliance. Wood argues that "the interest of small farmers and tenants in improved crediting and marketing facilities could do little to alleviate conditions for the black sharecroppers of the Colored Alliance, who had been reduced to the status of wage laborer by the Landlord-Tenant Act." As the CFA was composed of both tenants and croppers, "racial and economic cleavages overlapped."

C305. Woodward, C. Vann. *American Counterpoint: Slavery and Racism in the South Dialogue*. Boston: Little, Brown and Company, 1971. Mentions the role of Populism in the evolution of black civil rights. Woodward gives the Populists the benefit of the doubt, claiming that they gave "unexpected support for Negro rights." The party's approach to the issue was paternalistic and humanitarian but "more pragmatic and economic." The Populists "fought for Negro civil and political rights and offered the Negroes a warmer political fellowship and greater political equality than they had ever received before."

C306. _____. *The Burden of Southern History*. Rev. ed. Baton Rouge, LA: Louisiana State University Press, 1968. Reprints Woodward's "The Populist Heritage and the Individual" and "The Irony of Southern History."

C307. _____. *Origins of the New South, 1877-1913*. Baton Rouge, LA: Louisiana State University Press, 1951. The book that rekindled the continuing debate on the role of blacks in the Populist movement. Woodward argues that the Populists needed Southern blacks if they were to be politically successful, but that it was also the most problematic alignment. Populist journals scoffed at Democratic cries of "Negro domination," but they also realized the dangers of the issue. Rather than follow the vote-gathering route of Democrats and Republicans, Populists elected blacks to their councils and gave them a voice in the party organization. Woodward paints an overall benign portrait of the Populists and tends to give them more racially advanced credit than is due them, but Origins will continue to be the starting point for debate on the movement for years to come.

C308. _____. *The Strange Career of Jim Crow: a commemorative edition with a new afterword by William S. McFeely*. New York: Oxford University Press, 2002. A seminal work in so many areas--Southern history, African-American studies, economic history. As in *Origins*, Woodward tends to paint a more liberal picture of the Populists, especially compared to both Democrats and Republicans, than can easily be warranted. To Woodward, the Populists "steered clear of the patronizing approach" of the two major parties, finding a limited type of "equalitarianism" of want and poverty between poor whites and blacks. Woodward admits that their were "Negrophobes" within the movement, but the majority of the party members appeared anxious to work together in biracial harmony.

C309. _____. *Thinking Back: The Perils of Writing History*. Baton Rouge, LA: Louisiana State University Press, 1986. Woodward's own reconsideration of some of his most influential writings and theories. He acknowledges that his earlier portrait of Tom Watson's racial tolerance was perhaps "incautious" and went too far, although he later stated that Populist gains in interracial cooperation "were limited and that their significance is easily exaggerated." White Populists also "showed much more zeal for protecting the rights of black Populists than of black Democrats and could be as rough in intimidating those who voted the wrong way as were their opponents."

C310. _____. *Tom Watson: Agrarian Rebel*. New York: Rinehart and Company, 1938. Still the basic biography on Watson, despite decades of criticism on essential interpretations. Watson championed black and white rights through the Populist movement, but his frustration over lack of political success transformed him into a high-profile racist. Essential introduction to the man and his milieu.

C311. Wynes, Charles E., ed. *Forgotten Voices: Dissenting Southerners in an Age of Conformity*. Baton Rouge, LA: Louisiana State University Press, 1966. Reprints seven significant essays from the Populist era, including Cable's "The Freedman's Case in Equity," Watson's "The Negro Question in the South," and Lewis H. Blair's "The Southern Problem and Its Solution."

C312. _____. *Race Relations in Virginia, 1870-1902*. Charlottesville, VA: University of Virginia Press, 1961. Brief study of race relations during the Populist era. Wynes argues that "the small white farmer of Virginia knew that he had more in common with the Negro farmer than he did with the ruling element of the Democratic party, the opponent of Populism." But racist rhetoric "undoubtedly greatly reduced" the number of white farmers willing to join the movement. It is not surprising that Virginia blacks, discouraged by the Populists and with a virtually nonexistent Republican Party locally, turned to the Democrats in furtherance of their best interests.

D. PERIODICAL ARTICLES AND ESSAYS

D1. Abramowitz, Jack. "Agrarian Reformers and the Negro Question." *Negro History Bulletin* 11 (March 1948): 138-39. Brief summary article on the relationship between the Alliance and blacks. Notes a number of black Populists, including Laurent, Rayner, Warwick, Glopsy, Foster, and Doyle.

D2. _____. "John B. Rayner—A Grass-Roots Leader." *Journal of Negro History* 36 (April 1951): 160-93. Rayner spoke frequently at rallies throughout East Texas and wrote occasionally for the Southern Mercury, the state party organ. With the collapse of the state party, Rayner turned to a variety of projects aimed at improving black industrial and domestic education through self-help while maintaining goodwill with white Southerners. Abramowitz also discusses the Negro Farmers Improvement Society, which Rayner protégé Robert L. Smith oversaw in the twentieth century.

D3. _____. "The Negro in the Agrarian Revolt." *Agricultural History* 24 (April 1950): 89-95. One of the first articles to demonstrate the meaningful role black farmers played in the period 1876-1896. The formation of the Colored Farmers' National Alliance and Cooperative Union was a major step forward, with the group achieving a membership of 1,200,000 by some estimates. Abramowitz is an excellent source of names for many early leaders of these organizations.

D4. _____. "The Negro in the Populist Movement." *Journal of Negro History* 38 (July 1953): 257-89. One of the seminal articles in this field. Excellent overview of black involvement in the Populist movement, with discussion of state conventions, personalities, and varying degrees of fusion politics from state to state. Although regularly electing blacks to local political offices, the Populists by 1896 began to weaken, due to a combination of race-baiting and ticket-splitting. Democrats soon took over much of the South and brought about the disfranchisement of blacks and poor whites which would remain into the latter half of the twentieth century.

D5. Addams, Jane. "The Progressive Party and the Negro." *The Crisis* 5-6 (1912-13): 30-31. Almost twenty years after the collapse of the People's party, reformer Jane Addams found the same racial problems existing at the Progressive Party convention in Chicago. However, upon questioning the credentials committee, Addams discovered black delegates from West Virginia, Maryland, Tennessee, and Kentucky, which was viewed as a sign of progress.

D6. Ali, Omar. "Colored Farmers' Alliance." In Jack Salzman, Greg Robinson, and Thaddeus Russell, ed., *Encyclopedia of African-American Culture and History, Supplement.* New York: Macmillan Reference USA, 2001. Brief entry on the CFA notes it role as a forerunner to the Southern Tenant Farmers' Union and Alabama Sharecroppers Union in the 1930s. Also available online at http://www.tsha.utexas.edu/handbook/online/articles/view/ CC/aac1.html

D7. _____. "The Making of a Black Populist: a Tribute to the Rev. Walter A. Pattillo." *Oxford Public Ledger* 121 (28 March 2002). The Rev. Walter A. Pattillo was the leader of North Carolina's black Populists during the 1890s. Born into slavery, he later studied theology at Shaw University and became a prominent Baptist preacher in the area from 1874 onwards. Following his defeat for Register of Deeds, Pattillo grew active in the Colored Farmers Alliance, editing two newspapers (the *Alliance Advocate* and *Baptist Pilot*) which addressed concerns of the black community. Known for his efforts at uniting black and white in the agrarian crusade, Pattillo served as a delegate to the St. Louis and other conventions and was the first North Carolinian to call for creation of a third party. Article online at http://www.geocities.com/salika4/OxfordPublic Ledger RevWAP. html.

D8. Alvord, Wayne. "T. L. Nugent, Texas Populist." *Southwestern Historical Quarterly* 57 (July 1953): 65-81. Thomas Lewis Nugent was twice the Populist candidate for governor of Texas, in 1892 and 1894, desiring to alter the fundamental values by which men lived and the attitudes which controlled them. His particular brand of Social Christianity combined beliefs in the inherent goodness of wealth, hard work, and individualism with a low regard for established churches. Like many reformers of the period, Nugent was enamored of Swedenborgianism, which strengthened his belief that men must create harmony on earth in order for the great redemption to take place.

D9. Anderson, Eric. "The Populists and Capitalist America: The Case of Edgecombe County, North Carolina." In Jeffrey J. Crow, Paul D. Escott, and Charles L. Flynn Jr., ed. *Race, Class, and Politics in Southern History: Essays in Honor of Robert F. Durden.* Baton Rouge, LA: Louisiana State University Press, 1989. Edgecombe County, North Carolina was a center of power for the

Farmers' Alliance but not a Populist stronghold "of any kind." County Populists were at their peak in the summer of 1898, when they almost elected a number of officials to local office. Democrats warned of the danger of black electoral power, and the more opportunistic Populist leaders followed the white supremacy line to garner votes. The misgivings of ordinary Populists at the need for black voter support in part forced the collapse of the party.

D10. Argersinger, Peter H. "'A Place on the Ballot:' Fusion Politics and Antifusion Laws." *American Historical Review* 85 (April 1980): 287-306. The adoption of the antifusion laws altered the political behavior characteristic of the Gilded Age, with varying effects on the role of third parties, modes of political participation, and the electoral process. Implementation of the Australian ballot system throughout the states in part led to the collapse of the People's party, which needed fusion coalitions to succeed. A good article for understanding how the revised ballot system of the 1890s impeded third party success.

D11. Arnesen, Eric. "Following the Color Line of Labor: Black Workers and the Labor Movement Before 1930." *Radical History Review* 55 (winter 1993): 53-87. Arneson argues that black workers, particularly in the South, "developed a tradition of black labor activism that has yet to be made integral to either African-American or labor historiography." Although most workers of both races remained outside organized labor, a "significant number" of blacks embraced trade unionism for "practical and principles reasons." Before, during, and after the heyday of the Populist movement, Southern black workers organized, struck for better working conditions and higher wages, and participated in biracial events such as labor parades.

D12. _____. "Up from Exclusion: Black and White Workers, Race, and the State of Labor History." *Reviews in American History* 26 (March 1998): 146-74. Excellent review article on the state of labor history as it relates to the race question. Arnesen notes Letwin's *The Challenge of Interracial Unionism* (**C176**) as an examination of Alabama's coal miners during the post-Reconstruction era, along with studies by Alex Lichtenstein (**D248**) and Brian Kelly. Useful for understanding just how much research still needs to be done on black labor during the Populist era.

D13. Arnett, Alex M. "The Populist Movement in Georgia." *Georgia Historical Quarterly* 7 (December 1923): 313-38. The farm credit system in 1890s Georgia was no respecter of race—black and white farmers both suffered at the hands of creditors. The main cause of the farmers' perpetual state of debt was falling crop prices combined with the "appreciation of all standing obligations" such as the growth of the dollar. The coming of the Farmers' Alliance and People's party brought some legislative changes, but the problem of black voter participation was predominant.

D14. Atkins, Leah R. "Populism in Alabama: Reuben F. Kolb and the Appeals to Minority Groups." *Alabama Historical Quarterly* 32 (fall and winter 1970): 167-80. Alabama Populism can be separated into four distinct groups: Jeffersonian Democrats (a factional dispute within the Democratic Party), the "Black and Tans" and "Lilly Whites" of the Republican Party, and the fusion Jeffersonian-Democratic-Populists. Each of these groups contributed to the political force that empowered Kolb's political career in the late nineteenth century. Kolb started his political life as a Democrat, but after failing to win the Alabama governorship he became the third party candidate. Although Kolb believed in white supremacy, he eagerly sought black votes, simultaneously reluctant to include blacks in the party structure. In his speeches, Kolb stressed the common problems of black and white farmers; black leaders often spoke at his rallies. Democrats went on the offensive, appealing to black voters and reminding them of the benefits of a "peaceful, conservative" Democratic government. Although Kolb failed to win the election for the Populists, many blacks came to see the movement as their best chance at achieving active participation in Alabama.

D15. Bacote, Clarence A. "Negro Officeholders in Georgia Under President McKinley." *Journal of Negro History* 44 (July 1959): 217-39. In response to the threat of losing black voter support if he didn't provide sufficient federal patronage, President William McKinley attempted to install a number of black officials in federal posts, with little success. The appointment of I. H. Lofton as postmaster of Hogansville roused particular ire among area whites, and later state representative Hall offered a resolution condemning the move. The Committee on the State of the Republic, however, dominated by Populists, reported adversely on the bill. Democratic legislators ignored the recommendation and overwhelming passed the measure. Bacote also notes that so many Democrats and Populists were given preferment for federal patronage in 1898 that black Republicans passed resolutions condemning the practice.

D16. _____. "Negro Proscriptions, Protests, and Proposed Solutions in Georgia, 1886-1908." *Journal of Southern History* 25 (August 1959): 471-98. Bacote sees the strength of the Alliance in Georgia politics during the late 1880s as reflective of the growing antagonism between poor whites and blacks. Although the Alliance advocated a liberal platform for the time, including abolition of the convict lease system, it was also responsible for enacting many of the Jim Crow laws which further separated the races and kept the elite in power. Newspapers across the country noted how detrimental the Alliance-dominated legislatures were to black rights. In the 1892 gubernatorial race, blacks supported Governor Northen, despite the endorsement of state Republican leaders of the Populist candidate. The concurrent rise in lynchings and abuse of the convict lease system lead to three avenues of escape for Georgia blacks: the short-lived "back-to-Africa" movement, exodus to the North, and Western colonization.

D17. _____. "Some Aspects of Negro Life in Georgia, 1880-1908." *Journal of Negro History* 43 (July 1958): 186-213. Bacote notes that the Farmer's Alliance opposed black education in any form in Georgia, as white Alliance members blamed the lack of education for white children on blacks and Reconstruction. James Barrett, speaking at an Alliance convention, is quoted as stating that the more education blacks received, the greater menace they would be to Southern (i.e., white) institutions. Some Alliance legislators proposed a constitutional amendment which would require black schools to be supported from black assessments, a failed initiative which was revived in the 1900 session. Bacote is also useful for his identification of numerous black professionals, organizations, and developments during this period.

D18. Baggett, James Alex. "Origins of Early Texas Republican Party Leadership." *Journal of Southern History* 40 (August 1974): 441-54. Reconstruction brought both Northern carpetbaggers and Southern blacks to power in the Republican Party in Texas, but their impact was minimal, as most of the party leadership in the state at the time consisted of white men with pre-Reconstruction Unionist backgrounds. Baggett mentions a number of black Texas Republican leaders who would have some influence on the state's Populist movement, including Norris Wright Cuney and Frank "Parson" Green. Even these leaders must be viewed as collaborationists rather than controllers of the state party.

D19. Baggozi, Richard P. "Populism and Lynching in Louisiana." *American Sociological Review* 42 (April 1977): 355-68. Comments on Inverarity's first and second causal models (**D217**). Although Baggozi points out a number of methodological and conceptual problems in Inverarity's research, he also notes that a reanalysis of the data supports his theory to a greater extent than reported in certain instances. Worth examining by researchers interested in data analysis problems. See also critiques by Pope and Ragin (**D317**) and Wasserman (**D422**).

D20. Bagwell, David Ashley. "'The Magical Process': The Sayre Election Law of 1893." *Alabama Review* 25 (April 1972): 83-104. The Sayre Election Law of 1893 represents the first movement in Alabama political history to control by law the black voter. Following the "stolen election" of 1892, Populists began preparing for the 1894 races. When it became obvious that black voters would not align with poor whites, the Populist leaders sought to eliminate the black vote. However, the leadership also did not wish to eliminate the poor white vote, if possible. State representative Anthony D. Sayre chaired the Alabama House committee looking into the matter and proposed a bill which would institute use of the Australian "secret" ballot. Although many at the time argued that the Sayre bill was a move toward black disfranchisement, the bill actually sought to establish procedures which would allow election officials to place black votes in the conservative column.

D21. Bahjenbruch, Judith. "The Greenback Political Movement: an Arkansas View." *Arkansas Historical Quarterly* 36.2 (1977): 107-22. Demonstrating the strong support by blacks of the Greenback movement, the Arkansas state Green-back convention of July 1878 was seven-eighths black in composition, although their presence caused some dissension within the party. The convention was dominated by the Pulaski County Greenback Club, which was 75% black and controlled by Republicans. Little Rock Greenbackers nominated a full slate of black candidates for Pulaski County public office, including well-known local figures J. B. Atkinson, Isaac Gillam, Elias Rector, and Green Thompson, who went on to serve as a state legislator.

D22. Bailey, Fred Arthur. "Free Speech and the Lost Cause in the Old Domin-ion." *Virginia Magazine of History and Biography* 103 (April 1995): 237-66. In the postbellum years in Virginia, patriotic societies such as the United Daugh-ters of the Confederacy sought to establish a myth of Southern history that would support the power structure of the ruling oligarchy. By the end of the century, poor blacks and whites rebelled against the ruling class as part of the agrarian movement. Significantly, notes Bailey, the crusade for an elite South-ern interpretation of American history coincided with this class warfare. While states moved to disfranchise blacks and poor whites, the elite recognized that restrictions on civil rights must be intellectually and emotionally acceptable. An interesting look at how the ruling elite can rewrite history to suit its needs.

D23. Baker, Bruce E. "The 'Hoover Scare' in South Carolina, 1887: An At-tempt to Organize Black Farm Labor." *Labor History* 40 (August 1999): 261-82. Hiram F. Hover organized the Cooperative Workers of America (CWA) in the mid-1880s in upstate South Carolina. Although the organization was short-lived, it serves as an example of an early attempt to unite black and white work-ers in common cause. A former member of the Powderly's Knights of Labor, Hover split from that group on basic theoretical grounds. Blacks responded positively to the CWA, with a number of leaders rising from local ranks. The "Hoover Scare" of 1887 arose in part from media reports on black "Hoover Clubs," although the final violence came at the hands of fearful white residents.

D24. Baker, Riley E. "Negro Voter Registration in Louisiana, 1879-1964." *Louisiana Studies* 4 (winter 1965): 332-49. As the disfranchisement debate is a significant corollary issue to black populism, any document which provides reli-able statistics on voter registration is potentially extremely useful for the re-searcher. Baker notes that only Virginia and Louisiana centralized their voter registration records, and that the latter state's records are surprisingly complete and detailed from 1879 onward. Through a series of tables, Baker shows the relationship between population growth and voter registration, with a combination of a voter roll purge and new registration requirements forcing both white and black off the lists. Black registration dropped especially fast, from 44.3% of total registered voters in 1897 to 4.1% by 1899.

D25. Barnes, Donna. "Strategy Outcome and the Growth of Protest Organizations: A Case Study of the Southern Farmers' Alliance." *Rural Sociology* 52 (1987): 164-186. Sociologists are proposing rationalistic theories of protest development which posit that an organization must convince members of an aggrieved population that the benefits of participating in the protest outweigh the risks. Using longitudinal data on the Farmers' Alliance, Barnes explores the outcome of strategy crises and factors which effect it. The organization was fatally undermined by its support of the subtreasury plan and had little choice but to organize a third party. Alliance members saw no reason to continue paying dues when the new People's party, which had no dues requirement, supported their beliefs.

D26. Barr, Elizabeth N. "The Populist Uprising." In William E. Connelley, ed., *A Standard History of Kansas and Kansans*. Chicago: Lewis Publishing Co., 1918. Barr's early history of the Populist movement in Kansas is excellent--detailed in every way, with photos of major personalities and a separate biographical database. Barr pays particular attention to the formation of the People's party and the subsequent elections. Benjamin Foster is noted as a participant in the early days. The entire five-volume set is available online at http://skyways.lib.ks.us/genweb/1918ks/

D27. Barrows, Samuel J. "What the Southern Negro Is Doing for Himself." *Atlantic Monthly* 67 (June 1891): 805-15. Barrows' journey through the Deep South revealed numerous examples of black enterprise and advancement. "Great numbers" moved from the state of common laborer to farm owner on their own initiative, although high prices asked by merchants keep them in financial bondage. The influence of the new black schools—Hampton, Tuskegee, Atlanta—has also had a positive effect on developing tradesmen. The Farmers' Alliance is noted as attracting attention among blacks seeking relief from the mortgage system. A surprisingly upbeat, factual article that avoids every contemporary stereotype.

D28. Barton, D. Scott. "Party Switching and Kansas Populism." *The Historian* 52 (May 1990): 453-67. Barton uses multiple regression analysis to examine Kansas voting patterns during the Populist era and concludes that, although the Republican Party suffered election losses due to low voter turnout and the Populist fusion efforts, the coalitions did not last and a new electoral era was not founded. Interesting model for examining party alignment and fusion in other states, to test the strength of fusion politics.

D29. Baskett, Thomas S., Jr. "Miners Stay Away!: W. B. W. Heartsill and the Last Years of the Arkansas Knights of Labor, 1892-1896." *Arkansas Historical Quarterly* 42 (summer 1983): 107-33. Running parallel to the Alliance was the Noble Order of the Knights of Labor, which admitted blacks to its membership to improve labor conditions throughout the nation. Baskett quotes Turner and Rogers (**D343**) on the strike efforts of black Arkansas Knights, and also notes that the 1892 congressional campaign of organizer W. B. W. Heartsill revealed links between the Knights and the People's party in Arkansas.

D30. Baum, Dale and Worth Robert Miller. "Ethnic Conflict and Machine Politics in San Antonio, 1892-1899." *Journal of Urban History* 19 (August 1993): 63-84. The People's party had less direct effect in San Antonio than in Texas' other major cities. Baum and Miller compare voter registration and turnout for the period 1892-1899 and note that black voters tended to support Republicans or abstain from voting, thus sealing a Bourbon Democrat-Republican fusion deal. However, as the decade progressed, the Populists successfully wooed more black votes, to the detriment of the Republican Party.

D31. Baum, Dale and Robert A. Calvert. "Texas Patrons of Husbandry: Geography, Social Contexts, and Voting Behavior." *Agricultural History* 63 (fall 1989): 36-55. The Patrons of Husbandry, better known as the Grange, first organized a lodge in Texas in the summer of 1873. This early agrarian organization had no formal policy barring black farmers from membership, but "racist attitudes precluded them from joining." Southern Grangers proposed a separate black organization, the Council of Laborers. Estimates suggest that a sizable number of former Grangers voted for Populist candidates in 1892. Excellent article for understanding the racial sentiments of the future Alliance and Populist movements in the state.

D32. Beck, E. M. and Stewart E. Tolnay. "The Killing Fields of the Deep South: The Market for Cotton and the Lynching of Blacks, 1882-1930." *American Sociological Review* 55 (August 1990): 526-39. Using time series analysis techniques, Beck and Tolnay study the relationship between the cotton market and lynchings both before and after the Populist period. Lynchings were found to rise when the "constant dollar" price of cotton declined and inflationary pressure increased. The authors posit that Southern white mob violence toward blacks was thus strongly affected by the economy, particularly among the poorer white farmers. The Populist movement briefly united white and black farmers, but this racial alignment collapsed as the movement turned increasingly racist.

D33. _____, James L. Massey, and Stewart E. Tolnay. "Black Lynching: the Power-Threat Hypothesis Revisited." *Social Forces* 67 (March 1989): 605-23. One of the few "theory-driven" explanations for the Southern lynching phenomenon of the period employs Blalock's "power threat hypothesis" as a framework, arguing that Southern whites lynched blacks in order to retain political hegemony. The authors re-examine the empirical data of past studies and find a number of conceptual and methodological weaknesses. They finally determine that there is no support for the "power threat" explanation for lynching.

D34. _____, James L. Massey, and Stewart E. Tolnay. "The Gallows, the Mob, and the Vote: Lethal Sanctioning of Blacks in North Carolina and Georgia, 1882 to 1930." *Law and Society Review* 23 (1989): 317-31. The authors examine the relationship between lynchings and executions of blacks in North Carolina and Georgia in part during the Populist era. Analysis reveals that total lethal sanctioning (lynchings plus executions) declined in Georgia after several disfranchisement measures were implemented, although no similar effect was found for North Carolina.

D35. Bemis, Edward W. "The Discontent of the Farmer." *Journal of Political Economy* 1 (March 1893): 193-213. What is the cause of the current of farmer discontent? According to Bemis, the one fact complained of by farmer and wage-earner alike is "relative, not absolute, decline in the share of national income secured." An additional cause, especially in the South, is his "lack of thrift, energy and intelligence in adopting improved methods of farming." Bemis makes it a point throughout to note that the problems are caused by black and white farmers alike, although he also notes many statistical comparisons between the races, sometimes in favor of the black farmer.

D36. Biergert, M. Langley. "Legacy of Resistance: Uncovering the History of Collective Action by Black Agricultural Workers in Central East Arkansas from the 1860s to the 1930s." *Journal of Social History* 32 (fall 1998): 73-99. Central East Arkansas has long been a hotbed of unrest for black farm workers. Although the central focus of this article is the Southern Tenant Farmers Union (STFU), founded in 1934, Biergert discusses at length the ramifications of the Colored Farmers' Alliance and the failed strike of 1891. The author utilized local newspaper articles originally overlooked by William Holmes in his otherwise excellent article (**D200**).

D37. Billings, Dwight B., Jr. "Class and Class Politics in the Southern Populist Movement of the 1890s." *Sociological Spectrum* 1 (1981): 259-92. Billings offers a class-dialectical analysis of the Populist movement in North Carolina, arguing that elected Populist leaders, though reform oriented, represented the interests of the state's large farmers and planters while neglecting black and poor white farmers. The collapse of the party was therefore due partly to this class contradiction. According to Billings' statistical analysis, Populist leaders like Leonidas L. Polk chose to support their own positions of power rather than look out for the rights of their constituents. Populist leaders must also be faulted for their failure to warn against race-baiting in the election campaigns.

D38. Bishop, Joseph B. "The Secret Ballot in Thirty-three States." *The Forum* 12 (January 1892): 589-98. The rapidity with which ballot reform, especially the switch to the Australian system, has advanced is "without parallel in the history of reform movements in this country." Bishop includes a handy state-by-state chart showing type of ballot in use, method of voting, general character of the ballot, and the date of enactment.

D39. Black, Paul V. "The Knights of Labor and the South: 1879-1893." *Southern Quarterly* 1 (1963): 201-12. The Noble Order of the Knights of Labor, founded in 1869, was an ideal organization for the South, in that its "mixed" assemblies of artisans and unskilled workers embraced "abstract ideals of social reform" and gave the Order a "crusading fervor." By 1886 the once conservative union had become a "utopian reform society" with cooperatives and black assemblies. Black notes that "the most significant of all the Order's objectives in the South was inter-racial solidarity," and that the Richmond convention of 1886 was "widely attended by members of both races." The Knights and Populists also "frequently exchanged gestures of reciprocal support."

D40. Bland, Gayle K. "Populism in the First Congressional District of Kentucky." *Filson Club Historical Quarterly* 51 (1977): 31-43. Kentucky's First Congressional District in 1890 reported a population of 164,000, including 22,000 blacks (15% of the total). Most farmers worked small to moderate sized holdings, although the number of farm owners had fallen dramatically in the period 1880-1890. Although the Populists showed significant membership at first, enrollment dropped sharply as the move toward a third party took shape. Bland notes that in the 1892 election, Populist candidates did better in counties with low black populations. In contrast, Populists did poorly in the Seventh District, where there were more blacks in proportion to whites.

D41. Bloch, Herman D. "Labor and the Negro, 1866-1910." *Journal of Negro History* 50 (July 1965): 163-84. In his survey of the relationship between blacks and organized labor, Bloch makes an interesting point which is relevant to the Populist movement: the farther removed from the threats to self-interest (in the case of labor, job security), the less antagonistic is the person toward black acceptance. The national leadership of various unions and groups such as the Knights of Labor could speak broadly of bringing all workers, regardless of race, under one big umbrella, but at the local level the issue was clouded by the fear of potential loss of jobs. National constitutions could call for open membership regardless of race, but local practice often found ways of circumventing their charters.

D42. Bode, Frederick A. "Religion and Class Hegemony: A Populist Critique in North Carolina." *Journal of Southern History* 37 (August 1971): 417-38. Southern white churches regularly preached the gospel of the status quo, which left them open to Populist attacks during this time of discontent with the social order. Populists attacked the mainline Protestant churches for their lack of involvement in social reform, while Democrats exploited the race issue and the churches' toleration of chattel slavery. In a reversal of roles, the unlettered "revolutionary" Populists were able to brand the Democrats, the party of virtue and intelligence, as anti-intellectual and panderers to the prejudices of the masses.

D43. Boggs, Carl. "The New Populism and the Limits of Structuralist Reforms." *Theory and Society* 12 (May 1983): 343-64. Viewed in historical terms, the New Populism constitutes a species of structural reformism, with all of its characteristic dilemmas and limitations. New Populists espouse a theory whose core element is democratization—a process that would lead to expanded popular involvement in the workplace, political system, and community. New Populism reform seeks not only a reconstituted welfare state, but a more basic power shift back to "the people." New Populists participate "energetically" in the existing political-institutional system, making alliances with unions, political parties, and other organized groups as necessary. However, this "joining of several forces" is also the flaw of the movement—these mergers cannot sustain the Populist insurgency that modern leaders (e.g., Tom Hayden) espouse. For a critique of Boggs, see Mark E. Kann, "The New Populism and the New Marxism," *Theory and Society* 12 (May 1983): 365-73.

D44. Bonacich, Edna. "A Theory of Ethnic Antagonism: The Split Labor Market." *American Sociological Review* 37 (October 1972): 547-59. Bonacich argues that antagonism between ethnic groups is partially the result of a split labor market, in which there exists a large labor price differential for the same occupation. However, the price of labor is not a response to the race or ethnicity of labor market entrants, but rather a difference in resources and motives which may be correlates of ethnicity. A split labor market pits a business against two labor groups in a three-way conflict, with business seeking to hire the cheapest labor. The legislative history of the Deep South consists of regular attempts by higher priced white labor to ward off undercutting by cheaper groups, although businesses and plantation owners brought in non-Aryan ethnic groups (e.g., Italians and Chinese) to undercut free black wage earners.

D45. Bonner, James C. "The Alliance Legislature of 1890." In Bonner, James C., and Lucien E. Roberts, ed., *Studies in Georgia History and Government*. Athens, GA: University of Georgia Press, 1940. The Georgia Alliance grew rapidly just prior to 1890 and was able to wrest political power from the Bourbon elite as the decade opened, with thirty-one of the forty-four senators in the General Assembly Alliancemen. Bonner notes the presence of Lectured Crawford as the black assemblyman from McIntosh County. The *Athens Banner* newspaper, normally friendly to the Alliance, took issue with the organization because of "their very liberal attitude toward Negro education."

D46. Bovee, John R. "Doctor Huguet: Donnelly on Being Black." *Minnesota History* 41 (summer 1969): 286-94. Populist leader Ignatius Donnelly wrote three novels—Caesar's Column, Doctor Huguet, and The Golden Bottle—which focused on the plight of America's downtrodden. *Doctor Huguet*, published in 1891, has its white Southern protagonist miraculously exchange bodies with a local dissolute black man, which gives the author the chance to examine attitudes of both races. Although Donnelly's views on race were mixed—he argued throughout his career for tolerance and equal political rights while claiming blacks were intellectually and physically inferior to whites—his belief in the brotherhood of all men made him one of the most forward-thinking of all Populist leaders.

D47. Boyd, Herb. "Radicalism and Resistance: the Evolution of Black Radical Thought." *Black Scholar* 28 (spring 1998): 43-53. Although Boyd notes a number of black movements of the 1890s which arose "to challenge the entrenchment of white supremacy, disenfranchisement, lynching and bigotry," including the National Afro-American League and the American Negro Academy, no mention is made of the CFA or the efforts at biracial unionism during the period. The activities of the National Association of Colored Women and the Wells-Barnett's anti-lynching campaign during the 1890s are noted.

D48. Brady, Marilyn Dell. "Populism and Feminism in a Newspaper by and for Women of the Kansas Farmer's Alliance, 1891-1894." *Kansas History* 7 (winter 1984/85): 280-90. Poems in the *Farmer's Wife*, a Kansas Alliance newspaper edited by and written for movement women, addressed the issue of black male delegates to the 1892 national convention who opposed women's suffrage. One poem, by a white woman speaking as a black man, suggests that women's suffrage should "take second place to those issues about which laboring people could agree."

D49. Brandon, Ida. "The Tax Payers Union in Brazoria County." *Texas History Teachers' Bulletin* 14 (1926): 86-92. Brazoria County, Texas was a hotbed of agrarian activity, especially among black voters. In response, local whites organized The Tax Payers' Union--familiarly known as The White Man's Union--to prevent blacks from voting in primaries, holding elected office, and generally participating in the election procedure. Brandon includes the full text of the group's Constitution and By-laws from April 1919.

D50. Brewer, William M. "The Poll Tax and the Poll Takers." *Journal of Negro History* 29 (July 1944): 260-99. Disfranchisement restrictions, including the poll tax, stemmed in part from the growing Populist threat at the polls in the 1890s, although it was not always clear whether or not the leaders of the disfranchisement movement in the South meant to remove the vote from poor white as well as black voters also. Most useful for its historical overview of the problem and the impetus Populism gave to this particular discriminatory measure.

D51. _____. "Poor Whites and Negroes in the South Since the Civil War." *Journal of Negro History* 15 (January 1930): 26-37. Poor Southern whites had always had an antipathy towards blacks, starting during the slavery period and not ending with Reconstruction. That event, if anything, deepened racial hatred, as poor whites were suddenly on the same economic level as former slaves. Whites of all classes united to proscribe the position of Southern blacks through legislation. The growth of Southern industry and birth of the New South also held no promise for blacks. Political demagogues such as Tillman took advantage of the influx of capital into the region and contemporary Supreme Court decisions to further deprive blacks of civil and political rights. Poor white craftsmen also successfully sought to ban blacks from local trade unions.

D52. Brier, Stephen. "Interracial Organizing in the West Virginia Coal Industry: the Participation of Black Mine Workers in the Knights of Labor and the United Mine Workers, 1880-1894." In Gary M. Fink and Merl E. Reed, ed., *Essays in Southern Labor History: Selected Papers, Southern Labor History Conference, 1976*. Westport, CT: Greenwood Press, 1977: 18-43. The growth of the Knights of Labor as an organizational force in the Southern West Virginia coal fields in the 1880s and 1890s underscores the development of militant, interracial unions in the industry and the active participation of black mine workers in local and district trade union organizations in the state. Many blacks who came to this region seeking employment came from eastern Virginia, an area of strong Readjuster support from 1879-1881. The union from the beginning urged black miners to join, and by the 1890s some even held elective office in the interracial organization. Brier concludes that these black miners came to view interracial trade unionism as a vehicle through which they could achieve "liberation" as both workers and a race.

D53. Brinkley, Alan. "In Retrospect: Richard Hofstadter's The Age of Reform: a Reconsideration." *Reviews in American History* 13 (September 1985): 462-80. Although Hofstadter's The Age of Reform is one of the most influential books on twentieth century American history, its reputation has waned, especially compared to Woodward's *Origins of the New South*. Hofstadter in the end was caught between two competing visions of society, distrusting the politics of unrestrained popular will but simultaneously hoping for a better future.

D54. Broadway, Lilibel H. H. "Frank Burkitt: The Man In the Wool Hat." *Social Science Bulletin* 4 (April 1952): 20-23. Brief biography of Frank Burkitt, Mississippi editor, Populist candidate, and supporter of black civil rights.

D55. Brooks, Robert P. "A Local Study of the Race Problem: Race Relations in the Eastern Piedmont Region of Georgia." *Political Science Quarterly* 26

(June 1911): 193-221. Emancipation inflicted a heavier loss on the planters of the "black counties" of the Eastern Piedmont Region (Wilkes, Lincoln, Greene, Oglethorpe, and Taliaferro) than those of the "white counties." Confirming Census observations, as the percentage of blacks increases within a county, the percentage of landowners among them decreases. Most black county residents are renters. Brooks affirms, however, that blacks are most successful when guided by whites. Despite the writer's attitude toward blacks throughout, his article is still worth examining for its population tables.

D56. Brown, Thomas J. "The Roots of Bluegrass Insurgency: an Analysis of the Populist Movement in Kentucky." *Register of the Kentucky Historical Society* 78 (summer 1980): 219-42. Little has been written on the Populist movement in Kentucky. Brown notes membership in the Kentucky CFA at 25,000 in December 1890. Populist leader Thomas Pettit opposed the Separate Coach Bill, which evaporated the state's white support for the party. The threat of black voting power also proved a hindrance to Populist electoral success.

D57. Bryan, Ferald J. "Henry Grady and Southern Ideology: An Analysis of the Texas State Fair Address." In Charles W. Kneupper, ed., *Rhetoric and Ideology: Compositions and Criticisms of Power*. Arlington, TX: Rhetoric Society of America, 1989. Analysis of Henry Grady's famous Texas State Fair address of 1888 in Dallas. The South's greatest problem to overcome is the presence of "two separate races" of nearly equal population. White Southerners had nothing to fear physically from the former slaves, but whites must stand together and not split their votes, in order to maintain control. See also C134.

D58. Bryant, Girard T. "J. B. Rayner, A Negro Populist." *Negro History Bulletin* 3 (May 1940): 125-26. Brief article on John B. Rayner of Texas, although Bryant tends not to be terribly informative: "Just when he was born I do not know," "I do not know what happened to Rayner." Most useful are excerpts from Rayner's own writings--primarily accounts of his travels, although a front page letter from the *Southern Mercury* (12/12/95) is reprinted--and contemporary articles about him.

D59. Cable, George Washington. "The Convict Lease System in the Southern States." *Century Magazine* 27 (February 1884): 582-99. A central concern for the Populists at times was the convict lease system, a form of near-slavery active throughout the Deep South well into the 20th Century. Cable examines the system state by state in the region and finds it ranging from its most humane in Tennessee to its most degrading in Mississippi, Arkansas, and Louisiana. Little account is given to the different treatment of black and white prisoners.

D60. _____. "Does the Negro Pay for His Education?" *The Forum* 13 (July 1892): 640-49. Examining tax rates and per capita education spending throughout the South, Cable concludes that blacks and poor whites are being cheated out of an adequate education. For lack of pro rata distribution of funds, "hundreds of thousands" of Southern school children of both races are out of school, and "hundreds of thousands" more get "wretched" schooling.

D61. _____. "The Freedman's Case in Equity." *Century Magazine* 29 (January 1885): 409-18. Cable sees the presence of blacks in the U.S. as "the greatest social problem" of the day. Simply because a man is declared a freedman does not make him a free man under existing conditions. The solution will not come simply through politics, as existing laws already give black and white men equal rights. Until the "outraged intelligence of the South lifts its indignant protest" against those who keep blacks in semi-slavery, the situation will not improve for either race or the country at large. No mention is made by Cable of political movements. See also **C220, C311**.

D62. _____. "The Silent South." *Century Magazine* 30 (September 1885): 674-91. One of Cable's most famous and significant articles of the period, "The Silent South" addresses his desire to convince his fellow Southerners of the rights of the freedmen. The Southern mind has not come to grips with the definition of the black man's rights, with many white Southerners believing that the Civil Rights Bill under consideration by Congress would lead to social chaos. But civil rights should not be equated with social rights. To have peace, social relations must not impose on civil rights, and vice versa. But the political parties are not "solid" for the subservience of black civil rights to white domination, with the Republicans "grown fat and lazy" concerning civil rights and the Democrats working to eliminate regressive legislation at the state level.

D63. _____. "A Simpler Southern Question." *The Forum* 6 (December 1888): 392-403. Cable writes in response to several politicians who published earlier essays in *The Forum*, including Senators Wade Hampton, William E. Chandler, and J. B. Eustis. The major political parties must ask themselves, "do you advocate the Negro's enjoyment of each and every one of these rights under only and exactly the same protections and limitations he would be under if, just as he is in everything else, he were white?"

D64. _____. "What Shall the Negro Do?" *The Forum* 5 (August 1888): 627-39. The only one of Cable's addresses before a black audience to be published. Blacks must never draw the color line but must always strive for the benefit of both races. They must also develop their own leaders and never give up hope for the future. Blacks must also not overlook their power as individuals and the necessity of individual power to give power to numbers.

D65. Caffey, Francis G. "Suffrage Limitations at the South." *Political Science Quarterly* 20 (March 1905): 53-67. A 1903 report on suffrage in eleven Southern states by the committee on political reform of the Union League Club of New York City points out that suffrage is greatly restricted by law in the South ern states, and it is argued that "the restrictions constitute a denial of the right of citizens of the United States to vote within the meaning of the fourteenth amendment." The Southern white population is enjoying "an unfair advantage," and therefore Southern representation in the Electoral College should be reduced. Caffey argues that the authors of the report are rather unfair to Southerners, and that the constitutional suffrage restriction such as found in Alabama are "not selfish; it is merely practical." A fascinating, statistic-laden apologia for disfranchisement.

D66. Calista, Donald J. "Booker T. Washington: Another Look." *Journal of Negro History* 49 (October 1964): 240-55. By the time of Washington's Atlanta Exposition Speech of 1895, Populism was all but dead and a disfranchisement movement in full swing throughout the South. Reform from outside the South would be fruitless; Southern blacks must look to themselves for success. Despite the move toward re-assessment of Washington's role in the rapid loss of political and civil rights for blacks in the 1890s, his Atlanta Compromise had a number of positive results, including the psychological value of believing that even the lowest person on the economic ladder was in a bargaining position with the white world.

D67. Calvert, Robert A. "A. J. Rose and the Granger Concept of Reform." *Agricultural History* 51 (January 1977): 181-96. Rose was appointed by a Democratic governor to serve as Commissioner of Agriculture, Insurance, Statistics, and History for Texas in 1894 and, according to Calvert, was the most important Granger in the state at the time of the great Populist revolt. Although the state organization generally followed the political lead of the national body, Rose saw the growth of the more liberal Farmers' Alliance and People's party as dangerous and challenged the national leadership on free trade issues. Rose also opposed the Force Bill, as state Grangers were known to oppose black suffrage. A useful article for understanding the conflicts among local state agrarian reform organizations.

D68. _____. "Agrarian Texas." In Walter L. Buenger and Robert A. Calvert, ed., *Texas Through Time: Evolving Interpretations*. College Station, TX: Texas A&M University, 1991. In his brief historiographical essay, Calvert notes that "the relationship of black Texans to agrarian goals needs addressing." He cites works by Barr and Rice on the topic and suggests that it is unlikely that historians can put together a fuller account of the CFA other than the sketchy one that now exists "without some fortuitous discovery of documents."

D69. _____, and William Witherspoon. "Populism in Jack County, Texas." *Southern Studies* 25 (spring 1986): 31-66. Jack County, Texas is on the state frontier and is dominated by opposing forces of ranchers and farmers. Includes detailed demographic breakdown of Populists versus Democrats by birthplace, median age, years of county residence, occupation, tax renditions, individual landholdings by acreage, and platmaps of voting patterns.

D70. Cantrell, Gregg. "'Dark Tactics': Black Politics in the 1887 Texas Prohibition Campaign." *Journal of American Studies* 25 (April 1991): 85-93. Reprinted in Donald G. Nieman, *African-American Life in the Post-Emancipation South, 1861-1900*, vol. 6 (Hamden, CT.: Garland Press, 1993). The Texas prohibition referendum provides a case study of the choices state blacks faced after Reconstruction, during a decade often considered by historians as being relatively free of black political involvement. Although some black Republican leaders such as Cuney refused to take a stand on the issue, seeing political problems on both sides, John B. Rayner supported the Prohibitionists as a means of weakening the state Democratic Party. Rayner advised white leaders on how to gain support from black preachers and spent time stumping the state for the movement. Many of the central figures of this campaign would later join the state Populist party.

D71. _____. "John B. Rayner: a Study in Black Populist Leadership." *Southern Studies* 24 (winter 1985): 432-43. Rayner was Texas' foremost black Populist spokesman, sitting on the state party's executive committee and travelling as a fulltime lecturer. Although originally a Republican, he turned from the party apparently with the 1892 Texas gubernatorial race between James Hogg and George Clark. He became more involved in his local county organization and at the state level, delivering speeches throughout East Texas in 1895-96. Rayner continued to lecture on "The Negro's Place in Southern Politics" as late as the fall of 1898, but after the political violence in his county late that same year, he turned to fundraising for black education.

D72. _____. "John B. Rayner: No Outlet on the Road of Hope." In Ty Cashion and Jesús F. de la Teja, ed., *The Human Tradition in Texas*. Wilmington, DE: Scholarly Resources, 2001: 87-101. Rayner, as the leading black Populist in Texas during the 1890s, was first attacked by white Democrats who saw him and his party as dangerous to their existence, but also later by fellow blacks who disagreed with his post-Populist accommodationism. He later worked on gaining financial support from whites for Conroe College, a black industrial school, and Robert L. Smith's Farmers Improvement Society college.

D73. _____, and D. Scott Barton. "Texas Populists and the Failure of Biracial Politics." *Journal of Southern History* 55 (November 1989): 659-92. As with other Southern states, Texas Populists sought victory at the polls through fusion politics, uniting with the Republican Party to defeat Democrats. However, the party failed to overcome the racial animosity of the rank-and-file white party membership, who preferred white supremacy over a biracial coalitionist government. The authors utilize a combination of limited scope (Texas) and ecological regressions of county voting returns to focus on the issue of the racial aspects of Southern Populism, which enables them to estimate the true success or failure of fusion politics. Cantrell and Barton provide voting statistics not found elsewhere, courtesy of the Inter-University Consortium for Political and Social Research. See also **C159**.

D74. Carleton, William G. "The Conservative South: a Political Myth." *Virginia Quarterly Review* 22 (spring 1946): 179-92. Carleton argues that the myth of the Conservative South cannot be justified when one considers the rich tradition of liberalism there. The Populist experience "had a sobering effect upon liberal leaders in the South" when they saw poor whites withhold support if it meant more black political power. Liberals thus saw black disfranchisement as the means for poor whites to be successful.

D75. _____. "The Southern Politician: 1900 and 1950." *Journal of Politics* 13 (May 1951): 215-31. In terms of the questions of the day, politicians may be classed along a spectrum from left to right. Farther to the left in the practical politics of the South in 1900 would be the Populists, who derived their strength from small farmers, both white and black. Tom Watson might be considered the most extreme Southern Populist, with Marion Butler the more conservative. Following them on the left were the radical agrarians such as Ben Tillman and James K. Vardaman, who sided with the Populists on most economic issues but split with them over civil rights for blacks. But despite their political leanings, right or left, most Southern leaders sought to exclude blacks from the political realm following the rise and fall of Populism in the 1890s.

D76. Carlton, Frank T. "The South During the Last Decade, 1890-1900." *Sewanee Review* 12 (April 1904): 174-81. Brief summary article of the changes in economic and social conditions in five Southern states—Georgia, South Carolina, Alabama, Mississippi, and Louisiana—during the 1890s. Subject areas include population, manufactures, agriculture, wage-earners, and education. Carlton, a Northerner, notes the large black population mingled with the white, with the former concentrated in the future in the extreme Southern portion. In addition, blacks have moved from farm workers to farm owners, an improvement in status. Blacks must also follow the dicta of Booker T. Washington and "fit themselves for agricultural and mechanical pursuits." The problem is a Southern one and must be "worked out in and by the South," not by "theoretical and academic discussions in the North."

D77. Carter, Purvis M. "Robert Lloyd Smith and the Farmers' Improvement Society, a Self-Help Movement in Texas." *Negro History Bulletin* 29 (fall 1966): 175-76, 190. Brief history of the Farmers' Improvement Society, a black Texas agrarian self-help organization which flourished under the direction of state legislator Robert Lloyd Smith from 1890 through the 1920s. Carter argues that Smith sought, through cooperative effort, "to achieve an admirable objective the production of an effective citizenry, rather than the promotion of a prospective status for Negroes." Carter also states that many Texas inhabitants in or around small towns were not included in the membership of the Alliance or Populist movement.

D78. Casdorph, Paul. "Norris Wright Cuney and Texas Republican Politics, 1883-1896." *Southwestern Historical Quarterly* 68 (April 1965): 455-64. Cuney was, from 1883 through 1896, the leading black Republican in the state of Texas, although he never held elective office. As blacks dominated the party during that period, Cuney was de facto head of the statewide Republican Party until his ultimate conflicts with national party leaders. Appointed to the powerful position of Collectorship of Customs at Galveston in 1889, Cuney slowly lost control of the state party, which split into a black-dominated regular party and a "lily-white" faction.

D79. Cashin, Edward J. "Vann Woodward's 'Tom Watson': an Interpretation." *Georgia Review* 28 (1974): 519-31. Cashin's review essay of the Beehive Press edition (1973) of Woodward's biography, which includes a new preface by the author in which he asserts that he stands by what he wrote in the original edition. Watson's life was tragic not for Woodward's reasons—his crudity and cruelty and bigotry—but because "he was himself chronically miserable." Watson was the product of forces that ultimately defeated him.

D80. Cassity, R. O. Joe, Jr. "The Political Career of Patrick S. Nagle, 'Champion of the Underdog'." *Chronicles of Oklahoma* 64 (1986-87): 48-67. Patrick S. Nagle is one of the more fascinating characters of Oklahoma political history, beginning his career as a conservative Democrat and ending as a leading Socialist spokesperson. Throughout the 1890s, Nagle opposed most agrarian and Populist legislation, but by 1905 he championed the legislative proposals of the state's Farmers' Union. By 1910 he was a committed Socialist, arguing that the party was "honor bound" to defend the rights of blacks as members of the working class. He gave legal advise to blacks on voting procedure and also strongly supported suffrage for all women. Although not a Populist per se, Nagle was a significant voice of progressive politics in Oklahoma in the years immediately following the collapse of the Populist movement.

D81. Chafe, William H. "The Negro and Populism: A Kansas Case Study." *Journal of Southern History* 34 (August 1968): 402-19. Chafe questions the Populist assumption that blacks and whites shared a common self-interest and reassesses the widespread belief that white prejudice was the major reason behind the movement's failure. Kansas is chosen as a study because of the large number of newspapers controlled and edited by blacks, and the freedom from the post-bellum brand of Southern fusion politics found elsewhere. Many blacks

joined the Populists because the movement directly appealed to their own immediate self-interest--promises of protection and patronage. This theory follows
Woodward's thesis that blacks supported whichever political group--including
Democrats--would secure them upward mobility. White Populists, on the other
hand, stressed anti-big business/government issues, thus putting them in conflict
with black ideologies and goals. Once protection and patronage began to disappear, however, blacks turned from Populist politics but often found themselves
with nowhere to go.

D82. Chamberlain, Henry Richardson. "Farmers' Alliance and other Political
Parties." *The Chautauquan* 13 (June 1891): 338-42. Chamberlain seeks to explain the sudden appearance and strength of the farmers' movement, particularly
the Alliance. Mentions the CFA as part of the confederation. The conservative
Alliance leaders realized at the time of the Ocala convention that it was too soon
to form a third party. However, if the movement lasts, indications are that it
"will succeed in preventing either party from securing a majority in the Electoral
College" in the upcoming election.

D83. Chesnutt, Charles W. "The Disfranchisement of the Negro." In *The Negro
Problem*. New York: James Pott, 1903. As a prominent black author of both
fiction and non-fiction at the turn of the century, Chesnutt was well-tuned to the
problems of the day. Via a combination of means, blacks have been disfranchised throughout the Deep South, to the point where "the Negro is subjected to
taxation without representation, which the forefathers of this Republic made the
basis of a bloody revolution." The problem is not only moral but practical—the
United States can only be truly free if all of her people are given the same rights
and privileges. Nations are first free, and only then rich and prosperous. Chesnutt takes issue not only with white Southerners, but also with Northerners of
both races, and in particular Booker T. Washington, whose utterances on restricted suffrage have been applauded by white politicians. The direct remedy
for disfranchisement is in political action.

D84. Christensen, Lawrence O. "Race Relations in St. Louis, 1865-1916."
Missouri Historical Review 78 (January 1984): 123-36. St. Louis "evolved an
unusual pattern of segregation," in that the city's black leadership was able to
block most segregation measures. Although black residents never attained the
level of citizenship rights held by their Northern brethren, they also did not experience the level of disfranchisement and segregation found in other Deep
South cities. After 1870, the existence of a competitive two-party system in the
state helped black St. Louisans in their political struggles, and by 1890 it was
reported that they held the balance of political power in the city. No mention is
made of Populist activities.

D85. Clanton, Gene. "'Hayseed Socialism' on the Hill: Congressional Populism, 1891-1895." *Western Historical Quarterly* 15 (April 1984): 139-62.

Congressional Populists of the 52nd and 53rd Congresses (1891-95) represent a "missed opportunity of significant magnitude," in Clanton's mind. These representatives did not employ racist language in their speeches of the period, and Thomas Watson called for justice for black Americans during the second session of the 52nd Congress. Senator Peffer of Kansas presented what he called a "very timely" petition on behalf of "the colored people of Riley County, Kansas" who were protesting lynchings. Populist congressmen, however, also felt bound by the Omaha convention platform, which supported the Australian ballot system over federal intervention at the polls.

D86. Clevenger, Homer. "The Farmers' Alliance in Missouri." *Missouri Historical Review* (October 1944): 24-44. The Farmers' Alliance was strong in Missouri, although rather than follow the path to a third party, state farmers worked within the Democratic Party to effect change. The Missourians were initially associated with The Farmers' and Laborers' Union of America, a regional organization, before joining in convention in 1889 to form the National Alliance. The formation of the People's party proved the death blow for the state Alliance, however, with membership dropping precipitously. Clevenger notes that by 1894, almost every remaining Alliance member was now also a Populist. No mention of black activity during this period, although the author notes farmer support for the Australian ballot and other electoral reforms.

D87. _____. "The Teaching Techniques of the Farmers' Alliance: An Experiment in Adult Education." *Journal of Southern History* 11 (November 1945): 504-18. Education within the Farmers' Alliance took many forms, from the publication of numerous books and articles to bi-weekly/monthly meeting sessions at the local level. The "curriculum" centered on the platform of the organization, to indoctrinate the members into national economic questions. As it is unclear from Clevenger's article whether or not the Colored Farmers' Alliance modeled an educational program after their white counterparts, further investigation into this area would be fruitful.

D88. Collins, Robert M. "The Originality Trap: Richard Hostadter on Populism." *Journal of American History* 76 (June 1989): 150-67. Hofstadter's *Age of Reform* has long been considered not only as a major study of twentieth century U.S. history but also a highly controversial one. His critics, chief among them Norman Pollack, argued that Hofstadter reduced the Populists to a horde of "delusional cranks," although Collins believes Hofstadter's papers reveal his inability to convey his views effectively, which lead to misreadings. Unfortunately, Hofstadter's "striving for freshness" and originality caused him to sometimes overstate or misstate what he really meant to communicate.

D89. "Colored Farmers' Conventions." *The American Missionary* 18 (May 1894): 196-7. A brief report on the "colored farmers' conventions" held at Talladega, Alabama on 27 December 1893 and 4 February 1894. More than one hundred black farmers attended the first convention, which focused on issues of land ownership and the importance of education. Farmers are especially urged to avoid debt and mortgages. Seventy-five farmers met at the second convention, which focused on practical matters of husbandry. A constitution was adopted, officers elected, and future plans talked over. An interesting example of black farmer initiative outside the white sphere of influence.

D90. Connolly, Noreen R. "Attorney Lutie A. Lytle: Options and Obstacles of a Legal Pioneer." *Nebraska Lawyer* (January 1999): 6-12. Despite the relatively high estimated number of women in the agrarian movement, the literature is nearly silent as to the role of black women. Lutie A. Lytle, from Topeka, was a remarkable woman on all counts: first black woman to graduate from a Southern law school, first black woman admitted to the Tennessee and Kansas bars, and first woman law professor anywhere in the world. Born in 1871, Lytle was the daughter of prominent Topeka businessman J. R. Lytle, a leader in the Populist Flambeau Club, an arm of the People's Party, organized in 1893. As a result of her father's position, Lutie Lytle was engaged as the assistant enrolling clerk for the Populists in January 1895. That fall, she enrolled as a student at Nashville's Central Tennessee College, entered the Law Class in 1897, and was admitted to the bar that September. Moving back to Topeka, she considered several options for practicing law, but none were satisfactory. Lytle returned to Central Tennessee College's Department of Law as a teacher in the fall of 1898 but left to get married shortly afterwards. She continued to participate in the political scene and later became a vocal supporter of Marcus Garvey.

D91. Cooke, Jacob E. "The New South." In Donald Sheehan and Harold C. Syrett, ed., *Essays in American Historiography: Papers Presented in Honor of Allan Nevins*. New York: Columbia University Press, 1960. As Cooke argues, "the New South does not lend itself to a historiographical discussion, for few historians have presented a monistic interpretation which gives unity and meaning to the varied facets of the Southern experience." Useful for its overview of the creed that so affected Populism, particularly the relationship between blacks and the political structure, as seen by Woodward, Hicks, etc.

D92. Cooper, Arnold. "'Protection to All, Discrimination to None': The Parsons Weekly Blade, 1892-1900." *Kansas History* 9 (summer 1986): 58-71. The Parsons Weekly Blade, a black-owned and –operated newspaper in Parsons, Kansas, advocated black political independence and self-determination. Initially supportive of Republicans and anti-Populist, the Blade ultimately grew disenchanted with the party of Lincoln and threw its support to the Populists in 1898. See also **B17**.

D93. Cooper, Frederick. "Elevating the Race: The Social Thought of Black Leaders, 1827-1850." *American Quarterly* 24 (December 1972): 604-25. Black leaders of the ante-bellum period, writing particularly in *The Colored*

American and *Freedom's Journal*, placed their focus on the success of the race more on self-improvement than political action, especially as they viewed the northern abolitionists as more interested in slaves than the free population. Self-improvement could be achieved by black religious, fraternal, mutual relief, and educational organizations without the immediate intercession of white supporters, who would focus on improving black political strength. An important article for understanding the roots of post-bellum black self-help thought.

D94. Cooper, William J. "Economics or Race: an Analysis of the Gubernatorial Election of 1890 in South Carolina." *South Carolina Historical Magazine* 73 (October 1972): 209-19. The 1890 South Carolina gubernatorial election pitted the Populist Democrat Ben Tillman against a small group of ultra-conservative Democrats lead by Alexander C. Haskell, who felt that Tillman had done great harm to the state. Haskell openly courted black votes, whereas, as Cooper demonstrates, Tillman gained new support not primarily from share-croppers and farm renters but from a broader spectrum of the white population. The wealthy counties did not desert the Democratic Party because of Tillman, which suggests that his electoral strength cannot be argued along class lines.

D95. Corzine, Jay, Lin Corzine, and James Creech. "Black Concentration and Lynchings in the South: Testing Blalock's Power-Threat Hypothesis." *Social Forces* 61 (March 1983): 774-96. The authors claim that there is substantial evidence that the effect of percent black on discrimination is limited to the South. Examining the data through Multiple Classification Analysis and multiple regression analysis for the region during the rise and fall of the Populist movement, the authors test the the power-threat hypothesis to see if black concentration is related to level of discrimination. The hypothesis is supported for the South as a whole, with subregional variance.

D96. _____. "The Tenant Labor Market and Lynching in the South: a Test of Split Labor Market Theory." *Sociological Inquiry* 58 (summer 1988): 261-78. The authors investigate the threat to "high-priced" (white) labor from "cheap" (black) labor within the farm tenancy system of the postbellum South as an underlying cause of lynching. They conclude that racial violence is linked to economic competition between working-class whites and blacks primarily in that part of the South dominated by the plantation system.

D97. Cox, Oliver C. "The Leadership of Booker T. Washington." *Social Forces* 30 (October 1951): 91-97. Sociological examination of Washington as a black leader, especially in light of the New South developments; in many ways his speeches of the period mirror those of Henry Grady just a few years earlier. His leadership must be thought of as "spurious," in that his function was to control the masses, rather than lead them like Marcus Garvey. Cox views Washington as a puppet of the white elite with a mission to subdue the spirit of mass protest rather than supporting their causes.

D98. Crippen, Harlan R. "Conflicting Trends in the Populist Movement." *Science & Society* 6 (1942): 133-49. Crippen argues that an accurate analysis of Populism is possible only when the three categories--Southern, western, and wheat-belt--are considered separately. A provocative footnote states that "it is worth noting that most writers on Populism suffer from the same anti-Negro bias which undermined Southern Populism. Few of the studies of Southern Populism can be credited with objectivity." Populist action was "marked by unwise compromise, hesitation, and confusion."

D99. Crofts, Daniel W. "The Black Response to the Blair Education Bill." *Journal of Southern History* 37 (February 1971): 41-65. The Blair Education Bill swiftly became one of the lightning rod issues among black intellectuals in the late 1880s. The bill proposed to improve literacy by injecting $77 million over an eight-year period primarily to the Southern states, with each state matching federal assistance with at least an equal amount from its own resources. However, the bill also required each state to provide "free common schools for all its children of school age," regardless of race. Proponents claimed that most blacks favored passage of the bill, although leaders such as T. Thomas Fortune understood that it was no cure-all. Although Crofts does not bring Populism into the picture, his article is important for understanding the Southern attitudes toward federal intervention in state and local affairs.

D100. Crow, Jeffrey J. "Cracking the Solid South: Populism and the Fusionist Interlude." In Lindley S. Butler and Alan D. Watson, ed., *The North Carolina Experience: an Interpretive and Documentary History*. Chapel Hill, NC: University of North Carolina Press, 1984. Crow examines the myth of the postbellum "Solid South" in light of agrarian politics of the 1880s and 1890s. After the death of Polk, the mantle of North Carolinian Populist leadership fell on Marion Butler, who brought "a hard-headed pragmatism and organizing genius" to the movement. Crow includes excellent supporting documents on white supremacy and reform issues.

D101. _____. "'Fusion, Confusion, and Negroism': Schisms Among Negro Republicans in the North Carolina Election of 1896." *North Carolina Historical Review* 53 (October 1976): 364-84. The election in 1896 of Republican Daniel L. Russell to the North Carolina governorship revealed the differing attitude of black leaders toward Populism, racial tensions affecting white Southern Republicans, and the locus of issues that would shape the white supremacy campaigns through 1900. Russell's victory at the polls was a direct result of fusion politics, which came about as a result of the return of home rule to the counties, along with election reform laws. Conservative black leaders resented the insulting paternalistic attitudes of Russell, but black fusionists, including state assemblyman James H. Young, disregarded the candidate's lily-white rhetoric and urged friendly relations as more politic. Excellent article includes pictures of many state leaders from both races.

D102. Crowe, Charles. "Tom Watson, Populists, and Blacks Reconsidered."
Journal of Negro History 55 (April 1970): 99-116. In what is essentially a
strong critique of Woodward's *Tom Watson: Agrarian Rebel* (**C310**), Crowe
argues that the evidence is conclusive that Watson's political career prior to
1892 was to a degree as racist as his later years as a leading racist politician.
One fault of Woodward's book lies in its milieu of its conception and publication—the 1930s paean to agrarianism and the mythical Old South by Southern
intellectuals. When "the illusion of uniqueness has been stripped from Watson
and the Populists," some of Woodward's key arguments collapse. Crowe believes that Watson's alleged pro-black stance must have been the result of a
dramatic conversion and lasted only between 1892 and 1896.

D103. Cunningham, George E. "The Italian: a Hindrance to White Solidarity
in Louisiana, 1890-1898." *Journal of Negro History* 50 (January 1965): 22-36.
Italians started to arrive in Louisiana as early as 1865, as part of a planter
scheme to replace blacks laborers with "docile" whites. Their comparative lack
of racial prejudice led the Italians to work in the fields with blacks, although the
majority settled in New Orleans. The Italians were slow to assimilate into
Southern white culture, as reflected in mass lynchings in New Orleans in 1891.
A suffrage amendment put before a popular vote in 1896 sought to disfranchise
state blacks and thus destroy the Populist Party, but New Orleans Italians pa-
raded against the measure, opposing disfranchisement without recourse to a constitutional convention. The measure failed handily, demonstrating the power of
the Populists. Further legislation in 1896 put state voter registration under Democratic control, and their 1898 state convention focused on attempts to prevent
the Italian vote from growing in strength.

D104. Daniel, Lucia E. "The Louisiana People's Party." *Louisiana Historical
Quarterly* 26 (October 1943): 1055-1149. Still one of the best works on the
Louisiana People's party. Daniel examines in great detail every aspect of the
party, including providing detailed election returns by parish (and sometimes by
ward) for 1890-1900 and a list of officeholders elected in April 1896. Notes the
various fusion alignments and significant role of blacks in the electoral process.

D105. Dann, Martin. "Black Populism: A Study of the Colored Farmers' Alliance Through 1891." *Journal of Ethnic Studies* 2 (fall 1974): 58-71. Dann sees
the CFA as part of a tradition of black radical agrarianism that began in the
1870s and continued with the STFU, Alabama Sharecroppers' Union, and other
groups. Article contains some interesting obscure facts on Humphrey and useful excerpts from contemporary newspapers. Places Rayner (here mistakenly
named "James") as part of the late 1890s and early 20th century black agrarian
movement, with no mention of his early work.

D106. Davis, Harold E. "Henry Grady, The Atlanta Constitution, and the Politics of Farming in the 1880s." *Georgia Historical Quarterly* 71 (1987): 571-

600. As managing editor and part-owner of the Atlanta Constitution during the 1880s, Henry Grady was arguably the most prominent of the "New South" leaders of the post-Reconstruction era. Davis discusses the Intra-State Convention of August 1887 in Atlanta, attended by Macune (leader of the Farmers' Alliance, "an organization of unhappy people convinced that the system was abusing them"), among others. But Grady also understood the potential power of the black agrarian vote and sought to influence opinion which would keep his paper influential in state politics.

D107. Davis, Hugh C. "Hilary A. Herbert: Bourbon Apologist." *Alabama Review* 20 (July 1967): 216-25. Hilary A. Herbert served as congressman from Alabama (1876-1893) and Secretary of the Navy under Grover Cleveland and was long considered one of the leading apologists of the Bourbon regimes. His book *Why the Solid South?* (1890), written in response to the Force Bill, attacked the concept of "centralism," which he felt was dangerous to states' rights and a potential road to socialism. As early as 1890, Herbert denounced the Populist program in the South, which would put too much power in the hands of the federal government. With the help of naturalist Louis Agassiz and the skull measurement theories of Edward D. Cope, Herbert argued that blacks were naturally inferior to whites, although he also called for legal equality to prevent lynch law.

D108. Degler, Carl N. "Black and White Together: Bi-Racial Politics in the South." *Virginia Quarterly Review* 47 (summer 1971): 421-44. Degler comments on the Readjuster movement and particularly Mahone, who although not a racial liberal by modern standards was definitely willing and able to carry out his promise of bringing blacks into the political system—something the Populists could not say or do. The Readjusters must be considered the most successful effort at biracial Southern politics before the contemporary era.

D109. _____. "Racism in the United States: An Essay Review." *Journal of Southern History* 38 (February 1972): 101-08. In this positive review essay of George M. Frederickson's *The Black Image in the White Mind* (C117), Degler notes the author's argument that racism rarely appeared in print before 1830, but took flower when northern abolitionists opened their attack on slavery. The post-Reconstruction section of the book, however, is not as well argued as the first, and Frederickson takes no note of Populist ideas on blacks, despite the writings of Tom Watson and Marion Butler.

D110. Delap, Simeon Alexander. "The Populist Party in North Carolina." *Trinity College Historical Society (Durham, NC) Historical Papers* 14 (1922): 40-74. Detailed early account of the Farmers' Alliance and People's party in North Carolina from its antecedents through 1898. In addition to a discussion of the Democratic response to the black political threat after 1896, Delap quotes the Wilmington Star as saying the party in 1892 "was about equally composed of Republican whites and negroes and disappointed Democrats." Additionally, the "Populist candidate for Governor probably secured a large part of the negro vote" in 1896 due to Republican candidate Russell's racist statements.

D111. De Santis, Vincent P. "Negro Dissatisfaction with Republican Policy in the South, 1882-1884." *Journal of Negro History* 36 (April 1951): 148-59. The Arthur administration felt that the best way to gain political control of the South was to actively support independent movements and unite them with Republicans against the Bourbon Democrats. Black Republican leaders, however, were dismayed by many of Arthur's appointments and sought to organize a large-scale independent movement among black voters. One of the emergent leaders and strongest opponents to Arthur's plans was *New York Age* editor T. Thomas Fortune, who regularly attacked Administration policies towards blacks and set the stage for the split to come.

D112. _____. "President Arthur and the Independent Movements in the South in 1882." *Journal of Southern History* 19 (August 1953): 346-63. Arthur began his Southern campaign to crack the Democratic South by giving full support and assistance to the Readjusters, in particular William Mahone of Virginia. Other leaders, including James G. Blaine and Whitelaw Reid, sought difference approaches in opposition to the Administrations. By 1882 there arose an Independent movement calling for equal rights for all men, regardless of color. Republicans united with Independents with the backing of Arthur, although Florida and Louisiana did not see much Independent activity. To achieve its ends, however, the Administration often backed candidates antithetical to black leaders, which lead to a feeling of abandonment by black voters.

D113. _____. "Republican Efforts to 'Crack' the Democratic South." *Review of Politics* 14 (April 1952): 244-64. De Santis reviews the entire history of Republican efforts to win Southern voters away from the Democrats. The appearance of the Populists in 1892 brought problems and opportunities for the Republicans, who attempted to form coalitions with blacks to gain political strength.

D114. _____. "The Republican Party and the Southern Negro, 1877-1897." *Journal of Negro History* 45 (April 1960): 71-87. The alliance between Republicans and blacks would give each group what it wanted—black votes for the Republicans, and enforcement of the Fourteenth and Fifteenth Amendments for blacks. However, complications arose from the start, as blacks grew to suspect the aims of the Republicans. The coup de grace to the alliance came with the abandonment of the Force Bill by the Republican-controlled Congress, which De Santis argues was part of a well-planned policy that would remove the reliance on black support of the Party in the region while bolstering their opinion among Southern whites. It should also be pointed out that even some Southern blacks opposed the Force Bill, and only T. Thomas Fortune's paper condemned President Harrison and Congress for their failure of its passage.

D115. Dethloff, Henry C. "The Alliance and the Lottery: Farmers Try for the Sweepstakes." *Louisiana History* 6 (spring 1965): 141-59. The 1892 Louisiana Lottery campaign pitted anti-lottery Populists against pro-lottery Democrats, who also held power in primarily black parishes. Local newspapers argued that the lottery bill was supported by blacks, and that as long as the Louisiana Lottery Company controlled the state, there was no need for a Force Bill to ensure black voting rights.

D116. _____, and Robert R. Jones. "Race Relations in Louisiana, 1877-98." *Louisiana History* 9 (fall 1968): 301-23. Brief mention of the Populists as a factor in Louisiana politics. Black voter registration dropped dramatically between 1890 and 1900, with the subsequent voting strength of the Populists increasing. Louisiana Populists also approved of black disfranchisement but also did not want blacks to be counted as registered voters.

D117. Diggs, Annie L. "The Farmers' Alliance and Some of Its Leaders." *Arena* 5 (April 1892): 590-604. An excellent brief contemporary overview of the Farmers' Alliance and its most important leaders by one of the leading female Populists of the day. Features biographies of Leonidas L. Polk, Alonzo Wardall, H. L. Loucks, C. W. Macune, Marion Cannon (of the California Farmers' Alliance and Industrial Union), General James B. Weaver, and L. F. Livingston, along with photos of all but Polk. Diggs tends towards hagiography and spiritualism (a popular topic in the Arena). No mention of black suffrage or labor issues, although questions of free silver, women's suffrage, and prohibition are covered.

D118. Dillard, Tom. "To the Back of the Elephant: Racial Conflict in the Arkansas Republican Party." *Arkansas Historical Quarterly* 33 (Spring 1974): 3-15. One early symptom of the growing political independence of black voters from the Republican Party at the end of the nineteenth century was the rise of the Arkansas Populist and Greenback movements. Isaac Gillam and Green Thompson, two prominent black Little Rock politicians, were active in the local Greenback Party in the 1870s, Thompson serving as a state representative on that ticket. Elias Rector and P. M. E. Thompson both were active in the Pulaski County Populist movement. Teddy Roosevelt's Bull Moose Party attracted other prominent black Arkansas leaders, although by FDR's presidency most blacks had turned to the Democratic Party.

D119. Dillingham, Pitt. "Land Tenure Among the Negroes." *Yale Review* 5 (August 1896): 190-206. Dillingham quotes Van de Graaff (**C413**) that Southern blacks are migrating from the farm to mining communities and towns, and that this is the first step towards migration into the Northern cities and out of the

Black Belt. With the close of the Civil War and the end of the plantation system, a new relationship of crop-lien farming together with other agricultural and economic factors turned the former slaves into nothing more than tenants. The credit system will be the undoing of the South, however--"in the new rebellion the colored tenant will do his share of the fighting." Mentions the work of the Calhoun Settlement in Alabama as a black self-help plan for fighting back against the current system. A surprisingly sentient article for its time, although no mention is made of Populism or other agrarian movements.

D120. Doherty, Herbert J., Jr. "Voices of Protest from the New South, 1875-1910." *Mississippi Valley Historical Review* 42 (June 1955): 45-66. A number of "voices of protest" arose in the post-Reconstruction era in response to the developments of the "New South." T. Thomas Fortune, George Washington Cable, *Forum* editor Walter Hines Page, Edgar Gardner Murphy, and Tom Watson in particular addressed race issues, although each had his own solution to the dilemma. Despite their writings, most of these "voices" were not immediately influential in arousing support for change, and those calling for improved conditions for blacks were particularly unsuccessful.

D121. Douglass, Frederick. "The Negro Exodus from the Gulf States." *Frank Leslie's Popular Monthly* 9 (January 1880): 39-48. The black exodus from the Deep South into Kansas in particular is a cause for joy, especially as white Southerners now see that the prosperity of the region is dependent upon black men and women. If the landlords of the South adopt a course of fair treatment for their laborers, the exodus not only will stop but become undesirable.

D122. Drago, Edmund L. "The Black Press and Populism, 1890-1896." *San Jose Studies* 1.1 (1975): 97-103. By 1896, black newspapers were unanimous is their opposition to the Populists, favoring the presidential candidacy of William McKinley over William Jennings Bryan and remaining loyal to the Republican Party. Drago argues that black editors were most needed to give an intellectual foundation to the movement, but their petit bourgeois outlook made them unable to discern any alternative for advancement outside the status quo.

D123. Drew, Frank M. "The Present Farmers' Movement." *Political Science Quarterly* 6 (June 1891): 282-310. Drew begins his article with an overview of the various earlier and contemporary farmers reform groups, including the Colored Farmers' Alliance. Quoting its charter, Drew suggests that a reason 70% of black voters refrained from doing so in the 1890 election was that "they were busy making money." A letter from general superintendent Humphrey to Drew claims a CFA membership in 1891 of 1,250,000, of which 700,000 were adult males and 150,000 more males aged 18-21. In the South, Alliance membership is comprised of the "third estate": small farmers and mechanics. Drew goes so far as to chart both the comparative platforms of the six leading organizations (including the CFA), demonstrating the degree of unanimity of belief among the groups, and the success of the farmers in electing officials pledged to their needs.

D124. Du Bois, W. E. B. "Georgia: Invisible Empire State." In Ernest Gruening, ed., *These United States*. New York: Boni and Liveright, 1926. Du Bois takes issue with the then-current racial situation in Georgia, noting how much the situation had declined since the turn of the century. He also notes the influence of Tom Watson, who tried to unite labor and invited blacks to help in the organization of the Populist Party in Georgia. Populist opponents argued that blacks would take away white jobs, and the race difference grew until "in most cases the whole knowledge and thought of the workers and voters went in keeping Negroes down, rather than to raising themselves." The only way for Watson to survive politically "was to out-Herod Herod in his diatribes against Negroes. . . ."

D125. _____. "The Negro in the Black Belt: Some Social Sketches." *Bulletin of the Dept. of Labor* 22 (May 1899): 401-17. One of the early serious studies by Du Bois to ascertain the condition of rural Southern blacks. The field work was completed by his students at Atlanta University, but Du Bois based many of his conclusions on his personal knowledge rather than the raw data. Useful for understanding the post-Populist era. Published as a pamphlet.

D126. Elkins, F. Clark. "The Agricultural Wheel: County Politics and Consolidation, 1884-1885." *Arkansas Historical Quarterly* 29.2 (1970): 152-75. The Agricultural Wheel and the Brothers of Freedom successfully ran candidates in seven of the eleven counties in which they posted slates. Their similar goals and ideals resulted in a merger of the two groups in 1885. State blacks, barred from membership, formed the Sons of the Agricultural Star, with headquarters in Monroe County, that same year.

D127. _____. "The Agricultural Wheel in Arkansas, 1887." *Arkansas Historical Quarterly* 40.3 (1981): 249-60. Although the Wheel originally forbade black membership, by 1887 the organization began to open up its membership. Delegates to the Hollywood (Clark County) state convention voted to seat a black delegation of "Wheelers" from St. Francis County. Black leaders went on to establish Wheels in Hempstead and other Arkansas counties as a result. The Wheel finally merged with the Southern Farmers' Alliance in 1889.

D128. Emerick, C. F. "An Analysis of Agricultural Discontent in the United States. I." *Political Science Quarterly* 11 (September 1896): 433-63. The degree of agricultural discontent in the United States in 1896 is alarming and unusual, given the normal placid nature of the farm community. The relative growth of the urban population does not translate into an economic rural decline. However, three-fourths of the aggregate wealth of the U.S. is concentrated in cities, chiefly through the introduction of steam power and the factory system.

Also, the rise of modern transportation has caused a migration of agricultural industry, chiefly to the central and western states. The value of farm land in the older states has enormously decreased, primarily because of the cultivation of virgin soils.

D129. _____. "An Analysis of Agricultural Discontent in the United States. II." *Political Science Quarterly* 11 (December 1896): 601-39. In part two of his analysis, Emerick notes that the volume of mortgage debt is distributed according to the wealth, energy, and enterprise of the people, but also that the burden of debt has been increased by a decline in agricultural prices. In addition, a number of factors have contributed to the growth in the relative numbers of farm tenants. Four remedies for agricultural depression are considered: the free coinage of silver, a general property tax, an export bounty on agricultural staples, and a greater development of thrift among the farmers.

D130. _____. "An Analysis of Agricultural Discontent in the United States. III." *Political Science Quarterly* 12 (March 1897): 93-127. In the concluding portion of his analysis, Emerick underlines the importance of thrift for improving the rural condition, even quoting Booker T. Washington that "art and music for people who live in rented houses and have no bank account are not the most important subjects to which attention can be given." But agricultural discontent is also part and parcel with the spirit of the age; the wants and desires of the rural population have developed more rapidly than the means of satisfying them. The ostentatious show of wealth of the urban population gives the farmer the feeling that he is getting less than he deserves.

D131. Erlich, Howard S. "Populist Rhetoric Reassessed: a Paradox." Quarterly *Journal of Speech* 63 (April 1977): 140-51. "Populist rhetoric cannot be easily characterized or nicely pigeonholed without denying substantive elements within the movement." Populist leaders could attempt alliance with Southern blacks while simultaneously "exposing" conspiracies. The legacy of Populism is a "rhetoric of irrationality and provincialism competing with one of relative sophistication and concern for individual and social welfare."

D132. Ettinger, Brian Gary. "John Fitzpatrick and the Limits of Working-Class Politics in New Orleans, 1892-1896." *Louisiana History* 26 (fall 1985): 341-67. John Fitzpatrick became mayor of New Orleans when "the Ring," the city's political machine, ousted the Reform party lead by the New Orleans elite. Blacks played a significant part in electoral politics in this era on a number of fronts, including the powerful biracial dock unions and pro-Lottery black Republicans, both of whom favored Fitzpatrick's machine. The newly formed People's party also endorsed Fitzpatrick, but Ettinger notes the Populists "were virtually without support in the city." Their endorsement, however, showed the importance of "class" in the 1892 election. Fitzpatrick also gained black support by making "guarded statements" against the Mississippi form of disfranchisement.

D133. Ferguson, James S. "The Grange and Farmer Education in Mississippi." *Journal of Southern History* 8 (November 1942): 497-512. Early in its history, the Grange emphasized education for farmers. When the Republican-controlled government in 1870 established separate, free public schools, the Grange opposed the action partly on their unwillingness to pay separate taxes to the new bifarcate system. However, with cuts in expenditures Grangers became self-imposed guardians of the school system, even urging whites to teach in black schools. The group's primary interested in Mississippi, however, was in training farmers towards self-sufficiency, a measure that met with mixed success.

D134. Fields, Barbara J. "Origins of the New South and the Negro Question." *Journal of Southern History* 67 (November 2001): 811-26. In her fiftieth anniversary critical analysis of Woodward's *Origins*, Fields argues that "Woodward's refusal to jim-crow Jim Crow is the great gift that Origins has bestowed on the study of afro-Southerners." Woodward rightly points out that the question during the Populist era was not one of white supremacy, but of which whites should be supreme.

D135. Fingerhut, Eugene R. "Tom Watson, Blacks, and Southern Reform." *Georgia Historical Quarterly* 60 (winter 1976): 324-43. Fingerhut argues that Watson's relationship to blacks was one of political expediency. When the Southern black was a useful political ally, he courted their votes. When blacks were no longer useful, Watson disgarded them. "Their political rights were a means to an end. The changes in Watson's actions toward blacks were real. His consistency was as obvious."

D136. Fink, Leon. "'Irrespective of Party, Color or Social Standing': the Knights of Labor and Opposition Politics in Richmond, Virginia." *Labor History* 19 (summer 1978): 325-49. The Knights of Labor found Richmond, Virginia an excellent spot for recruiting industrial laborers of both races just prior to the rise of Populism. In the summer of 1885, the Order opened membership to black recruits, and within a year thirty-five local "assemblies" had been chartered in Richmond and neighboring Manchester. A Reformist faction within the Orders ranks formed a biracial coalition with a platform calling for "a general understanding and cooperation of the toiling masses, irrespective of party, color, or social standing." A fascinating article on local black/white power struggles in the late 1880s which laid the groundwork for agrarian politics a few years later.

D137. Finnegan, Terence. "Lynching and Political Power in Mississippi and South Carolina." In W. Fitzhugh Brundage, ed., *Under Sentence of Death: Lynching in the South*. Chapel Hill, NC: University of North Carolina Press, 1997. Finnegan argues that the white elite disfranchised blacks "because of their supposed inferiority, but they lynched when African Americans challenged the myths that sustained white supremacy and refused to accept the social, economic, and political constraints that white racism demanded." Notes the Leflore County Massacre of 1889, which saw the apprehension of forty black Alliance leaders and murder of twenty-five blacks.

D138. Fishel, Leslie H., Jr. "The Negro in Northern Politics, 1877-1900." *Mississippi Valley Historical Review* 42 (December 1955): 466-89. While the efforts of the Alliances and other farmers' movements had little influence among northern blacks during the 1880s-90s, black leaders followed their own paths towards self-determination through economic and political organization. Editor T. Thomas Fortune planned to unite the diverse northern and western groups under the umbrella of an Afro-American National League that sought to influence opinion and legislation after the manner of farm and labor movements, by moving outside of the existing political structure. The parallel failure of both the Alliance and League appears to result in part from their move away from initial non-political status into that of a political organization.

D139. Fleming, Walter L. "Pap Singleton, the Moses of the Colored Exodus." *American Journal of Sociology* 15 (July 1909): 61-82. One of the first great migrations of Southern blacks was to Kansas, under the guidance of Benjamin "Pap" Singleton, a former slave who insisted on the title "The Moses of the Colored Exodus." After little success in acquiring land for Tennessee blacks, Singleton turned his attention to Kansas, where he was able to settle numerous "exodusters" in the colonies of Nicodemus, Dunlap, and Singleton between 1876-78. By 1885, Singleton had organized his United Transatlantic Society as a "back to Africa" movement, with little success. Ultimately, he distrusted fellow black leaders and saw little hope of successful integration of the races in the United States.

D140. Flower, Benjamin O. "The Burning of Negroes in the South: a Protest and a Warning." *Arena* 7 (April 1893): 630-40. Flower, an Arena editor and Southerner, places much of the blame for lynching on the presence of federal troops who upheld government by "half-savage" blacks and aliens in the South after the Civil War. White Southern savagery was awakened by the treatment of the states during Reconstruction, and as horrible and unjust as lynching was, it was also to be expected. Using the lynching of Henry Smith in Paris, Texas as his focal point, Flower argues that only the rigorous and impartial enforcement of the law, rather than vigilantism, will save the South from catastrophe.

D141. Flynn, Charles L., Jr. "Procrustean Bedfellows and Populists: An Alternative Hypothesis." In Jeffrey C. Crow, Paul D. Escott, and Charles L. Flynn, Jr., ed. *Race, Class, and Politics in Southern History: Essays in Honor of Robert F. Durden*. Baton Rouge, LA: Louisiana State University Press, 1989. Flynn takes to task both Woodward and Shaw's thesis on the nature of Southern populism, arguing that party organization became the issue dividing Georgia Populists and Democrats. A division over political tactics became a fight over "the substance of democracy." Flynn notes, however, that democratic rights, "universally celebrated in the abstract" by Populists, were denied by these same men to many in practice.

D142. Folmsbee, Stanley J. "The Origin of the First 'Jim Crow' Law." *Journal of Southern History* 15 (May 1949): 235-47. Although much 'Jim Crow' legislation did not appear until the late 1880s and early 1890s, Folmsbee traces the history of an aborted 1881 Tennessee bill which would have required railroads to provide separate cars or compartments for blacks and whites. Curiously, the bill was enacted by a Republican-controlled legislature which included four black members, two who did not vote on the issue. Because of the rampant political corruption of the time and the number of counties with large black populations, Democrats and Republicans competed for black votes. A 'Jim Crow' law in 1891 was unanimously opposed by Republican legislators, although Democrats under the control of the Farmers' Alliance supported the measure.

D143. Ford, Lacy K. "Rednecks and Merchants: Economic Development and Social Tensions in the South Carolina Upcountry, 1865-1900." *Journal of American History* 71 (September 1984): 294-318. Ford argues that the South Carolina Upcountry was dramatically transformed from 1850 to 1900 as the commercial and industrial revolutions swept into the region. As economic development continued, farmers grew hostile toward the special tax exemptions granted for capital investment and publicly financed railroads. Many farmers complained against the growing power of the lien merchant and laws, which they felt put too much power in the hands of local blacks. From these beginnings grew the local Farmers Alliance movement, which saw the region's problems in terms of class struggle.

D144. Forsythe, Harold S. "African American Churches, Fusion Politics in Virginia, and the Repbulican Gubernatorial Campaign in 1889." In John Saillant, ed., *Afro-Virginian History and Culture*. New York: Garland, 1999. Forsythe questions why blacks were willing to ally themselves with native Southern whites to make effective political coalitions in Virginia. He points to the efforts of William Mahone, who specifically appealed to black church leaders to help his 1889 gubernatorial campaign. Rural and urban black clergy spread the word for politics free of race-baiting and white supremacy, but the Southern white churches countered that their black counterparts had no business meddling in politics.

D145. Franklin, John Hope. "'Legal' Disfranchisement of the Negro." *Journal of Negro Education* 26 (summer 1957): 241-48. In his overview article to this special issue of JNE on "The Negro Voter in the South," Franklin notes that far from having disappeared from the political scene by 1890, Southern blacks were still voting and even electing black representatives to state legislatures. The radical agrarian movement attracted followers from both races who even agreed on a number of the same goals, despite maintaining separate organizations. But even as these biracial coalitions developed, they had within them the seeds of their own downfall. Whites who joined the movement only had to have their racial antipathies aroused to not only desert but also turn against their black allies. By the late 1890s, many Southern states had enacted constitutional provisions which served to disfranchise black voters.

D146. Franzoni, Janet Brenner. "Troubled Tirader: a Psychobiographical Study of Tom Watson." *Georgia Historical Quarterly* 57 (winter 1973): 493-510. Franzoni notes Woodward's hint at Watson's mental troubles as a starting point for her brief psychobiography of the Georgia politician. The components of Watson's youth, including his encounters with death, predisposed him to an adult neurosis, but it remained for Watson to find suitable outlets for his unmet needs. The maturing man found it increasingly difficult to cope with circumstances which tended to foster rather than retard symptoms of mental disorder.

D147. Gaither, Gerald H. "Blacks and the Southern Farmers' Alliance Movement." *East Texas Historical Journal* 14 (Spring 1976): 24-38. Brief overview of the relationship between blacks and the Southern Alliance. While "organically separate, the order was ideologically in tune with the aims of the total agrarian movement." Gaither calls into question reported CFA membership statistics, noting discrepancies among reports by Alliance leaders.

D148. _____. "The Negro Alliance Movement in Tennessee, 1888-1891." *West Tennessee Historical Society Papers* 27 (1973): 50-62. Although it remained organically separate, the Tennessee Colored Farmers Alliance and Wheel "were ideologically in tune with the broad aims of the state's agrarian movement; philosophically and financially, however, they relied heavily upon the organizations of their white counterparts, and as such were regarded as little more than dependent allies."

D149. Garland, Hamlin. "The Alliance Wedge in Congress." *Arena* 5 (March 1892): 447-57. Although Garland notes that nearly fifty congressmen have Farmers' Alliance leanings, only nine form a separate organization: Jerry Simpson, John G. Otis, John Davis, Benjamin H. Clover, William Baker, O. M. Kem, W. A. McKeighan, Thomas E. Watson, and K. Halvorsen. The article includes photographs of each congressman. No mention is made of racial issues, but Garland's is a useful article nevertheless for its summation of the relative strengths and weaknesses of Alliance leadership in Washington.

D150. Garvin, Roy. "Benjamin, or 'Pap,' Singleton and His Followers." *Journal of Negro History* 33 (January 1948): 7-23. Although Benjamin, or "Pap" Singleton was not the sole individual responsible for the mass exodus of blacks from the Deep South into Kansas and other Midwestern states, he is probably the most famous, having founded eleven colonies in that state between 1873 and 1880. Wyandotte, Kansas saw a significant influx of blacks during the period, including future ambassador to Liberia C. H. J. Taylor. Garvin's article focuses primarily on the immigrants themselves, rather than Singleton, and gives an idea of the importance the "exodus" would have on black Kansas and the future of the Populist party and fusion politics in that region.

D151. Gavins, Raymond. "Gordon Blaine Hancock: a Black Profile from the New South." *Journal of Negro History* 59 (July 1974): 207-27. The racial and economic philosophy Gordon Blaine Hancock, interracialist educator, minister, and journalist from South Carolina, developed progressively over time, using his base first at Seneca Institute and later at Virginia Union University and elsewhere to foster belief in "upward striving" among blacks. A prolific and scholarly sociologist who combined the self-help philosophy of Booker T. Washington with the scientific inquiry of Du Bois, Hancock believed that much racial conflict was economic, pitting immigrants and other low-paid workers against blacks. His "Double-Duty-Dollar" theory, which urges black community economic self-reliance, was an early theorization of Du Bois' "group economy" and "Buy Black" campaigns.

D152. _____. "The Meaning of Freedom: Black North Carolina in the Nadir, 1880-1900." In Jeffrey J. Crow, Paul D. Escott, and Charles L. Flynn, Jr., ed, *Race, Class, and Politics in Southern History: Essays in Honor of Robert F. Durden*. Baton Rouge, LA: Louisiana State University Press, 1989. Middle class black leaders in North Carolina voiced mixed strategies of accommodation and protest to counter the rise of disfranchisement and lynching, but also to instill group pride and solidarity. Gavins notes the presence of the Colored Farmers' Alliance, with fifty-five thousand members, and the black assemblies of the Knights of Labor in fifty counties.

D153. Gay, Dorothy A. "Crisis of Identity: the Negro Community in Raleigh, 1890-1900." *North Carolina Historical Review* 50 (April 1973): 121-40. Excellent study of one Southern city during the Populist era. Black political participation revealed a divided leadership, not loyal to any single party or united with the Republican party itself. Dissent became obvious at the state Republican convention of 1896, when black leaders split on their support of gubernatorial candidate Daniel L. Russell.

D154. Gladden, Washington. "The Embattled Farmers." *The Forum* 10 (November 1890): 315-22. The American farmer is up in arms over redress of his grievances, and he is turning to agrarian movements and other radical means for help. Several results may come of the farmers' uprising, including securing discussion of important economic issues, loosening the bonds of partisanship, and helping to bring an end to sectionalism.

D155. Glasrud, Bruce A. "William M. McDonald: Business and Fraternal Leader." In Alwyn Barr and Robert A. Calvert, ed., *Black Leaders: Texans for Their Times*. Austin, TX: Texas State Historical Association, 1981. Brief biography of William M. "Gooseneck Bill" McDonald, who for thirty years oversaw the Texas Republican Party and fought against the insurgent black Populists. The Populist era is quickly glossed over, and there is little sense of the bitter struggles between McDonald, Cuney, and other black Texas leaders.

D156. Godshalk, David F. "William J. Northen's Public and Personal Struggles against Lynching." In Jane Dailey, Glenda Elizabeth Gilmore, and Bryant Simon, ed., *Jumpin' Jim Crow: Southern Politics from Civil War to Civil Rights*. Princeton, NJ: Princeton University Press, 2000. After his election as Georgia governor in 1890 with the support of the Farmers' Alliance, Northen turned his back on many of his friends who switched from the Democrats to the Populists. Northen flatly rejected uniting black and white voters in common cause, although he won re-election with the support of black voters who favored his anti-lynching stance. After his loss in the 1894 general assembly election, he came to distrust black voters, but he continued his anti-lynching crusade.

D157. Going, Allen J. "The Agrarian Revolt." In Arthur S. Link and Rembert W. Patrick, ed., *Writing Southern History: Essays in Historiography in Honor of Fletcher M. Green*. Baton Rouge, LA: Louisiana State University Press, 1965. Going notes that, at the time of his writing, "the agrarian background of Populism was still incomplete," and that scholars are in need of biographies of Kolb and Macune, among others. Useful general overview of much of the research in this bibliography.

D158. _____. "Alabama Bourbonism and Populism Revisited." *Alabama Review* 36 (April 1983): 83-109. Going examines the literature of post-Reconstruction Alabama in the thirty years since the publication of his *Bourbon Democracy in Alabama* (University, AL: University of Alabama Press, 1951). Although he does not dwell on any one topic, including Populism, Going comments on a number of interesting dissertations and papers which would have some bearing on the study of blacks and Alabama politics. He also notes the works of Hackney and Rogers on the role of blacks in Alabama Populism.

D159. _____. "Critical Months in Alabama Politics, 1895-1896." *Alabama Review* 5 (October 1952): 269-81. Considering the state of Republican Party affairs around 1890, it is no wonder that blacks joined the CFA or listened to the "blandishments" of Black Belt Democrats. However, as the free silver issued threatened to cause a major rift in the Democratic machinery, Populists stepped into the breach in a fusion campaign with Republicans. State Republicans, at the same time, split over the fusion question, with blacks splitting over the issue themselves. Ultimately, state Democrats withstood the Populist threat after the poor showing of the Populists.

D160. _____. "The South and the Blair Education Bill." *Mississippi Valley Historical Review* 44 (September 1957): 267-90. The history of the Blair Education Bill, an attempt by the federal government to improve education primarily throughout the Deep South, is instructive for understanding Southern attitudes towards federal interventionist policy during the rise of Populism. Going notes that Redeemers usually supported the bill, while the "agrarians" opposed it on the grounds of unconstitutionality, extravagance, expense, and other reasons. Southern Democratic and Republican state party platforms endorsed the bill, but Going is not specific regarding Alliance support (or lack thereof). He further argues that "the lack of progress and of hope for Negro education may have furthered measures to disfranchise the Negro."

D161. Goodwyn, Lawrence C. "Populist Dreams and Negro Rights: East Texas as a Case Study." *American Historical Review* 76 (December 1971): 1435-1456. To shed light on the interracial politics of late nineteenth century Populism, Goodwyn examines the example of Grimes County, in east Texas. Populism there endured for more than a generation following Reconstruction, with the county sending black legislators to Austin well after the Democrats took control. The racial coalition brought electoral victory to the Populists in the 1896 and 1898 elections. Success came from a combination of the power of the local white Populist sheriff (who hired black deputies), black political goals, and the economic goals of white farmers. However, a backlash in the form of the White Man's Union and its campaign of terror ultimately lead to the destruction of the People's party in the county.

D162. Grantham, Dewey W., Jr. "The Contours of Southern Progressivism." *American Historical Review* 86 (December 1981): 1035-59. In this review essay on Populism and Progressivism in the South, Grantham discusses numerous post-Origins studies on the movements and notes needs for further research. He also notes that Southern Democrats were "genuine advocates of reform" who increasingly accepted the Populist concept of a positive state. White consensus during the Populist era reflected a widespread conviction that disfranchisement was one element of the formula toward greater social stability and public calm in the region.

D163. _____. "Georgia Politics and the Disfranchisement of the Negro." *Georgia Historical Quarterly* 32 (March 1948): 1-21. The Populist movement proved that the black vote was capable of serving as a deciding factor in Georgia elections. After initial success, the party fell into swift decline after 1896, as white Populists returned to the Democratic Party folds. To many Populists, the presence of a black voting bloc was an excuse for the Democrats to practice widespread fraud, and not until the black vote was eliminated would Tom Watson and white Populists hold power in the state. Watson and Hoke Smith took up the disfranchisement banner, although most Democrats and major state newspapers came out against it.

D164. _____. "The Progressive Movement and the Negro." *South Atlantic Quarterly* 54 (October 1955): 461-77. Despite its comprehensive program of reform, the Populist Movement and its liberal supporters gave little attention to the status of black Americans. Grantham notes that, in many ways, "the thirty-year period after 1877 was an era of retrogression" for blacks. The problem lay in part in the progressive emphasis on municipal reform—railways, taxation, corruption in government. Blacks were "incidental" to other reforms at the city level, although they would naturally have a share in the positive effects felt also by whites. Southern reformers such as Hoke Smith were often progressive on many levels, but they attained power as Negrophobes with the support of white Populists. Their democracy was for whites only and harmed relations between the races.

D165. _____. "Negro Disfranchisement in Arkansas." 26 (autumn 1967): 199-255. Race relations in post-Civil War Arkansas *Arkansas Historical Quarterly* differed significantly from the rest of the South in part because of the economically conservative "Redeemers," New South leaders who directed the movement to expel the carpetbaggers. Many shared office with black political leaders through the "fusion principle," which would in part present both white and black candidates for upcoming elections. With falling cotton prices, however, white and black farmers turned to Populism, with eleven black representatives among party convention delegates in 1892. However, the party's liberal racial attitudes, including condemnation of lynching, lead to strong Democratic race-baiting and the destruction of the fusion system. As a result, within the next two years blacks were eliminated from nearly all public offices and essentially lost the vote to new poll taxes after 1891.

D166. Green, James, and Paul B. Wortham. "Black Workers in the New South, 1865-1915." In Nathan I. Huggins, Martin Kilson, and Daniel M. Fox, ed., *Key Issues In the Afro-American Experience, Volume 2.* New York: Harcourt, Brace, Jovanovich, 1971. Overview of both agricultural and industrial black laborers during the period. The authors notes that "some black farmers joined with their white counterparts to seek relief" from oppressive credit and marketing systems through "collective action and cooperative marketing schemes." Rebellious black farmers joined with whites in the Populist party, despite "disagreements."

D167. Greene, Larry A. "Black Populism and the Quest for Racial Unity."
Telos 103 (spring 1995): 127-42. The failure of Reconstruction and the Populist movement in the 1890s lead to the failure of a biracial democracy in the
South. The "stock law" struggles in 1880s Georgia demonstrated that black and
white farmers could transcend racial divides for the betterment of the class.
Some anti-stockers went on to become Populist leaders. On the surface, Populists appeared to promote racial harmony, but the movement also failed to repu-
diate white supremacy and advocate an egalitarian biracial Southern society.
Greene traces the demise of Populism through the mass emigration of blacks to
the North and the struggle for black leaders to find their voice. Contemporary
Populists must address the racial dimension of economic issues honestly to build
successful coalitions.

D168. Greer, Colin, and Barry Goldberg. "Populism, Ethnicity, and Public
Policy: an Historical Perspective." In Harry C. Boyte and Frank Riessman, ed.,
The New Populism: the Politics of Empowerment. Philadelphia: Temple University Press, 1986. The ethnic revival of the 1970s, although significant and
shortlived, helped shaped the modern view of democratic empowerment. Populism in the modern era is a response to antidemocratic corporatist tendencies of
the "progressive" state, but this thinking too often leads to a supposition of government as the source of domination. Since the great ethnic revival of the
1950s, there has grown within the politicized economy the notion of public ethnicity, which has helped define contemporary curriculums, domestic spending
patterns, and pluralism. Populism has the potential to advance the struggle for
the public ownership of the state, but only if the ethnic working class' historic
tie to the need for and growth of the state is realized.

D169. Grimshaw, Allen D. "Lawlessness and Violence in America and Their
Special Manifestations in Changing Negro-White Relationships." *Journal of
Negro History* 44 (January 1959): 52-72. Save for a short period following the
Civil War, U.S. black-white relations have followed the standard accommoda-
tive pattern of superordination-subordination, with whites continually in the
dominant position. Grimshaw outlines the history of violence in race relations,
noting that a tenuous alliance existed for a brief time with the rise of the Populist
movement. After the breakdown of the alliance, however, there arose a classic
period of repression and lynching. Of most importance for its attempt to demonstrate that racial antagonism is part of the American tradition of lawlessness
and violence.

D170. Grob, Gerald N. "Organized Labor and the Negro Workers, 1865-1900."
Labor History 1 (Spring 1960): 164-76. In his brief article, Grob outlines the
general history of the relationship between blacks and organized labor in the
postbellum years. The success of the Knights of Labor is noted, and in the
South "the Negro local was a familiar sight." Grob also cites the difficulties
Samuel Gompers had in inducing industrial unions to accept black workers on

an equal basis. Part of the blame for the failure of biracial unionism, particularly in the South, falls upon the Populists, whose involvement in race-baiting elections resulted in the rise of Jim Crow laws and disfranchisement legislation.

D171. _____. "Terence V. Powderly and the Knights of Labor." *Mid-America* 39 (January 1957): 39-55. Terence V. Powderly was arguably the most well-known and powerful labor leader in the United States, until the rise of Samuel Gompers. Although he developed nothing original in the way of organizational policy or technique, he drew attention to the nascent American Labor Movement. In a major break from other reform leaders of the period, Powderly believed that race was not a qualification for union membership. He also argued that cheap black labor had to be eliminated if white labor was to effectively organize. However, he also recognized the problems of the Deep South's relationship to blacks, noting that it was better for blacks to have separate organizations.

D172. Gross, George Wellington. "The Negro as a Factor in Kansas Politics." *Agora* 2 (1893): 166-70. The authors were unable to examine this article, but Gross' article casts additional light on the role of blacks in a state where they played an active leadership role in the Populist movement.

D173. Gutman, Herbert G. "Black Coal Miners and the Greenback-Labor Party in Redeemer Alabama, 1878-1879." *Labor History* 10 (summer 1969): 506-35; rpt in Donald G. Nieman, ed., *African Americans and Non-Agricultural Labor in the South, 1865-1900.* New York: Garland, 1994: 18-47. This collection of letters written between 1878-1879 to the unionist *National Labor Tribune* reveals in part the early growth of black labor unionism and the often uneasy relationship between black and white coal miners of the region. Writers also note the interest among northern and Southern black workers in the Greenback-Labor Party, the precursor in many ways to the Knights of Labor and Farmers' Alliance. Gutman suggests that such letters open, in an unusual way, the world of these workers just after Reconstruction, especially as they name previously unknown strikes and other events.

D174. _____. "The Negro and the United Mine Workers of America: The Career and Letters of Richard L. Davis and Something of Their Meaning, 1890-1900." In Donald G. Nieman, ed., *African Americans and Non-Agricultural Labor in the South, 1865-1900* (New York: Garland, 1994): 49-138. Paralleling the rise of the blacks in the agrarian reform movement was their arguably even more significant role in the growth of labor unionism in the coal industry. Richard L. Davis, a black miner, attended the UMW's founding convention and was elected to Ohio's District 6 Executive Board in 1890 and was twice elected to the UMW National Executive Board, in 1896 and 1897. A longtime proponent of interracial unionism, Davis often found mistrust and conflict among both races. Gutman briefly compares the role of blacks in the UMW and Populist movement and notes the more enlightened attitude of the former over the latter.

D175. Haas, Edward F. "John Fitzpatrick and Political Continuity in New Orleans, 1896-1899." *Louisiana History* 22 (winter 1981): 7-30. The 1896 mayoral election saw the stunning defeat of the Regulars, lead by Mayor John Fitzpatrick, by the reformists Citizens' League. However, through careful maneuvering, the machine was able to place influential members in patronage and nonofficial positions. Governor Murphy Foster also threw his support to the Regulars, as he feared the continued alliance of Populists, Republicans, and the League. The Regulars also were central to the disfranchise movement, arguing that blacks were a corrupting influence in elections. In the end, New Orleans voters returned the Regulars machine to power in 1899, where it remained for the next fifty years.

D176. Hackney, Sheldon. "Origins of the New South in Retrospect." *Journal of Southern History* 38 (May 1972): 191-216. For Hackney, Woodward's work is both Beardian and Faulknerian. In the first analysis, *Origins* is concerned with the cynic's question of who is in control and what are they after? Woodward seems to accept the dualistic world view of the Populists themselves, that of a world as arena between the forces of class vs. mass, or business vs. the people. But it also addresses the tragic Faulknerian version of the South of decay, opportunism, and nobility. A good analytic piece on Woodward combined with a Populist historiography.

D177. Hahn, Stephen. "Common Right and Commonwealth: the Stock-Law Struggle and the Roots of Southern Populism." In J. Morgan Kousser and James M. McPherson, ed., *Region, Race, and Reconstruction: Essays in Honor of C. Vann Woodward*. New York: Oxford University Press, 1982. The stock-law controversy was one of the great struggles in the 1880s rural South which lead to the rise of Populism. Locals complained that blacks tended to vote "No Fence." Hahn quotes the use of fraud and coercion to gain black votes, including promises to pay taxes and chartering trains to Atlanta on election day.

D178. Halsell, Willie D. "The Bourbon Period in Mississippi Politics, 1875-1890." *Journal of Southern History* 11 (November 1945): 519-37. The period of Bourbon power in Mississippi began roughly around 1875 with the defeat of the Democratic Party reactionaries and ended after a period of decline in the 1890s. The rise of the Farmers' Alliance and Populist party in part contributed to the decline of this faction. During the early 1880s, the Greenback Party stood in opposition to the Bourbons. Halsell discusses some of the major Bourbon elected officials in Mississippi and compares their interests and power to that of their Georgia counterparts of the same name.

D179. Hamm, Walter C. "The Three Phases of Colored Suffrage." *North American Review* 168 (March 1899): 285-96. Hamm divides the development of black suffrage into three distinct periods. The first phase lasted ten years, until the spring of 1877, in which brute force was used to coerce black voters.

The second phase began with "white control in every Southern state and determined to perpetuate that control"—the period of the rise of Populism and the disfranchise movement. The third phase follows the "one straight road out of the embarrassments into which colored suffrage has brought the country"—a constitutional amendment making suffrage contingent on literacy, and literacy the basis for the apportionment of House membership and Electoral College votes. The "experiment in colored suffrage" is vital to the survival of both races, although Hamm fears the white race will deteriorate with continued intimate contact with the black.

D180. Hammond, Marcus B. "The Southern Farmer and Cotton." *Political Science Quarterly* 12 (September 1897): 450-75. Agricultural discontent in part stems from localized crop price problems, and in the Deep South that crop is cotton. After the Civil War, the plantation system was in shambles, and the wage-system used to hire the new freedmen did not work for a number of reasons. By 1876, only 5% of freedmen had become landowners. The South finally adopted the sharecropping system, which allowed the tenant to rent land and receive part of the crop. Simultaneously there developed a "crop lien" system, wherein the merchant secured at the beginning of the season a chattel mortgage from the farmer in exchange for necessary supplies; this system was more prevalent with black than with white farmers. Despite Hammond's racial generalizations as to the quality of black farmers and sharecroppers, his article is useful for its contemporary overview of the economics of a one-crop system.

D181. Hampton, Wade. "The Race Problem." *Arena* 8 (July 1890): 132-38. South Carolina's Senator Wade Hampton believes that blacks are incapable of self-government, and that the "Constitution was violated when the negro was allowed to vote." Since politicians are too cowardly to do the right thing—deprive blacks of their citizenship—the next best thing would be mass deportation to where blacks would not come into contact with whites at any level.

D182. Hargis, Peggy G. "Beyond the Marginality Thesis: the Acquisition and Loss of Land by African Americans in Georgia, 1880-1930." *Agricultural History* 72 (spring 1998): 241-63. Of central import to understanding Populism's potential lure for Georgia blacks is an analysis of land ownership. Drawing on county-level data, Hargis notes that, in Georgia, rural blacks acquired title to slightly more than one million acres by 1900. One of the main factors influencing land purchase was local white attitudes, which would vary from county to county. Hargis further argues that the marginality thesis as an analytical explanation for black land ownership is a "vacuous dead end."

D183. Harper, Roland M. "Development of Agriculture in Lower Georgia from 1890 to 1920." *Georgia Historical Quarterly* 6 (December 1922): 323-54. Excellent source of statistical information on the condition of black farmers during the Populist era. Includes a nice graphical chart showing the percentage of black farmers 1870-1920 broken down by region (e.g., Red Hills).

D184. Harrington, Wynne P. "The Populist Party in Kansas." *Collections of the Kansas State Historical Society, 1923-1925.* Topeka, KS: Kansas State Printing Plant, 1925. Extremely detailed but often amusing account of the rise and fall of Populism in Kansas, told by a delegate to the Populist national convention in 1900. Lists the Kansas slate for state office for 1890, including "auditor, B. F. Foster (colored)."

D185. Harris, D. Alan. "Campaigning in the Bloody Seventh: The Election of 1894 in the Seventh Congressional District." *Alabama Review* 27 (April 1974): 127-38. The 1894 Seventh Congressional District race between Populist Milford Wriarson Howard and William Henry Denson was one of the most notorious in the mountain region's history. Howard, author of the popular *If Christ Came to Congress*, was charged by Democrats with a number of crimes, including gambling with blacks, leading a mob which kept them from voting, and paying five dollars to have a black Republican assaulted. After Howard won the election, Republicans turned against him, in fear of losing political power.

D186. Harris, W. T. "Education of the Negro." *Atlantic Monthly* 69 (June 1892): 721-36. Harris foresees the resolution of "the Negro Problem" without recourse to violence once all blacks are educated in schools and become newspaper readers; have all forms of industrial training accessible to them, with a quota of skilled black men and women in manufacturing; have black ministers educated in Christian theology interpreted in the missionary spirit, and finding its auxiliaries in modern science and literature. Mutual respect for moral and intellectual character will lead to civil and political recognition for blacks. Harris includes the comments of a number of advance readers of his article, including J. L. M. Curry of the Slater Fund.

D187. Haygood, Atticus G. "The South and the School Problem." *Harper's New Monthly Magazine* 79 (July 1889): 225-31. Haygood considers the question of common schools—mostly found in rural areas and small villages—in the wake of Reconstruction. Although often in poor condition, these small schools have shown steady improvement, especially as the South awakens to the realization that the ignorant classes, both white and black, must be educated. The greatest achievement, however, is in black education, from the primary grades to higher education. Haygood includes many statistics to bolster his arguments, particularly that there is "substantial progress" in educating blacks. A useful article for understanding literacy in the region during the Populist movement.

D188. Haynes, Frederick Emory. "The New Sectionalism." *Quarterly Journal of Economics* 10 (April 1896): 269-95. The "new sectionalism" represents a cleavage between the older, wealthy states of the East and the poorer and/or newer Southern and Western states.   The Farmers' Alliance and Populist Party represent most completely the ideas behind this concept, particularly as regards economic issues.   Article includes state-by-state breakdown of Populist vote for 1892 and 1894. Haynes notes the role of fusion politics in Populist campaigns and the growing influence of socialism--and that the basic attitude of Populists is socialistic.

D189. Henningson, Berton E., Jr. "Northwest Arkansas and the Brothers of Freedom: the Roots of a Farmer Movement." *Arkansas Historical Quarterly* 34.4 (1975): 304-24. The Brothers of Freedom organized as a class-oriented movement and soon grew to 40,000 strong within Arkansas. In 1885, it merged with the Agricultural Wheel. Both groups initially excluded women and blacks, opening membership solely to white males who believed in a supreme being and had a strong moral character.   However, by 1886 the Wheel opened to black male members.

D190. Hicks, John D. "The Birth of the Populist Party." *Minnesota History* 9 (September 1928): 219-47.   Hicks considers the Populist Party as the most "outstanding" to date of all third party movements, primarily because it forced the major parties to take cognizance of issues they had previously ignored or dodged. He notes the existence of the CFA, which carried the principles of the Southern Alliance to Southern blacks, but also notes the problematic question of black membership in the larger proposed organziation. Hicks additionally mentions the participation of the CFA with other groups in the formation of "The Confederation of Industrial Organizations." The section on the St. Louis convention is especially detailed and often amusing.

D191. _____. "The Farmers' Alliance in North Carolina." *North Carolina Historical Review* 2 (April 1925): 162-87. Hicks outlines the numerous successes of the Alliance in North Carolina, including improving the education of farmers and driving from power "the ruling caste of elderly politicians" who thwarted progress. To achieve their goals, the "Republican party was permitted to gain control of the State through negro votes."

D192. _____, and John D. Barnhart. "The Farmers' Alliance." *North Carolina Historical Review* 6 (July 1929): 254-79. The decision to launch a third party was the death blow for the Farmers' Alliance, as most Southern Alliancemen, "in common with other Southern whites, believed in one party for white men and one party only." The authors also note the existence of a "strong" Colored Farmers' Alliance, although it remained under the thumb of the Southern Alliance even after the St. Louis convention.

D193. Higgs, Robert. "Race, Tenure, and Resource Allocation in Southern Agriculture, 1910." *Journal of Economic History* 33 (March 1973): 149-69.

Taking 1910 as his target year, Higgs studies the relationship between racism and sharecropping and concludes that discrimination might have had a "direct but relatively small influence" in the determination of farm size. Additionally, he finds that racial discrimination had little or no effect in determining the division of farm rental contracts between fixed- and share-rent forms, although risk played a major role. But Higgs also underlines the difficulty in making solid judgments in this area, considering the myriad variables. See also **D452**.

D194. Hild, Matthew. "Organizing Across the Color Line: The Knights of Labor and Black Recruitment Efforts in Small-Town Georgia." *Georgia Historical Quarterly* (summer 1997): 298-305. The Knights of Labor, the largest labor organization of its kind at the time, had only limited success in organizing blacks in small-town Georgia. Organizers were faced with threats and violence, but some small assemblies were formed, which demonstrated that some white Georgians understood the common class interests that could be addressed by an all-inclusive organization such as the Knights.

D195. Hill, Herbert. "In the Age of Gompers and After: Racial Practices of Organized Labor." *New Politics* 4 (spring 1965): 26-46. Hill's essay, a critical analysis of the racial practices of organized labor, was the opening salvo in a battle which long filled the pages of academic journals. Although Samuel Gompers himself initially urged the formation of biracial unions, local chapters and groups wishing to affiliate with the AFL openly banned blacks from membership in the late 1890s, paralleling the rise of disfranchisement in Southern states.

D196. Himelhoch, Myra. "St. Louis Opposition to David R. Francis in the Gubernatorial Election of 1888." *Missouri Historical Review* 68 (1974): 327-43. David R. Francis, elected governor of Missouri as a Democrat in 1888, failed to win the majority of votes in his home city of St. Louis, even though he had been mayor. Democrats blamed in part black Republicans for overvoting; with 6% of the vote, blacks maintained the balance of electoral power. The evidence, however, does not support the contention of illegal voting. The Union Labor and Prohibition parties were also on the ballot but failed to draw much support.

D197. Hoar, George Frisbie. "The Fate of the Election Bill." *The Forum* 11 (April 1891): 127-36. Hoar was Senate floor leader for the bill. He notes the possibility of a deal between the "silver bill" congressmen and Force Bill opponents. A good overview of the congressional history of this bill.

D198. Holmes, George K. "The Peons of the South." *Annals of the American Academy of Political and Social Science* 4 (September 1893): 265-74. The black tenant farmer is in a worse position than under the slave system, for then he was better fed and housed, had the best medical attention in the area, and was restrained from doing harm to both himself and his master. Blacks favor tenancy to selling their labor for wages, and in some regions white planters find they can only hire inferior laborers, because the superior prefer tenancy. It is up to the Southern plantation owner to help his region escape the thrall of the crop-lien system.

D199. _____. "Tenancy in the United States." *Quarterly Journal of Economics* 10 (October 1895): 34-53. Examining census records for farm tenancy, Holmes demonstrates that the influence of the South upon the average for the United States is "very great," with tenant farmers in the South Atlantic states at 45.84% of total farm families and in the South Central states 48.27%. However, the farm tenants of the South, especially blacks, live in extraordinary poverty, al-though they could without much effort own small farms. Farm tenants are better off than farm laborers, but farm tenancy also represents a loss to society, as its agriculture is inferior, and "the independence of the owner is poorly replaced by the tenants proprietorship." Holmes does not take into account other societal variables in Southern black farm ownership, believing instead that hard work will pay off.

D200. Holmes, William F. "The Arkansas Cotton Pickers Strike of 1891 and the Demise of the Colored Farmers' Alliance." *Arkansas Historical Quarterly* 32 (summer 1973): 107-19. Formed in Houston County, Texas, in 1886 by a group of black sharecroppers, the Colored Farmers' Alliance by 1891 claimed a national membership of 1,200,000 and organized exchanges in major Southern port cities. Although disagreeing with the white Southern Alliance on specific issues such as the single tax, the CFA frequently worked cooperatively with other Alliance groups. General Richard M. Humphrey, a white Southerner who served as general superintendent of the Colored Farmers' Alliance, urged a gen-eral cotton pickers' strike across the region, but only the pickers in the Arkansas delta followed through in what became a bloody clash. The resultant discredit-ing of Humphrey is at least partially to blame for the organization's demise.

D201. _____. "Demise of the Colored Farmers' Alliance." *Journal of South-ern History* 41 (May 1975): 187-200. Founded in 1886 in Houston County, Texas, the Colored Farmers' Alliance spread across the South, ultimately claim-ing a membership of 1,200,000. From the start, however, competition from rival black farm organizations, including chapters of the Agricultural Wheel and the National Colored Alliance, dampened the power of the group. In addition, the leadership of the Colored Farmers' Alliance was divided between blacks and whites, with the latter, particularly General Richard M. Humphrey, sometimes taking a paternalistic view of the membership. Repeated incidents of white vio-lence, mismanagement of exchanges, and other incidents further hampered the organization's operations, and the ill-fated Cotton Pickers' Strike of 1891 sealed its doom.

D202. _____. "Ellen Dortch and the Farmers' Alliance." *Georgia Historical Quarterly* 69 (1985): 149-72. Ellen Dortch was a fascinating character in the story of Georgia Populism. As editor of the Franklin County Tribune, she was a strong proponent of women's suffrage and equality of men and women in the professions. However, she distrusted the Farmers' Alliance and continually battled it, even arguing that women should not join. When the People's party officially organized in the county in 1892, she criticized white Populists who attempted to recruit black voters: "the white man who engages in such work is infinitely lower in the social and moral scale than the vilest negro in the land."

D203. _____. "The Georgia Alliance Legislature." *Georgia Historical Quarterly* 68 (Winter 1984): 479-515. The Georgia Farmers' Alliance was successful up until the point when it began to develop into a third party. Holmes tallies the voting record for Alliance officeholders and notes that J.W. Carter, the state's CFA president, was allowed to address the legislature concerning a proposed Jim Crow railcar bill.

D204. _____. "The Leflore County Massacre and the Demise of the Colored Farmers' Alliance." *Phylon* 34 (September 1973): 267-74. The Leflore County Massacre of 1889 occurred when local whites became enraged by CFA attempts to boycott local merchants. Soon afterwards, many white planters held a meeting and subsequently ordered Alliance stores to cease doing business with the CFA and editors of the *Colored Farmers' Alliance Advocate* to stop mailing the newspaper. The CFA in Leflore collapsed soon afterwards.

D205. _____. "Populism in Black Belt Georgia: Racial Dynamics in Taliaferro County Politics, 1890-1900." *Georgia Historical Quarterly* 83 (summer 1999): 242-66. Good local study of the relationship of the Populist movement to black farmers. Holmes notes that black and white Populists called for fair elections during the period. By 1895, the People's party understood the importance of blacks in winning elections and began to appoint them to racially balanced local committees.

D206. _____. "Populism: In Search of Context." *Agricultural History* 64 (Fall 1990): 26-58. Although more scholarship on Populism has appeared since the end of the sixties than in any previous era, the proliferation of works and perspectives have left Populist historiography without a clear, overall context, according to Holmes. Woodward's view of a passive role for Southern blacks during the Populist era has been challenged repeatedly recently, as scholars reveal the activist role many blacks took in the movement and party. Holmes also suggests that Barbara J. Fields' theory that race is purely an ideological construct strongly influenced by a given time and place as well as the particular people who employ it will lead to a deeper understanding of the subject.

D207. _____. "The Roots of Southern Populism." *Georgia Historical Quarterly* 67 (winter 1983): 489-502. In his review essay of Hahn's *The Roots of Southern Populism* (**C143**), Holmes argues that this work is the most important book on Southern Populism since Woodward's *Tom Watson* (**C310**). Post-Civil War conditions in the Georgia Upcountry left very few blacks as either landowners or sharecroppers. The failure of the Populists to address the problems of blacks and landless whites reflected one of the major weaknesses of the movement.

D208. _____. "The Southern Farmers' Alliance and the Georgia Senatorial Election of 1890." *Journal of Southern History* 50 (May 1984): 197-224. An examination of the Georgia senatorial election of 1890 can better illuminate the reasons why the state legislature of that fall, dominated by Alliancemen, failed to enact reform programs. Holmes outlines the backgrounds of the legislators and notes that they were a fairly diverse group, economically and philosophically. Although united in common cause on agrarian issues, they factionalized along conservative and radical ranks on most other issues, particularly the subtreasury plan and railroads. The article also notes the relationship between Populist newspapers and their changing owners, which goes far to explain the lack of cohesion at the editorial level.

D209. _____. "The Southern Farmers' Alliance: the Georgia Experience." *Georgia Historical Quarterly* 72 (winter 1988): 627-52. By the time of the aborted Cotton Pickers' Strike of 1891, the Colored Farmers' Alliance had begun to decline and soon disappeared, although it never had much organizational success in Georgia to begin with. As Holmes puts it, "Given the growing strength of white supremacy and the desperate economic status of most blacks, that should not be surprising." Good brief discussion of the relationship between the white and black alliances in the state.

D210. _____. "Whitecapping: Agrarian Violence in Mississippi, 1902-1906." *Journal of Southern History* 35 (May 1969): 165-85. Holmes notes that one of the unexamined areas of study concerning the Populist Era is the "existence of dirt-farmer organizations that violently manifested the forces of both agricultural distress and anti-Negro sentiment." The popular name for such groups was Whitecaps, which in Mississippi focused on groups that forced blacks from their homes and property. Whitecaps modeled themselves on earlier white terrorist groups, such as the Klan, but there is no evidence that the groups wore distinctive costumes. Much of the initial violence in 1892 and 1893 derived from the practice of merchants placing black tenants as caretakers on foreclosed lands. Small farmers resented what they saw as growing control of their land by bankers and black laborers. Interestingly, James K. Vardaman, one of the most racist of Mississippi's leading politicians, lent his strong support to the drive to end the practice after 1900.

D211. _____. "Whitecapping in Mississippi: Agrarian Violence in the Populist Era." *Mid-America* 55 (April 1973): 134-48. "Whitecapping" was a dirt farmers' movement that arose in Mississippi in the 1890s as a terrorist campaign primarily against blacks working on land acquired by merchants through mortgage foreclosures and against blacks working for lumber companies. Holmes notes that although the Alliance flourished in southwest Mississippi, the state's white farmers sought more radical and violent means of protecting themselves from a system that kept them in perpetual debt. Many state blacks believed there was a relationship between whitecapping and Populism, and for that reason they refused to vote the Populist ticket.

D212. Horton, Paul. "Testing the Limits of Class Politics in Postbellum Alabama: Agrarian Radicalism in Lawrence County." *Journal of Southern History* 57 (February 1991): 63-84. The rise and fall of the Agricultural Wheel in 1880s Alabama mirrors what would later befall the Populists and Jeffersonians in their efforts to form biracial political coalitions. Horton examines the political and agricultural history of Lawrence County, Alabama—the birthplace of the state Wheel—to study the direction the movement took. As one of the last counties to utilize fertilizer in crop production, Lawrence County saw a decline in farm productivity which, coupled with the growth of the crop-lien system, the push towards farm tenancy, and rising farm prices, resulted in local unrest. The Wheel, like the Knights of Labor, saw the farmers as a class, and the State Wheel under the direction of editor J. W. Allen sought to create a brotherhood of black and white laborers. However, the interest in biracial coalition politics could not overcome the history of racial politics supported by the Democrats.

D213. Hovland, Carl Iver, and Robert R. Sears. "Minor Studies of Aggression: VI. Correlation of Lynchings with Economic Indices." *Journal of Psychology* 9 (1940): 301-10. The authors hypothesize that the strength of instigation to aggression varies directly with the amount of interference with the frustrated goal-response. Examining black lynchings between 1882-1930, a correlation appears between the number of black lynchings and the farm value and per-acre value of cotton. During periods of depression, lynching is high; during periods of prosperity, lynchings decline. See also Mintz (**D282**).

D214. Humphrey, Richard M. "History of the Colored Farmers' National Alliance and Cooperative Union." In Nelson A. Dunning, ed., *The Farmers' Alliance History and Agricultural Digest*. Washington, DC: Alliance Publishing Co., 1891. All research on the Colored Farmers' Alliance ultimately must refer back to this central article by Humphrey, the Superintendent of the organization. Although extremely brief, the article includes the group's seven point "declaration of principles," signatories, incorporation and chartering information, one of the few photographs of Humphrey, and the "Declaration of Purposes" of the CFA. Also in this volume, and often overlooked, is J. H. Turner's article, "The Race Problem," which quotes at length an article by black Ocala delegate Rev. J.

L. Moore on race relations and the CFA, and the text of the Ocala agreement between the NFA and CFA.

D215. Hunt, James Logan. "The Making of a Populist: Marion Butler, 1863-1895." *North Carolina Historical Review* 62 (January 1985): 53-77 (part I); (April 1985): 179-202 (part II); (July 1985): 317-43 (part III). Butler's early views on blacks were on a course with those of his fellow North Carolinians and most Populists: "Whatever Butler had to say about blacks reflected his desire that they stay out of political office and remain socially separate." He softened his stance somewhat during his fusionist years as a Populist, but he occasionally returned to standard white supremacist rhetoric.

D216. Ingle, H. Larry. "A Southern Democrat at Large: William Hodge Kitchin and the Populist Party." *North Carolina Historical Review* 45 (spring 1968): 178-94. Except for the period 1894-96, when he worked for the Populists, Kitchin was an active member of the Democratic Party in North Carolina. A leading white supremacist spokesman in the state, Kitchin swung to the Populists when he felt unappreciated by the Democrats. He only sought black voters whenever he felt they were needed for his party's victory.

D217. Inverarity, James M. "Populism and Lynching in Louisiana, 1889-1896: a Test of Erikson's Theory of the Relationship Between Boundary Crises and Repressive Justice." *American Sociological Review* 41 (April 1976): 262-80. Sociologist Erik Erikson posited in his 1966 study *Wayward Puritans* that a disruption in solidarity—a "boundary crisis"—produces a sudden and dramatic increase in repressive justice—a "crime wave." Inverarity believes this theory flawed in three basic ways but seeks to overcome these problems with an analysis of lynching in Louisiana in the late nineteenth century. The Populist revolt during this period is a ideal example of a boundary crisis, combining an elevation of the formerly disenfranchised with the collapse of Southern white solidarity. The author suggests a corollary to Erikson: "the extent to which a community responds to a boundary crisis with the exercise of repressive justice depends directly on the magnitude of mechanical solidarity in that community." See also Baggozi (**D19**), Pope and Ragin (**D317**), and Wasserman (**D422**).

D218. Jackson, Harvey H. "The Middle-Class Democracy Victorious: the Mitcham War of Clarke County, Alabama, 1893." *Journal of Southern History* 57.3 (August 1991): 453-78. Southern violence can be attributed to a number of factors, individually and collectively, ranging from class struggle to the weather. Too often in studies of this phenomenon, the victors are treated like opponents, and their victory is assessed in that context. Jackson's study of The Mitcham War of 1893 examines both winners and losers, in a county embroiled by the rise of the Farmers' Alliance and a faltering economy. In the wake of the violence, both blacks and poor whites were disenfranchised by the victorious white Democrats, the middle class elite.

D219. _____. "The Mitcham War." *Alabama Heritage* 25 (summer 1992): 32-43. A popular account of a series of violent events, including murder, in Clarke County, Alabama, centering on the 1892 gubernatorial election. In the Mitcham Beat area, Democrats struggled to regain control from carpetbaggers, Republicans, and scalawags. The area was also a hotbed of Southern Alliance activity, and Alliancemen reportedly gathered "for the purpose of whipping" blacks who helped defeat Kolb.

D220. James, David R. "The Transformation of the Southern Racial State: Class and Race Determinants of Local-State Structures." *American Sociological Review* 53 (April 1988): 191-208. Theories of the state are unable to explain instrastate variation in policy implementation because they ignore local-state institutions. James asks, to what extent did rural class relations, especially those associated with tobacco and cotton production, account for the regional variation in Southern race relations? During the Populist era, planters sought to reduce the electoral strength of black tenants through disfranchisement. Since blacks could not vote, they could not sanction state officials through routine political processes. Elimination of blacks from the electoral equation would also eliminate party competition and maintain the ruling elite.

D221. Johnson, Guion Griffis. "The Ideology of White Supremacy, 1876-1910." In Fletcher Melvin Green, ed., *Essays in Southern History (James Sprunt Studies in History and Political Science, Volume 31)*. Chapel Hill, NC: University of North Carolina Press, 1949. Useful overview of Southern political and sociological thought concerning race and white supremacy during the period. Notes the effect of white supremacist thought on Tillman and Grady, in addition to the efforts of Cable and others to speak out against the caste system.

D222. Johnston, James Hugo. "The Participation of Negroes in the Government of Virginia from 1877 to 1888." *Journal of Negro History* 14 (July 1929): 251-71. Johnston believes that a study of the Readjuster Movement in Virginia politics suggests that blacks and whites can work together politically for the common good of a Southern state, that blacks played an effective and intelligent role in the movement, and that the work of William Mahone proves that there are Southern white men ready to utilize the black vote. During this period, a number of reform measures either passed the state legislature or were at least introduced, including the abolishment of the capitation tax designed to reduce the number of black voters, and the improvement of the school systems.

D223. Johnston, Robert D. "Peasants, Pitchforks, and the (Found) Promise of Progressivism." *Reviews in American History* 28 (September 2000): 393-8. An extended positive review of Elizabeth Sanders' *Roots of Reform* (**C258**). Johnston praises Sanders for her "historian's masterpiece," a "refreshingly uncynical book" which argues that citizens elect legislators "to represent both their interests and their dreams for a better world." Rather than argue that farmers were doomed from the start and later faded away, Sanders believes that they survived to fight more battles after the decline of the People's party and can be considered the "chief architects of the modern American state."

D224. Jolley, Harley E. "The Labor Movement in North Carolina, 1880-1922." *North Carolina Historical Review* 30 (July 1953): 354-75. Notes the activities of the Knights of Labor within North Carolina from 1884-1894. State membership was reportedly large and open to men and women of all races. The Knights are given credit for the April 1887 strike of black laborers against the Raleigh City Waterworks for a pay increase.

D225. Jones, Allen W. "Political Reforms of the Progressive Era." *Alabama Review* 21 (July 1968): 173-94. As a result of Populist activities in Alabama during the early 1890s, Democratic and other state officials ultimately limited the suffrage to the "intelligent and virtious" (sic) white males as a means of achieving "an incorruptible electorate and good progressive government." Paradoxically, they denied the ballot to many citizens, including blacks and women, but gave more participation in government to those with the right to vote. Interesting for the legacy of Populism on electoral reform.

D226. Jones, Thomas Goode. "The 1890-92 Campaigns for Governor of Alabama." *Alabama Historical Quarterly* 20 (Winter 1958): 656-83. Written by former Alabama Governor Thomas G. Goode for the Montgomery Advertiser on 17 September 1911, this article argues that Goode was elected by "the will of the people" fair and square. One of the "controlling issues" of the campaign was the candidates' attitudes towards the Ocala and St. Louis platforms, and Goode was perhaps the most outspoken on that matter. Goode comments especially on the attempt of the "opera house ticket" to sway black voters against him and notes that it was impossible for black voters in the Black Belt to have decided the governor's race between the state's white voters. An essential article for understanding a central Populist campaign.

D227. Justesen, Benjamin R. "George Henry White, Josephus Daniels, and the Showdown over Disfranchisement, 1900." *North Carolina Historical Review* 77 (January 2000): 1-33. The battle between the nation's only black congressman, George Henry White, and North Carolina journalist Josephus Daniels came to a head in the campaign of 1899-1900. Daniels, an avowed white supremacist, attacked White repeatedly for his attempts to stop the move towards disfranchisement of North Carolina blacks and to institute a national anti-lynching law. Republican leaders left voter registration to the Populists, who were only minimally successful in the wake of widespread violence. The resulting vote ended black electoral power in the state and partly can be blamed for White's decision to withdraw from politics.

D228. Kann, Kenneth. "The Knights of Labor and the Southern Black Worker." *Labor History* 18 (winter 1977): 49-70; rpt in Donald G. Nieman, ed., *African Americans and Non-Agricultural Labor in the South, 1865-1900* (New York: Garland, 1994): 169-90. The history of the Knights of Labor demonstrates that biracial coalitions could be formed in the South on common matters, although it can also be argued that by entangling themselves in racial matters, the Knights were doomed to failure. The first successful Southern inroads were made as early as 1885, and nearly 25,000 blacks had joined the Knights by 1887. However, locals were allowed the option of forming separate black and white assemblies. Numerous joint strikes were called, and both Birmingham and Dallas saw large biracial workers parades.

D229. Kantor, Shawn Everett. "Supplanting the Roots of Southern Populism: the Contours of Political Protest in the Georgia Hills." *Journal of Economic History* 55 (September 1995): 637-46. Kantor focuses on Hahn's claim in his *The Roots of Southern Populism* (**C143**) the stock law controversy not only anticipated the social and political contours of the Georgia Upcounty, but also "helps elucidate the cultural and ideological contours as well." Drawing on the results from nine "Populist elections" between 1892 and 1898, Kantor tests four factors that might have influenced Populist voting in the region. Using regression analysis, however, Kantor suggests that it is difficult to generalize about Populism in the region, as comparisons between Carroll and Jackson Counties reveal different socioeconomic factors producing the era's political divisions.

D230. _____, and J. Morgan Kousser. "Common Sense or Commonwealth? The Fence Law and Institutional Change in the Postbellum South." *Journal of Southern History* 59 (May 1993): 201-42. The "fence law" involves the right of crop owners to fence out other people's cattle and swine to protect their crops. Such concerns play a major role in the history of the South and West, dividing farmers from ranchers and often leading to range wars. The authors test Hahn's hypothesis (**C143**) that the fence law contests in the Georgia Upcountry "paved the road to Populism." Statistical analyses support their interpretation that voters in districts where the objective benefits of the stock law were high were likely to support new institutional arrangements sooner than those where the benefits were lower or negative. The fence law controversy, at least in the Upcountry, was a struggle not of cultures but of interests.

D231. Kantrowitz, Stephen. "Ben Tillman and Hendrix McLane, Agrarian Rebels: White Manhood, 'The Farmers,' and the Limits of Southern Populism." *Journal of Southern History* 66 (August 2000): 497-524. J. Hendrix McLane, "South Carolina's most successful proponent of interracial agrarian radicalism," stood in direct opposition to Ben Tillman, the anti-Populist Democrat and white supremacist. Kantrowitz posits that a close examination of McLane's rise and fall suggests "that not simply race, but a racialized conception of manhood," shaped the efforts of each man.

D232. Katz, William. "George Henry White: A Militant Negro Congressman in the Age of Booker T. Washington." *Negro History Bulletin* 29 (March 1966): 125-26, 134. Brief biography of George Henry White, first elected to Congress from North Carolina's Second Congressional district under the fusion ticket of 1896. White had the distinction of being the last ex-slave to sit in the U.S. Congress and the first black to serve in the twentieth century.

D233. Kazin, Michael. "Hofstadter Lives: Political Culture and Temperament in the Work of an American Historian." *Reviews in American History* 27.2 (1999): 334-48. Although Richard Hofstadter was once one of the most admired historians in the United States, his reputation among many critics is now that of "an elegant ruin from a benighted age." Rather than portray the Populists as lacking in rational causes for revolt, he examined the contradictions between the "hard" and "soft" faces of the movement. Fresh interpretations of the movement illustrate the shift in thinking about collective motives and behavior, much as Hofstadter's thinking shifted as he evolved politically.

D234. Kendrick, Benjamin B. "Agrarian Discontent in the South, 1880-1900." *Annual Report of the American Historical Association for the Year 1920.* Washington, DC: Government Printing Office, 1925: 267-72. The causes of agrarian discontent in the South from 1880-1900 were both economic and social. Kendrick only addresses two issues: the "lowly social status of the Southern farmer in 1890," and the lien law system. After the Civil War, according to Kendrick, blacks were demoralized and "disinclined to work for wages." Matters improved somewhat under the "cropping system." Notes the rise of the Farmers' Alliance and Populist Party as a result of agrarian discontent.

D235. Kessler, Sidney H. "The Organization of Negroes in the Knights of Labor." *Journal of Negro History* 37 (July 1952): 248-76. The Knights of Labor more than any other union of the period understood the need for organizing black workers, although Kessler asserts that it was as much out of fear of black-white labor competition as goodwill of its leaders, particularly Terence V. Powderly and Uriah Stephens. Local option left it to communities whether they wanted to form separate or mixed groups, but even all-black groups reported receiving and accepting white applicants. The strongest opposition to black unionists and their organizers occurred in South Carolina, where black organizers were urged to be "shot without trial." An excellent source of information on local black leaders and movement strength.

D236. Kirshenbaum, Andrea Meryl. "'The Vampire That Hovers Over North Carolina': Gender, White Supremacy, and the Wilmington Race Riot of 1898." *Southern Cultures* 4 (1998): 6-30. The Wilmington Race Riot of 1898 was one of the most violent episodes in Populist history. Newspaper editors used stories of white women endangered by black men to stir up the white populace and end

the black city fusionist government of Wilmington, North Carolina. Article includes excellent reproductions of anti-black period newspaper cartoons.

D237. Korobkin, Russell. "The Politics of Disfranchisement in Georgia."
Georgia Historical Quarterly 74 (spring 1990): 20-58. The Georgia disfranchisement battle was long and complicated, with Tom Watson arguing as late as
1904 that state Democrats would never eliminate black voters because they
needed them to win elections. The Georgia Populist party platforms of 1892 and
1894 are also "remarkable" in that they do not address race relations. Korobkin
argues that issues of race were unimportant to Watson in his Populist years.

D238. Kousser, J. Morgan. "A Black Protest in the 'Era of Accommodation': a
Document." *Arkansas Historical Quarterly* 34 (summer 1975): 149-78.
Woodward, among others, argued that black resistance to white aggression had
essentially ceased long before 1890. However, Kousser presents documents
noting organized and highly vocal black resistance to restrictive measures of the
period, particularly the Tillman Separate Coach bill.

D239. _____. "Progressivism for Middle Class Whites Only: North Carolina
Education, 1880-1910." *Journal of Southern History* 46 (May 1980): 169-94.
One of the negative outcomes of the progressive movement was the growing
inequality of funding for black and white schools. Distribution of taxes and
expenditures varied systematically with wealth and race, and the changes mir-
rored political, not economic conditions. Blacks in particular suffered after disfranchisement and the growth of the one-party system, particularly in those regions where before 1900 their votes had bought disproportionately high levels of
service. Kousser demonstrates that the negative correlation between black and
white tax rates reached statistical significance only during the period of Populist-Republican fusion.

D240. Kyriakoudes, Louis M. "Southern Black Rural-Urban Migration in the
Era of the Great Migration: Nashville and Middle Tennessee, 1890-1930." *Agricultural History* 72 (spring 1998): 341-51. The period 1890-1930 saw a mass
rural-to-urban migration of Deep South blacks, and Kyriakoudes uses his ongoing studies of Nashville and Middle Tennessee to survey the context and character of that migration. Black farmers made up roughly one-fifth of Middle Tennessee's rural population in 1890, and many owned their own land. A combination of pressures—population, rising land values, limited off-farm opportunities,
and rising tenancy—sent many farmers to the city. However, racial employment
patterns were clearly delineated in Nashville, which kept the former black farmers in menial, low-paying urban jobs.

D241. Lanier, Sidney. "The New South." *Scribner's Monthly* 20 (October
1880): 840-51; rpt. *Centennial Edition of the Works of Sidney Lanier* (1945).
Lanier anticipates the goals and aims of the Farmers' Alliance and People's party

in his call for biracial agrarian cooperation. "In the identical aims of the small-farmer class, whatever now remains of the color-line must surely disappear out of the Southern political situation."

D242. Lester, Connie L. "'Let Us Be Up and Doing': Women in the Tennessee Movements for Agrarian Reform, 1870-1892." *Tennessee Historical Quarterly* 54 (summer 1995): 80-97. Passing reference is made to the existence of 421 subordinate unions of the CFA in Tennessee, although Lester makes no specific mention of the role of black women in the movement.

D243. Letwin, Daniel. "Interracial Unionism, Gender, and 'Social Equality' in the Alabama Coalfields, 1878-1908." *Journal of Southern History* 61 (August 1995): 519-54. Alongside the agrarian reformers of the period there arose an interracial movement among Alabama's coalfield workers, first under the banner of the Greenback Party, later the Knights of Labor, and ultimately the United Mine Workers. Letwin explores how self-interest, solidarity, and accommodation related to the larger question of Southern race relations and argues that in workplaces occupied solely by men, the sight of blacks and whites working together was less challenging to Southern whites than where interracial association involved both sexes. While white and black miners organized and led their own local bodies, interaction between the groups was routine and extensive. During the state elections of 1890, 1892, and 1894, large numbers of miners of both races supported Reuben Kolb, whose platform addressed miners' concerns.

D244. Lewinson, Paul. "The Negro in the White Class and Party Struggle." *Southwestern Political and Social Science Quarterly* 8 (March 1928): 358-82. On a regular basis, the Southern Bourbon elite has used the "bogey of the negro" to unite fractioned white voters into a coalition which ousted Republicans, third partyites, and blacks from government and maintained the status quo of the ruling class. Lewinson cites three "highly significant sets of circumstances" that marked the rise and fall of the agrarian uprising, including the development of statutory suffrage-restriction codes, charges and countercharges of election fraud and corruption, and an unwillingness among Southern whites to go further with disfranchising measures, which manifested itself chiefly among "the politically irregular."

D245. Lewis, Elsie M. "The Political Mind of the Negro, 1865-1900." *Journal of Southern History* 21 (May 1955): 189-202. From 1877 to 1900, black leaders grew disgruntled over the failure of the Republican Party to grant them offices and a share of the patronage, and the failure of the federal government to guarantee their political and civil rights. But black leaders also split on the means of achieving success, with T. Thomas Fortune advocating an independent black political movement, Frederick Douglass arguing that such a move was worthless, and other leaders pushing the concept of fusion politics in the South.

D246. Lewis, J. Eugene. "The Tennessee Gubernatorial Campaign and Election of 1894." *Tennessee Historical Quarterly* 13 (June 1954): 99-126; (September 1954): 224-43; (December 1954): 301-28. The 1894 Tennessee gubernatorial election was one of the closest in state memory, with a large Populist turnout. Both the Republican and Populist platforms condemned Democratic campaign reforms, including the poll tax. Papers reported great interest among black voters in this election.

D247. Lewis, Ronald L. "Job Control and Race Relations in Coal Fields, 1870-1920." *Journal of Ethnic Studies* 12 (1985): 35-64; rpt. in Donald G. Nieman, ed., *African Americans and Non-Agricultural Labor in the South, 1865-1900*. New York: Garland, 1994: 245-74. Race relations among black and white coal miners followed different patterns throughout the South, particularly from the vantage of job control. In northern Alabama, inclusion was the normal practice, whereas exclusion was the key elsewhere. Black miners were crucial to the growth of labor unions in Southern West Virginia in the 1890s, although operators even there sought ways of using one group against another to weaken the organizational threat.

D248. Lichtenstein, Alex. "Racial Conflict and Racial Solidarity in the Alabama Coal Strike of 1894: New Evidence for the Gutman-Hill Debate." *Labor History* 36 (winter 1995): 63-76. The author examines the daily Pinkerton detective agency reports sent to Governor Thomas G. Jones of Alabama during the four-month coal strike in that state in 1894. The reports indicate "both the potential fault lines of racial cooperation and the possibilities for solidarity," with numerous examples of black workers willing to overlook the racism of their white counterparts and stick with the union.

D249. Lightfoot, B. B. "The Human Party: Populism in Comanche County, 1886." *West Texas Historical Association Yearbook* 31 (October 1955): 28-40. Comanche County, Texas was the site of one of the first farmers' protest movement in the U.S., the Human Party, which organized shortly after armed mobs drove all of the blacks out of the county. The party ultimately merged with the People's party, which saw great success in local elections into the 1900s.

D250. Link, Arthur Stanley. "The Progressive Movement in the South, 1870-1914." *North Carolina Historical Review* 23 (April 1946): 172-95. Link's oft-quoted review essay makes claims for a well-organized progressive movement in the South aimed at remedying the region's economic and social ills. Southern editors in particular paid scant attention to the growing problems in agrarian culture, and hardly any openly called for black political rights. One significant point of the Populist movement is that it forced the Democrats to move towards a reformist platform. Although short-lived, the Populist movement must be seen as having had a strong influence on Southern life and politics.

D251. Lloyd, Henry Demarest. "The Populists at St. Louis." *Review of Reviews* 14 (September 1896): 278-83. This oft-reprinted article on the 1896 convention is a good summary view of the membership of the reform movement at century's end: "handsome farmer" Marion Butler, anti-monopolist Ignatius Donnelly; Eugene V. Debs, et al. But Lloyd notes that "the most eloquent speeches" came from both white and black orators, who explained the situation in the South. "A delegate from Georgia, a coal-black Negro," told how the People's party "gave full fellowship to his race" after its abandonment by the Republicans and betrayal by the Democrats. Southern white Populists, in turn, pleaded with conventioneers not to be left to "the tender mercies of the Democrats" by accepting Democratic nominees without certain pledges and conditions. See also **C283**.

D252. Lloyd, Peggy S. "The Howard County Race Riot of 1883." *Arkansas Historical Quarterly* 59 (winter 2000): 353-87. Although not dealing specifically with the Populist movement, Lloyd's article shows how growing agricultural discontent combined with significant shifts in black/white population ratios could inflame an otherwise simple matter into a race riot. More importantly for Populist studies, however, is Lloyd's contention that Arkansas blacks found less tolerance and more suspicion among white Republicans and Greenbackers in the towns of Hope and Prescott than they did among the old slaveholding elites of the city of Washington.

D253. Lodge, Henry Cabot, and Terence V. Powderly. "The Federal Election Bill." *North American Review* 151 (September 1890): 257-73. Lodge, the congressman from Massachusetts, and Knights of Labor leader Powderly offer their perspectives separately on the Federal Election Bill. For Lodge, the shibboleth "force bill" is completely off the mark, as this in reality is an "anti-force" bill designed to stop the exercise of illegal force by those who use it at the polls anywhere in the U.S. Powderly, however, envisions bayonets encircling ballot boxes, and he rightly believes that the bill is directed particularly at the South. The real danger is illiteracy; the only thing that will prevent disfranchisement of citizens, white and black, is education.

D254. Logan, Frenise A. "The Colored Industrial Association of North Carolina and Its Fair of 1886." *North Carolina Historical Review* 34 (January 1957): 58-67. An interesting example of early black self-help efforts in the South, the Colored Industrial Association's 1886 fair serves as an example of other fairs of its kind throughout the South. Logan notes that the CIA was a major economic force for the state's black population. T. Thomas Fortune and Booker T. Washington lent their support for the effort, although support among state blacks was not universal.

D255. Love, John L. "The Disfranchisement of the Negro." In *The American Negro Academy Occasional Papers 1-22*. New York: Arno Press, 1969. Originally published in pamphlet form in 1899, Love's piece surveys the recent trend towards disfranchisement throughout the South, with special attention paid to Louisiana and South Carolina. Using numerous quotes from politicians of the day, Love concludes that "Southern white people, by permitting a few desperate politicans to outlaw the Negro, find themselves at the mercy of an oligarchy which has everything its own way."

D256. Mabry, William Alexander. "Ben Tillman Disfranchised the Negro." *South Atlantic Quarterly* 37 (April 1938): 170-83. Overview of the political machinations behind the rise of Ben Tillman and the disfranchisement of South Carolina blacks during the Populist era. In the midst of calls for election reform, and with the threat from Democrats to legislate white supremacy, blacks met in convention in Columbia in 1895 and called on their compatriots to "register to a man" and to "vote for any set of men regardless of their party name, who are in favor of an honestly managed government and opposed to radical, class, or impractical measures being encouched in the new Constitution."

D257. _____. "Disfranchisement of the Negro in Mississippi." *Journal of Southern History* 4 (August 1938): 318-33. The movement to disfranchise Mississippi blacks through revision of the state constitution caused friction within the state Democratic party. The threat of continued federal election intervention through the proposed Force Bill of 1890 spurred state leaders to seek local legal means of removing black voters. However, "black belt" Democrats were willing to sacrifice illiterate white voters to an educational clause if it meant disfranchising black voters also, but "white county" Democrats felt that the clause would remove too many voters of both races from the rolls. Payment of a poll tax also became a voting prerequisite at this time.

D258. _____. "Negro Suffrage and Fusion Rule in North Carolina." *North Carolina Historical Review* 12 (April 1935): 70-102. Though the black vote did not contribute significantly to the fusionist victory in the 1894 North Carolina elections, the overthrow of the Democratic majority gave new political power to state blacks. Notes the number of positions held by blacks in the years 1894-98, including city councilmen, police, postmaster, and collector of customs at the port of Wilmington.

D259. _____. "'White Supremacy' and the North Carolina Suffrage Amendment." *North Carolina Historical Review* 13 (January 1936): 1-24. The success of the Populist campaigns in North Carolina brought over a thousand blacks into elected and patronage positions in the state, much to the resentment of local whites, particularly in the eastern part of the state. The subsequent battle over disfranchisement ultimately resulted in North Carolina being a "one-party state."

D260. Macune, Charles W., Jr. "The Wellsprings of a Populist: Dr. C. W. Macune Before 1886." *Southwestern Historical Quarterly* 90 (October 1986): 139-158. Fascinating insight into one of the most enigmatic figures in the agrarian movement, by his great-grandson. As editor of the *Burnet (TX) Bulletin*, Macune wrote in 1875 that the reason for his adopted state's success was that it was a "white man's state."

D261. Mandel, Bernard. "Samuel Gompers and the Negro Workers, 1886-1914." *Journal of Negro History* 40 (January 1955): 34-60. The policy of Samuel Gompers' American Federation of Labor towards black workers represents a backwards step from the more unitarian one of the Knights of Labor. In the early 1890s, Gompers stressed that all local chapters under his union were not to be designated as "white" and "colored." But in the interest of the struggle for unionization of industry, he slowly yielded to exclusionist policies which kept black workers out of locals. Mandel sees the simultaneous deterioration of Southern race relations and the A.F. of L.'s abandonment of a policy for equal status for black workers from 1899 to 1902 as significant. In the long run, Gompers sacrificed his earlier principles in an attempt to organize the greater body of white workers throughout the nation.

D262. Marable, W. Manning. "Black History and the Vision of Democracy." In Harry C. Boyte and Frank Riessman, ed., *The New Populism: the Politics of Empowerment*. Philadelphia: Temple University Press, 1986. The central theme of African American political history, according to Manning, is how oppressed people come to terms with their exploitation. Newly freed slaves understood that "freedom" meant the absence of human exploitation and engaged in various activities in the ante-bellum South to precipitate that freedom. During Reconstruction, freed blacks attempted to become landowners and joined the Populist Party along with whites. However, after the collapse of the movement in the 1890s, economic self-sufficiency for blacks became a dead end by the latter part of the twentieth century.

D263. Marcus, Irvin M. "The Southern Negro and the Knights of Labor." *Negro History Bulletin* 30 (March 1967): 5-7. Brief overview notes the minor inroads made by the Knights of Labor in biracial cooperation to achieve workers' unity. The Knights, however, allowed Southern locals to maintain racially segregated lodges.

D264. Martin, Roscoe C. "The Greenback Party in Texas." *Southwestern Historical Quarterly* 30 (January 1927): 161-77. The Greenback Party flourished in Texas primarily from 1876-1884 and was part of the broader range of agrarian crusade movements across the United States. The first state convention was held in Austin in 1878, although it adjourned without making any nominations for public office. A subsequent convention in Waco issued a platform, including the repeal of convict labor law and the establishment of a free school system. In response, state Republican leaders, including black politicos Norris Wright Cuney and Dick Allen, called for support of independent candidates-- those who were not Democrats. The Greenbackers went on record as supportive of this plank, although the election results were unfavorable to both parties.

D265. Matthews, Donald R., and James W. Prothro. "Political Factors and Negro Voter Registration in the South." *American Political Science Review* 57 (June 1963): 355-67. The authors attempt to determine the relationships between political and legal factors and variations in the state black voter registration rates in the South. The very division of the region into eleven distinct states is the single most significant political factor in the equation, although formal voter registration requirements, state factional systems, and amount and kind of racial organizations in the counties play a part. Suffrage restrictions date back to the rise of populism, seen as a threat. However, black voter registration is normally higher in areas where both blacks and whites are organized, a result of the "boomerang effect" which draws blacks closer together.

D266. Mayhew, Anne. "A Reappraisal of the Causes of the Farm Protest in the United States, 1870-1900." *Journal of Economic History* 32 (June 1972): 464-75. Economic historians have generally explained the farm protest movement of the period as a result of low agricultural prices and high costs of inputs resulting from supplier monopolies. Examining farm conditions in the Midwest, Mayhew concludes that, despite true economic conditions, farmers felt interest rates were "too high" and that they were locked into a system where failure or success depended on prices. Farmers were no longer exempt from the rapidly developing commercialization of agriculture.

D267. McKelway, Alexander J. "The North Carolina Suffrage Amendment." *Independent* 52 (16 August 1900): 1956-57. McKelway, a Southern Presbyterian minister, was a leading opponent of child labor exploitation throughout the region. Although one of the region's leading reformers of the period, McKelway advocated white supremacy and strongly supported black disfranchisement. An illiterate white was always a more intelligent voter than a literate black.

D268. McKinney, Gordon B. "Southern Mountain Republicans and the Negro, 1865-1900." *Journal of Southern History* 41 (November 1975): 493-516. The Mountain Republicans of the Upper South were the only regional population to consistently support the Party during the Reconstruction Era and beyond. Between 1865 and 1900, a coalition of blacks and mountain whites was a powerful force in the states in this area. The defeat of the Force Bill opened a rift between the two groups, but careful politicking by Republicans allowed them to continue receiving black votes while permitting Democrats to exclude blacks from political office.

D269. McLaurin, Melton A. "Early Labor Union Organizational Efforts in South Carolina Cotton Mills, 1880-1905." *South Carolina Historical Magazine* 72 (January 1971): 44-59. Discusses the efforts of the Knights of Labor in the 1880s and National Union of Textile Workers to organize the cotton mills during the height of Populism. The Knights came under attack for their willingness to organize black artisans and farmers, although in separate assemblies.

D270. _____. "The Knights of Labor in North Carolina Politics" *North Carolina Historical Review* 49 (July 1972): 298-315. Organizing with increased speed after 1886, black Knights of Labor assemblies included domestic and industrial workers, in addition to farmers, in their ranks; some of the local assemblies were mixed race. Initially non-political, the local Knights assemblies ultimately joined the political fray, even electing some blacks to office. However, as more blacks joined the Knights, white members fled to the new Alliance.

D271. _____. "Knights of Labor: Internal Dissensions of the Southern Order." In Gary M. Fink and Merl E. Reed, ed., *Essays in Southern Labor History: Selected Papers, Southern Labor History Conference, 1976*. Westport, CT: Greenwood Press, 1977: 3-17. The internal dissensions which lead to the final collapse of Terence V. Powderly's Knights of Labor in the South mirror problems which would arise in other interracial groups. Besides the usual petty bickering found in any organization, the Southern Knights were faced with the race issue, with some black members resenting white dominance of locals and wishing to split off into separate black districts. Some whites, in turn, feared that the relatively liberal national policies of the national order would result in social equality between the races. By 1889, the Knights had ceased to exist save among black day laborers who still saw Powderly as their economic savior.

D272. _____. "The Racial Policies of the Knights of Labor and the Organization of Southern Black Workers." *Labor History* 17 (fall 1976): 568-85. The Knights of Labor faced the basic problem of all groups attempting biracial cooperation in the South: formulating a workable approach to the racial problem. The Knights sought a two-pronged approach, arguing that the race issue had no place in the economic struggle while allowing Southern states to form racially separate locals. Neither policy proved effective, and whites began to leave the organization as more blacks joined and clung to the group as their only hope of economic salvation.

D273. McMath, Robert C., Jr. "C. Vann Woodward and the Burden of Southern Populism." *Journal of Southern History* 67 (November 2001): 741-68. In his ffitieth anniversary critique of Woodward's *Origins*, McMath argues that "the unity of all producers" concept trumpeted by Populists and Progressives was little more than a slogan by the 1890s. White agrarians, even when they recognized the production capabilities of their fellow black farmers, were unwilling to united in common accord due to racial misgivings.

D274. _____. "Southern White Farmers and the Organization of Black Farm Workers: a North Carolina Document." *Labor History* 18 (winter 1977): 115-19. The relationship between the Southern and Colored Farmers' Alliances was shaky at best, as white farmers were hesitant about making common cause with blacks. But before the Alliances came the Knights of Labor, to which North Carolina blacks were attracted for years after the decline of the national organization. The "document" to which McMath refers is a fragmentary memorandum noting John Bryan Grimes' efforts to infiltrate a black Knights assembly. McMath argues that the document "suggests the need for caution in perceiving Southern white farmers as a monolithic interest group" whose members were inclined to cooperate with blacks.

D275. Meier, August. "The Negro and the Democratic Party, 1875-1915." *Phylon* 17 (summer 1956): 173-91. Useful overview article demonstrates that no one party held total control over the black voter, including the Populist. Meier mentions black self-help groups, including the Colored Independent Party of Pennsylvania, that formed throughout the period to discuss and lobby for political rights. Blacks switched their allegiance from the Republicans to the Democrats in large part after the Republicans failed to support their civil rights and Democrats made an effort to solicit black votes.

D276. _____. "Toward a Reinterpretation of Booker T. Washington." *Journal of Southern History* 23 (May 1957): 220-27. Although Washington minimized the significance of political and civil rights, he worked behind the scenes in the late 1800s against disfranchisement. His public statements could be construed to support anti-suffrage legislation, but he simultaneously worked with Northern philanthropists to raise money to fight the measures.

D277. Miller, Floyd J. "Black Protest and White Leadership: a Note on the Colored Farmer's Alliance." *Phylon* 33 (June 1972): 169-74. Miller addresses the anomaly of why the Colored Farmers' Alliance allowed whites to serve as its chief spokesmen. Although Alliance legislators repeatedly supported anti-black legislation, the CFA retained Humphrey in a leadership role partly because of his ability to support black economic demands.

D278. Miller, Kelly. "Forty Years of Negro Education." *Educational Review* 36 (December 1908): 484-98. Miller, of Howard University, offers a more enlightened analysis of black education than many of his contemporaries. The "forty years" of the title cover the period from the end of Reconstruction to the present writing. After the Civil War, the first educators to arrive from the North brought an almost missionary zeal, although they also often lacked the essentials of pedagogical skills. Education tended to follow the top-down approach, with black colleges formed to produce black teachers and other professionals. Black education must also recognize the differing needs of the rural and urban communities to succeed. However, people must realize that education is not the sole answer to the race problem, but it will at least help both races to accept and understand each other in the long run.

D279. Miller, Worth Robert. "Building a Progressive Coalition in Texas: The Populist-Reform Democrat Rapprochement, 1900-1907." *Journal of Southern History* 52 (May 1986): 163-82. To stem a conservative onslaught in Texas, former governor James Stephen Hogg reached out to white Populists in an effort to return them to the Democratic Party ranks. Voting records suggest that Hogg was successful in his efforts, as Democratic tallies rose significantly between 1900-1902. However, the increase also hinged upon the size of each county's black population, which generally could not vote in the Democratic primary. During Populism's heyday, Democrats sought both white and black voters. But the collapse of the People's party, the passage of a statewide poll tax, and the rise of the white primary effectively eliminated black political participation.

D280. _____. "A Centennial Historiography of American Populism." *Kansas History* 16 (spring 1993): 54-69. A good starting point for an overview of the Populist movement and its critics. Miller notes that Populism does not fit easily in either the capitalist or socialist camps, but a mixture of both. Blacks have received a good deal of special attention by movement historians, including Woodward, Kousser, Chafe, Abramowitz, and Saunders. Also posted at Miller's website, http://history.smsu.edu/wrmiller/Populism/Texts/historiography.htm/

D281. _____. "Harrison County Methods: Election Fraud in Late Nineteenth-Century Texas." *Locus* 7 (spring 1995): 111-128. Excellent local study of election fraud and the Populist movement, this time in Harrison County, Texas, one of three black-majority counties in the far northeastern part of the state. The disappearance of the People's party and adoption of the poll tax essentially ended voter fraud in Harrison County, but black voters were also effectively disfranchised. Miller finds that the level of elector tampering was "substantial enough to detroy any challenge to Democratic hegemony no matter how popular it was with the electorate."

D282. Mintz, Alexander. "Re-examination of Correlations between Lynching and Economic Indices." *Journal of Abnormal and Social Psychology* 41 (1946): 154-60. Commentary on Hovland and Sears (**D213**). Mintz argues that the trends exhibited by the numbers of lynchings and the total value of cotton were not found to be linear. Suggests comparisons with British crime rates as reported by D. S. Thomas.

D283. Mitchell, H. L. "The Founding and Early History of the Southern Tenant Farmers Union." *Arkansas Historical Quarterly* 10 (1973): 342-69. Mitchell founded the Southern Tenant Farmers Union in 1934 with seven black and ten white farmers as an independent organization of sharecroppers and tenant farmers on Southern cotton plantations. Influenced by Norman Thomas, Mitchell joined with a biracial group of local farmers and businessmen in 1934 to appeal to Washington to ensure the rights of sharecroppers under the Agricultural Adjustment Administration. The group coalesced into the Southern Tenant Farmers Union, with a membership of 31,000 during the Depression. After World War II, the STFU became the National Farm Labor Union.

D284. Moger, Allen W. "The Rift in Virginia Democracy in 1896." *Journal of Southern History* 4 (August 1938): 295-317. The Readjuster period of Virginia history prepared the ground for the growth of the state's Populist movement, which coupled with economic hardship and state financial problems intensified the radicalism of Virginia's Democratic Party in the 1890s. The free silver issue, prominent in the Populist platform, took hold of most Democrats, which led to a factional split as the "National Democratic" party organized to support sound money policy. By the 1896 elections, blacks tended to vote the Republican ticket, but Democrats adopted methods in black counties to eliminate or control their votes, with fraud generally acknowledged.

D285. Moneyhon, Carl H. "Black Politics in Arkansas During the Gilded Age, 1876-1900." *Arkansas Historical Quarterly* 44 (autumn 1985): 222-45. The central focus of black politics during the last quarter of the nineteenth century was at the local level. Fusion politics, which aligned black and white Republican officeholders with disaffected Democrats throughout the state, generally assured blacks safety from white violence. Although the majority of blacks remained loyal to the Republican Party, the party itself backed the Greenback Party in 1878 and 1880. The biracial nature of the state Agricultural Wheel was advantageous to an alliance with the Republicans in 1888 and 1890, with blacks throwing their support to compromise candidates. The backlash by Democratic representatives and voters lead to increasing segregation of facilities and declining power of the black electorate.

D286. Montgomery, David. "On Goodwyn's Populists." *Marxist Perspectives* 1 (spring 1978): 166-73. Review article of Goodwyn's *Democratic Promise* (**C129**). Montgomery finds that the racial attitudes of the Black Belt Democrats combined with an elitist political ideology that viewed the lower classes as necessarily subordinate.

D287. _____. "Violence and the Struggle for Unions in the South, 1880-1930." In Merle Black and John Shelton Reed, ed., *Perspectives on the American South: an Annual Review of Society, Politics, and Culture, Volume 1*. New York: Gordon and Breach, 1981. Despite a long history of violence against unionization, occasional interracial attempts were made to improve the condition of Southern workers. Montgomery notes that the Southern Alliance "ardently courted" the support of the CFA and black assemblies of the Knights of Labor to support legislative programs of common interest, but their "solicitude turned to rage" when the CFA called the Cotton Pickers' Strike of 1891.

D288. Moore, James Tice. "Agrarianism and Populism in Tennessee, 1886-1896: an Interpretive Overview." *Tennessee Historical Quarterly* 42 (spring 1983): 76-94. Notes that the CFA mustered only scattered support among black Tennesseans. Despite open solicitation in Texas and Georgia of black members, the Alliance lawmakers in Tennessee sought to reinforce old and current anti-black legislation and create new discriminatory measures. Alliancemen were also hostile to the needs of labor.

D289. _____. "Black Militancy in Readjuster Virginia, 1879-1883." *Journal of Southern History* 41 (May 1975): 167-86. The Readjuster Movement in Virginia history was brief, under the leadership of William Mahone, and the scholarly record almost completely ignores the role of black Readjusters, who are usually referred to as pawns in Mahone's political game. However, Moore suggests that Virginia's 100,000 black voters played a "crucial role" by reshaping the movement in their own image. With the Conservative split in 1879, state blacks found themselves courted by Mahone's Readjusters and fused with them to take control of the state legislature. However, blacks regularly refused to join in support of Mahone until a series of maneuvers in 1881 lead to a workable coalition on their terms. "Reform followed reform" through the next few years until the Danville Riot of 1883 marked the return of white supremacy to state politics and the collapse of the Readjusters.

D290. _____. "Redeemers Reconsidered: Change and Continuity in the Democratic South, 1870-1900." *Journal of Southern History* 44 (August 1978): 357-78. Woodward was a major influence on revisionist interpretation of the Redeemer period of Southern history, but Moore argues that a careful examination of the evidence suggests a revision of that revision. Rather than a major paradigm shift, a number of factors point to a continuity of thought and practice in Old and New South politics, in opposition to revisionist writing on Redeemer origins and views. Southern Democrats neither abandoned the farmers nor embraced Whiggery after the collapse of the Confederacy, but continued to view the capitalistic North with trepidation. Redeemers tended to follow the path of the western rather than northern politicians.

D291. Moore, John Hammond. "James Gaven Field: Virginia's Populist Spokesman." *Virginia Cavalcade* 9 (spring 1960): 35-41. Popular brief biography, with nice illustrations, of the 1892 People's party vice-presidential candidate. While campaigning, Field spoke out against the Force Bill, "a mere skeleton to frighten people."

D292. Morgan, John Tyler. "The Danger of the Farmers' Alliance." *The Forum* 12 (November 1891): 399-409. Such efforts as the Farmers' Alliance advocate agitate the "deep-rooted convictions" of Southern farmers. The move of the Alliance to form a third party is a "serious misadventure" that is harmful to both the organization and the U.S. "The politicians of all parties will, after a while, annoy the farmers with constant disputes with their laborers, in their efforts to gain the votes of the negro race by interfering with them. In such disputes, the men who instituted negro alliances and the Ocala platform will become 'a thorn in the flesh' of the cotton-growers."

D293. Moseley, Charlton. "Latent Klanism in Georgia, 1890-1915." *Georgia Historical Quarterly* 56 (1972): 365-86. Although the Georgia Ku Klux Klan remained dormant during the Progressive Era, the period was characterized by an increased number of lynchings and the growth of legal disfranchisement of blacks. Moseley relies heavily on Woodward's delineation of Populism and blacks in the period before discussing Tom Watson and the Democrats of the early 1900s. Watson supported Hoke Smith's "Populist reform movement" which went even further toward eliminating black rights. The anti-black and anti-Semitic principles found in Populist rhetoric of the period are a forerunner of Klan ideology.

D294. Murray, George Washington. "What Should Be the Negro's Attitude in Politics?" In Daniel Wallace Culp, *Twentieth Century Negro Literature*. Naperville, IL: J. L. Nichols and Co., 1902. As one of the last and most influential of the black congressmen from the Carolinas, George Washington Murray was positioned perfectly to theorize on the role of politics in the lives of his people. "It was a serious blunder," claims Murray, to allow the freedmen, without education into the workings of government, into a position that would make him responsible for the government. The paramount issue for Southern blacks should not be the attainment of political office, but rather attaining of such political influence as is necessary for the protection of life and property. The "Negro's Attitude in Politics" should be "whatever attitude would prove most beneficial to him . . . until he shall have acquired sufficient strength along all lines to occupy and maintain an independent position, and shape the course of action to suit his fancy and convenience." A photo and brief biography of Murray accompany his article.

D295. Naison, Mark. "Black Agrarian Radicalism in the Great Depression: the Threads of a Lost Tradition." *Journal of Ethnic Stu*dies 1 (fall 1973): 47-65. Black agrarian radicalism traces its roots to the Colored Farmers' Alliance, formed in Texas in 1886. Although the historical record of this group is weak, Naison posits that the movement was strongest among the middle levels of the black farm population—tenants, renters, and small farmers. The CFA's most extensive records are in Texas and Kansas, with other activity reported in the Deep South in 1891, as rumors of a cotton pickers' strike spread to the newspapers. With the collapse of the CFA in the mid-1890s, no other black agrarian protest movement rose up until the Great Depression, with the formation of the

Alabama Sharecroppers Union in 1931 and the Southern Tenant Farmers Union in 1934.

D296. Neal, Diane. "Agrarian Reform Versus Bourbon Democracy: The South Carolina Gubernatorial Campaign of 1890." *Proceedings of the South Carolina Historical Association* (1983): 5-14. Brief overview of the 1890 gubernatorial campaign. Most useful is Neal's breakdown by county and race of election returns, with a separate chart showing the increase in real estate mortgages over the decade. Black voters had little to choose from between Tillman and opponent Alexander C. Haskell.

D297. _____, and Thomas W. Kremm. "Challenges to Subordination: Organized Black Agrarian Protest in South Carolina, 1886-1895." *South Atlantic Quarterly* 77 (winter 1978): 98-112. Between 1886 and 1895, South Carolina black farmers repeatedly tried collective measures to improve their economic well-being, particularly via the CFA. The authors note especially the secretive Cotton Pickers' League, which Humphrey organized to lead the proposed 1891 strike in the state. Some black farmers joined both organizations.

D298. Nelson, Richard Wayne. "The Cultural Contradictions of Populism: Tom Watson's Tragic Vision of Power, Politics, and History." *Georgia Historical Quarterly* 72 (spring 1988): 1-29. Nelson argues that Watson's career might be understood using the Machiavellian or republican paradigm developed by J. G. A. Pocock, along the lines approached by Steve Hahn and Bruce Palmer. Watson's pessimism about preserving political virtue in the modern world and his efforts to contain the contradictions he saw in modern political life were dictated by his loyalty to the republican tradition identified by those authors.

D299. Nixon, Herman C. "The Cleavage Within the Farmers' Alliance Movement." *Mississippi Valley Historical Review* 15 (June 1928): 22-33. Lines of internal cleavage within the Farmers' Alliance organizations tended to split the movement in two, with the Middle West on one side and the South on the other. Nixon addresses the question of why, despite strong effort, the factions failed to join forces at the St. Louis convention in December 1889. Part of the answer lies with the existence of the CFA and the question of black membership in the general body, and part lies with the ties between the Southern Alliance and the Knights of Labor, which pushed the Alliance into a more militant politics. Much of the fractionalization must be laid down to the Conger Lard Bill, strongly supported by the Northern Alliance (and particularly the Iowa chapters) but denounced by the Southern Alliance (particularly the Colored Farmers' Alliance) as a "fraud" pitting "western hog against Southern negro."

D300. Nolan, Terence Hunt. "William Henry Skaggs and the Reform Challenge of 1894." *Alabama Historical Quarterly* 33 (summer 1971): 116-34.

Skaggs was an unusual choice to lead Alabama Populists in 1892, as he was a young, wealthy banker. However, he was considered very liberal for his time regarding race relations, although he urged the removal of black Populist leader William J. Stevens from the party convention of 1894 on the grounds that he could not be trusted. Although he campaigned for Reuben Kolb, he thought him a "necessary evil." Interestingly, in an effort to prevent election fraud, Skaggs issued a circular urging blacks not to register to vote.

D301. Nussbaum, Raymond O. "'The Ring Is Smashed!': The New Orleans Municipal Election of 1896." *Louisiana History* 17 (summer 1976): 283-97. Nussbaum argues that, while there was a relationship between New Orleans reformers and rural agrarians, it was a tenuous one based on practical politics and very little on ideology or genuine commitment. The Regulars, the machine party, claimed that their opponents, the Citizens League, had allied themselves with Republicans and Populists, which would bring back scalawag rule and black domination. The Regulars also considered the Populists absurd, influenced by "long-haired men and short-haired women of Kansas."

D302. Olzak, Susan. "The Political Context of Competition: Lynching and Urban Racial Violence, 1882-1914." *Social Forces* 69 (December 1990): 395-421. Olzak's research suggests that economic and political factors shaped regional and temporal variation in lynching and urban violence against Southern blacks at the close of the century. Event-history and time-series analysis show that violence rose during periods of economic slumps, especially those affecting the least-skilled workers. Olzak also argues that lynching was related to the Populist challenge to one-party rule as well as by changing economic conditions.

D303. Page, Thomas Nelson. "The Disfranchisement of the Negro: One Factor in the South's Standing Problem." *Scribner's Magazine* 36 (July 1904): 15-24. Restrictions placed on black suffrage in the South, according to Page, were a positive step towards ending electoral fraud and abuse of the system. He recognizes the difference between black educated and illiterate classes and suggests that the suffrage amendments will allow the educated elite to separate themselves from the others. However, the race consciousness urged by some blacks (and their northern allies) would only succeed in keeping blacks down, and that it would be best to follow Booker T. Washington's advice.

D304. _____. "The Lynching of Negroes: Its Cause and Its Prevention." *North American Review* 178 (1904): 33-48. Page, a white Virginian, argued that the rise of lynching following the Civil War was due to growing hostility between blacks and whites fueled by an increase in the rate of black men raping white women. Rapes would decrease if black leaders were held accountable for members of their race, and lynchings would decrease if law officers who allowed lynchings were removed from office. Mary Church Terrell, a leading black reformer of the period, would answer him in a subsequent issue (**D402**).

D305. Paisley, Clifton. "The Political Wheelers and Arkansas' Election of 1888." *Arkansas Historical Quarterly* 25 (spring 1966): 3-21. Debt and low cotton prices lead to the rise in the early 1880s of the Agricultural Wheel, including roughly 200 local black Wheels. Much of the leadership of the nonpartisan Arkansas Wheel also made up the leadership of the Union Labor Party of Arkansas, which for all practical purposes served as their political arm, although the average members were Democrats. In the resultant three-way race of 1888, the race card was played to fend off any alliance between black Republican and white Wheel voters. Despite massive Democratic Party election fraud, the Wheelers did very well.

D306. Parsons, Stanley B., Karen Toombs Parsons, Walter Killilae, and Beverly Borgers. "The Role of Cooperatives in the Development of the Movement Culture of Populism." *Journal of American History* 69 (March 1983): 866-85. The authors examine the role of cooperatives in the development of the Populist culture by using Lawrence Goodwyn's scenario of farmers joining the Alliance to participate in the cooperative movement and create "the world's first large-scale working class cooperative." However, the evidence suggests that many of Goodwyn's contentions do not stand, in that the Alliance cooperatives never attained large enough numbers to effect any change.

D307. Patterson, John. "From Yeoman to Beast: Images of Blackness in Caesar's Column." *American Studies* 12 (1971): 21-31. Ignatius Donnelly's best-selling novel *Caesar's Column* (1890) is useful for understanding the racial thinking of this leading Populist theorist. Patterson argues that the author's images of black revolt and the characterization of his protagonist connect the novel with the emotional appeals of late nineteenth century Southern white supremacists and the fictional world of Thomas Dixon's *The Clansman*. Although Donnelly sought a biracial coalition and worked against the loss of black civil rights, his fiction provides "a telling glimpse of the practical limitations inherent in his vision of a Populist alliance of blacks and whites."

D308. Peal, David. "The Politics of Populism: Germany and the American South in the 1890s." *Comparative Studies in Society and History* 31 (April 1989): 340-62. Whereas earlier articles viewed racism exclusively as a psychological aberration, Peal compares the agrarian movements of the 1890s in the American South and Germany and notes that racism was too pervasive in both regions not to infuse the Populist political movements in both countries. Black emancipation did not imply social acceptance in the South any more than did Jewish emancipation in Germany, but both countries saw political interests unite factions against the insurgents.

D309. Peffer, William Alfred. "The Farmers' Defensive Movement." *The Forum* 8 (December 1889): 464-73. Of the 4,500,000 U.S. farmers, "at least one million" are organized by late 1889, and with the general union of all the various agrarian organizations within the current year, membership will "fall little, if any, short of 4,000,000." Peffer includes brief histories of the Grange, Alliance, and Farmers' Mutual Benefit Association, but no mention of the CFA.

D310. ____. "The Passing of the People's Party." *North American Review* 166 (January 1898): 12-24. Peffer, former Populist senator from Kansas, addresses two issues at the end of the Populist Era: why is it going, and where. Summarized, the People's Party platform was "equal rights and opportunities to all: let the people rule." Although the campaigns began in earnest, by the 1896 elections the Populists agreed to form fusion tickets with the Democrats, "and now the People's party is afflicted with political anemia." The debates between fusionists and anti-fusionists have split the party, with the fusionists joining forces with William Jennings Bryan. The People's Party will not go to the Republicans, because its principles are diametrically opposed to those of the Populists. A new party, merged with advanced Democrats and other reformers, would be ideal, but the Democrats are opposed to that idea. More than likely, the party will splinter and its work accomplished by men active in other areas.

D311. Peterson, John M. "The People's Party of Kansas: Campaigning in 1898." *Kansas History* 13 (1990-91): 235-58. While People's party activities had pretty much died out in the rest of the nation, Kansas remained a political hotbed which crossed racial and gender lines in its campaigns. In his excellent overview of the 1898 campaigns, Peterson notes that in Independence, "a good colored speaker" was needed, while another "black orator" spoke in Arkansas City. John W. Leedy, the Populist governor elected in 1896 and renominated in 1898, was regarded favorably by black leaders because of his appointment of black officers to black volunteer regiments and tripling the number of blacks in patronage positions. Numerous black Kansas campaigners are named, along with breakdowns of voting statistics, making this a surprisingly rich source of information on black populism.

D312. Pfeifer, Michael J. "Lynching and Criminal Justice in South Louisiana, 1878-1930." *Louisiana History* 40 (spring 1999): 155-77. The relationship between the rise of Populism and lynching has been examined repeatedly, and Pfeifer takes a closer look at lynching as it related to the "Sugar Bowl" economy of the twelve parishes of South Louisiana. The dynamics of the sugar economy were different from those of the cotton economy, in that the former relied on gang labor on a wage basis, which lead to occasional work stoppages, labor riots, and strikes. Republican-Populist fusion tickets could also be quite competitive with Democratic slates in the region's elections, in that until 1900 most black males enjoyed unencumbered voting rights, officeholding, and jury duty. Lynchings were less common in this region than in North Louisiana for a variety of reasons, although legal hangings were not uncommon.

D313. Pierce, Michael. "Farmers and the Failure of Populism in Ohio, 1890-1891." *Agricultural History* 74 (winter 2000): 58-85. Despite a large farming population and a strong history of agrarian organization, including the Grange, the Farmers' Alliance and People's party failed to elect local officials to political office. One problem was that it was often difficult in the campaigns to distinguish the Democrats from the People's party, as many of their reform platforms were identical. Although no mention is made of the role of blacks in Ohio campaigns, Pierce is useful for his statistical breakdowns of rural voting and the role of non-Ohioans in the campaigns.

D314. Poe, Clarence H. "Suffrage Restriction in the South: Its Causes and Consequences." *North American Review* 175 (October 1902): 534-43. Poe, editor of North Carolina's agrarian paper Progressive Farmer, considers the results of the recent suffrage amendments. Following the implementation of new restrictions of black voting, the South is going through "a gradual recovery from our nearly four decades of bondage to the race issue." Simultaneously, black education levels have increased, to the point where future black voters "will act more sensibly than the old."

D315. Pollack, Norman. "Hofstadter on Populism: A Critique of 'The Age of Reform'." *Journal of Southern History* 26 (November 1960): 478-500. In this seminal critique of Hofstadter's work, Pollack argues that the five dominant Populist themes outlined in *The Age of Reform* offer a "particularly weak foundation," in that they consider the movement only on an ideological level and neglect the historical and sociological factors. Pollack examines each of Hofstadter's themes in turn and concludes that the reader must question the validity of his methodology and scholarship, as too often Hofstadter cites rare examples from the Populist literature while ignoring the vast body of differing opinion.

D316. _____. "Ignatius Donnelly on Human Rights: A Study of Two Novels." *Mid-America* 47 (1965): 99-112. As a major figure in the national Populist movement, Donnelly's thoughts and writings on human rights, particularly towards Jews and blacks, cannot be ignored. His 1891 novel *Doctor Huguet* places its protagonist, a white Southern doctor, in the body of a poor black man. Donnelly suggests that man must look beyond skin color in the area of political rights, but he follows the thinking of many other white intellectuals of his period in that political equality does not equal social equality. By novel's end, Donnelly calls for political unity between blacks and poor whites, while Pollack suggests Donnelly's rhetoric might have encouraged the trend which culminated in the People's party successes.

D317. Pope, Whitney, and Charles Ragin. "Mechanical Solidarity: Repressive Justice and Lynchings in Louisiana." *American Sociological Review* 42 (April 1977): 363-68. Comments on Inverarity (**D217**). The authors reject Inverarity's claim of the existence of a solid white South broken by a wave of agrarian radicalism, believing that Durkheim's theory of the gradual recession of mechanical solidarity debunks that concept. Additionally, Inverarity employs concepts from both Durkheim and Erikson without always accurately indicating whose ideas are whose. Pope and Ragin believe that Inverarity's article does not show how the relationship between Louisianaa lynching and Populism can be explained under the terms he employs. See also Baggozi (**D19**) and Wasserman (**D422**) for additional critiques.

D318. "The Presidential Campaign in America." *Progressive Review* (London) 1 (1896): 117-32. In an overview of the campaign, the anonymous correspondent for this Fabian journal notes that the Populists gave "Negroes of the South a political fellowship which they never had obtained, not even from their saviors, the Republicans."

D319. Proctor, Samuel. "The National Farmers' Alliance Convention of 1890 and Its 'Ocala Demands'." *Florida Historical Quarterly* 28 (January 1950): 161-81. An excellent "everything you wanted to know about Ocala" article, with some attention paid to local non-convention events and peripheral issues. Proctor details the organization of the convention, groups in attendance, presented reports, and other happenings of the event, with numerous quotes from the local Ocala Banner newspaper. Problems involving the Southern Alliance and its efforts not to split the Southern white vote are delineated. The Colored Farmers' Alliance is mentioned as one group which agreed to the St. Louis Demands of 1889. The final Ocala Demands are also posted.

D320. Pruett, Katharine M., and John D. Fair. "Promoting a New South: Immigration, Racism, and 'Alabama on Wheels'." *Agricultural History* 66 (winter 1992): 19-41. To promote immigration and improve Alabama's economy, agriculture commissioner Reuben Kolb devised 'Alabama on Wheels,' a whistlestop campaign throughout the Midwest in 1888. However, the racial preconceptualization that persisted in that part of the country, particularly among new immigrants, precluded positive results.

D321. Pruitt, Paul M. "A Changing of the Guard: Joseph C. Manning and Populist Strategy in the Fall of 1894." *Alabama Historical Quarterly* 40 (spring and summer 1978): 20-36. Only twenty-four years old in 1894, Joseph C. Manning became a decisive force for unity in the People's Party Alabama gubernatorial campaign of that year. Known as the "Evangel" because of his zealotry, Manning sought non-violent means to capture the statehouse for the Populist cause. His campaign plan combined an incorporation of fusionist politics (with Kolb's Jeffersonian Democrats) with his great personal popularity among the rank and file of the movement and an attack on election fraud. The successes of 1894 were not transferable to the campaigns of 1896, which saw divisions among the agrarian leadership on the free silver issue.

D322. _____. "Defender of the Voteless: Joseph C. Manning Views the Disfranchisement Era in Alabama." *Alabama Historical Quarterly* 43 (fall 1981): 171-85. Manning remained a strong (if not always consistent) advocate of black voting rights during the Populist era and the years up until his death in 1925. Disfranchisement keeps the Democratic elite in control in Alabama, argues Manning, while simultaneously ensuring that the agrarian poor black and white classes will not unite.

D323. Rabinowitz, Howard N. "More than the Woodward Thesis: Assessing *The Strange Career of Jim Crow*." *Journal of American History* 75 (December 1988): 842-56. Rabinowitz considers three of Woodward's contributions: the Woodward thesis on Jim Crow; the concept of the Second Reconstruction; and the final chapter of the 1974 edition, which Rabinowitz feels points up some of the limitations of the earlier sections and editions of the book. Although Woodward himself saw this work as a "period piece," Rabinowitz feels it is a pathbreaking work whose essence has yet to be faulted. His commentary on the 1974 new chapter is especially thought-provoking.

D324. Ramage, Thomas W. "The Bloody Tenth Congressional Election of 1892." *Richmond County History* 7 (1975): 65-75. The congressional election of 1892 in Georgia's "bloody" Tenth District was one of the most hotly contested of the period, pitting Populist Tom Watson against Democrat James C. C. Black. The Populists hoped to build on their core of white farmers with a percentage of the large number of black voters and Augusta city workers. Watson addressed blacks with the argument that their economic concerns were the same as their white counterparts, but the *Augusta Chronicle* in turn claimed that he permitted blacks to address him as "Jesus" and "Savior." Despite contrary newspaper claims, Watson denied trying to destroy the color line.

D325. Ransom, Roger L., and Richard Sutch. "The Ex-Slave in the Post-Bellum South: a Study of the Economic Impact of Racism in a Market Environment." *Journal of Economic History* 33 (March 1973): 131-48. The authors focus on the "costs of information underlying decisions in the labor market" to partly explain how racism can have a profound and lasting effect on the market even in the face of competitive pressures. If a black sharecropper decided to move on to a new farm and a new landlord, he was more often than not confronted with the white landlord's attitude that he was "let go" as an unreliable worker, although statistically black farm laborers gained from experience and did reasonably well. Although self-interest theory suggests that blacks would have achieved greater economic success as an organized group, the authors posit that black farmers could only imperfectly perceive the benefits, and they were increasingly disfranchised via quasi-legal means. See also **D452**.

D326. Redding, Kent. "Failed Populism: Movement-Party Disjuncture in North Carolina, 1890 to 1900." *American Sociological Review* 57 (June 1992):

340-52. Using county-level data on North Carolina Farmers' Alliance membership and People's party votes to test theories on the socio-structural bases of the two organizations and gauge the relationship between them, Redding demonstrates a disjuncture between membership and support. As a result, he notes that as early as 1892 the Populists lacked internal cohesion. The Alliance and the People's party had significantly different mobilization techniques and organizational characteristics, and thus the transition from movement to party undercut Populism.

D327. Reed, John Shelton. "Percent Black and Lynching: a Test of Blalock's Theory." *Social Forces* 50 (March 1972): 356-60. Hubert Blalock in his 1967 book *Toward a Theory of Minority-Group Relations* argues that the occurrence of lynching in Southern communities correlates proportionately to the size of the black population. Reed refines the argument by including factors for both the black and white populations. Although the rate varies from state to state, Reed argues that variations could be directly related to historical and governmental properties of the states.

D328. Reed, Thomas B. "The Federal Control of Elections." *North American Review* 151 (June 1890): 671-80. At the time of this writing, Reed was Speaker of the U.S. House of Representatives. Reed suggests that the Southern justification for white election fraud and violence against blacks is a false one; there is no real threat of black domination at the Federal level. But fraud, be it gerrymandering or ballot-stuffing, is rife throughout the South. This state of affairs is not good for the nation, and federal supervision of local elections is called for when necessary.

D329. Reid, Debra A. "African Americans, Community Building, and the Role of the State in Rural Reform in Texas, 1890s-1930s." In Catherine McNicol Stock and Robert D. Johnston, ed., *The Countryside in the Age of the Modern State: Political Histories of Rural America.* Ithaca, NY: Cornell University Press, 2001. With black agrarians "formally powerless" through racism and disfranchisement, they adopted fundamentally economic goals, working to strengthen the family farm to achieve independence and obtain land. Reid discusses the work of Robert Lloyd Smith and the Farmers' Improvement Society as one formal means during the Populist era at black self-help, although she notes that most black farmers sought public rather than private help for their betterment.

D330. Reid, George W. "Congressman George Henry White: His Major Power Base." *Negro History Bulletin* 39 (March 1976): 554-55. Brief biographical article on Reid, black Republican representative from North Carolina's Second Congressional District. Notes the role of the Negro State Council of North Carolina in promoting White's candidacy for the district. Reid concludes that White's major power base was not the Republican Party, but rather the black community.

D331. Reid, Joseph D. "Sharecropping as an Understandable Market Response: the Post-Bellum South." *Journal of Economic History* 33 (March 1973): 106-30. To what extent did racism play a role in the rise of the number of black sharecroppers in the post-bellum South? Reid argues that racism and "land thirst" are demonstrably less significant as factors than most historians and economists assume. Rather, it is a redistribution of risk between landlord and labor, a possible increase in agricultural productivity from varying the intensity of managerial attention to labor, and increased competition for the landlords' attention which underlie the shift in ownership practices. See also **D325**.

D332. Ridge, Martin. "Populism Redux: John D. Hicks and The Populist Revolt." *Reviews in American History* 13 (March 1985): 142-54. In his fine retrospective essay, Ridge argues that Hicks' work, far from being the last word on Populism, proved a catalyst to a variety of further cases studies, from Goodwyn, Hahn, Hofstadter, Bogue, and Saloutos, among others. In his treatment of blacks within the movement, however, Hicks is very much a man of his times, using stereotypes to bolster his arguments. His contemporary reviewers commented favorably on Hicks' demonstration of the corrosive influence of race on the reform movement of the 1890s.

D333. Roberts, Frances. "William Manning Lowe and the Greenback Party in Alabama." *Alabama Review* 5 (April 1952): 100-21. The Greenback Party under Confederate veteran William Manning Lowe was one of the first strong independent agrarian political movements in Alabama's postbellum years with a degree of biracial unity. However, after Lowe's death, many of his followers returned to the Democratic and Conservative Party, "probably because the insurgency movement had become a threat to white supremacy." They had been willing to vote with blacks for Lowe, but not for other candidates, especially when blacks started to seek public office.

D334. Robison, Daniel M. "Tennessee Politics and the Agrarian Movement, 1886-1896." *Mississippi Valley Historical Review* 20 (December 1933): 365-80. The agrarian revolt in Tennessee was marked by moderation throughout, with the Populists making their strongest showing in the 1892 elections. The race question did not dominate the political scene, although it acted as a deterrent to extreme divisions among white voters.

D335. Rodabaugh, Karl. "Agrarian Ideology and the Farmers' Revolt in Alabama." *Alabama Review* 36 (July 1983): 195-217. The Farmers' Alliance "espoused a compelling agrarian ideology that stressed the value of the small farmer's lifestyle." The rural way of life was ordained by God and should be small and self-sufficient. Because this ideology lacked clarity, its proponents had the greatest impact by conjuring up the evils of the urban-industrial world. The Alliance also raised "divisive economic issues that weakened the political impact of racism" but simultaneously stirred doubts as to whether the small farmers could generate enough political bargaining power to be successful.

D336. _____. "The Alliance in Politics: The Alabama Gubernatorial Election of 1891." *Alabama Historical Quarterly* 36 (spring 1974): 54-80. In Alabama, the rise of the Populist movement came in part because of the unwillingness of entrenched Bourbon leaders to admit agrarians such as Kolb to leadership ranks. The influential *Montgomery Advertiser* editorialized that "the white alliance will have no lot or part in the colored alliances," and even that city's Alliance Journal assured its readers that the separate alliances would not intermingle. The *Advertiser* in particular drew attention to the dangers of uniting the two alliances throughout the campaign.

D337. _____. "Fusion, Confusion, Defeat, and Disfranchisement: The 'Fadeout of Populism' in Alabama." *Alabama Historical Quarterly* 34 (summer 1972): 131-53. Rodabaugh argues that Woodward's claim that the Populist party must be held accountable for disfranchisement needs clarification. Although Populists blamed blacks for their final defeat, Alabama protestors had blamed blacks after every state election during the 1890s. Also, the Populists despaired of attracting black voters and sought to prevent them from participating effectively in politics. Appeals to black voters were opportunistic and not markedly different from those made by Democrats. The link between the party and disfranchisement can only be guessed at.

D338. _____. "'Kolbites' Versus Bourbons: the Alabama Gubernatorial Election of 1892." *Alabama Historical Quarterly* 37 (winter 1975): 275-321. Newly-elected Bourbon Governor Thomas Goode of Alabama presided over a state legislature with a large Alliance contingent supported by Kolb's disaffected agrarians. Although Goode was more progressivism than many in his views toward education of both races and the elimination of some of the more grievous wrongs, the Bourbon press used race baiting to attack the Kolb political threat. The "Kolbites," on their part, claimed among other things that Goode had ridden in a parade with blacks and thus tried to distance themselves from being seen as favorable to the race.

D339. _____. "The Prelude to Populism in Alabama." *Alabama Historical Quarterly* 43 (summer 1981): 111-52. Rodabaugh argues that a series of events first had to occur before state farmers politicized and fought for improvements. Notes the appearance, "despite severe hardships," of numerous black farm organizations in Alabama, including the CFA. Good quotes from various small-town Alabama newspapers on the presence of black Alliancemen and their relationship to the Southern Alliance.

D340. Rogers, William Warren. "The Agricultural Wheel in Alabama." *Alabama Review* 20 (January 1967): 5-16. The Agricultural Wheel was founded in February 1882 near Des Arc, Arkansas. As one of the early agrarian organizations, it spread rapidly to other states, and many Wheelers were also Alliancemen. In 1887, a number of Wheelers, including black delegates, met in Birmingham to form the Union Labor Party. The next year, the Lawrence County Wheel approved a motion to admit black members to segregated seats as silent members. The convention also adopted a resolution declaring that any political action taken by the white Wheel be passed on to the black Wheel.

D341. _____. "The Farmers' Alliance in Alabama." *Alabama Review* 15 (January 1962): 5-18. The first Alliance in Alabama was founded in Beech Grove, Madison County, in March 1887. Rogers notes the interest of ministers in the Alliance, and that once the organization entered politics, people without agricultural connections supported it, "but in general the response to the Alliance was confined to farmers, white and black, with both large and small farmers joining in large numbers." The weakest support came from the Black Belt, which was largely farmed by blacks, who did not have equal status to whites.

D342. _____. "The Negro Alliance in Alabama." *Journal of Negro History* 45 (January 1960): 38-44. Although logic suggests that blacks would support Populist candidates, who supported unfettered suffrage, in Alabama the Bourbon politicians who controlled the election machinery used the black vote to fraudulently win elections. State newspapers report the formation of a Negro Alliance early in 1889, although no mention is made of a statewide alliance to mirror that of the white farmers. By the summer of 1889, Humphrey estimated that there were 50,000 Negro Alliance members in Alabama alone. A Negro Alliance exchange was formed in Mobile that same year. A combination of poor statewide communications, some conservative Alliance backlash, and the entrance of the group into politics lead to the demise of the organization.

D343. _____. "Negro Knights of Labor in Arkansas: A Case Study of the 'Miscellaneous' Strike." *Labor History* 10 (summer 1969): 498-504. The Knights of Labor had active black and white assemblies in Arkansas during the 1880s, but strikes were a rarity. Rogers examines what one Arkansas government document dubbed a "miscellaneous strike" by state agricultural workers in 1886, which was actually a strike for higher wages by the Negro Knights of Labor on Tate's Plantation near Little Rock. The strike failed and the participants were brought to court, but Rogers notes that it was a "courageous, if foolhardy, action" destined for failure from the beginning. See also **D29**.

D344. _____. "Reuben F. Kolb: Agricultural Leader of the New South." *Agricultural History* 32 (April 1958): 109-19. Rogers' article focuses on Kolb's agricultural accomplishments rather than his run for governor of Alabama in 1892 and 1894.

D345. _____, and Wayne Flynt. "Reform Oratory in Alabama, 1890-1896." *Southern Speech Journal* 29 (winter 1963): 94-106. Interesting brief article on how the oratory of Manning, Kolb, and *Greenville Living Truth* editor James M. Whitehead stirred the masses for Populism. Whitehead spoke before black Alliancemen and was attacked by the conservative *Talladega News-Reporter* for doing so. Peyton G. Bowman, chairman of the Jeffersonian faction of the party, is cited as "the most persuasive speaker on the subject of Negro rights" (Flynt and Rogers give a brief sample of his fiery rhetoric).

D346. _____, and Jerrell H. Shofner. "Joseph C. Manning: Militant Agrarian, Enduring Populist." *Alabama Historical Quarterly* 29 (spring and summer 1967): 7-37. Manning was truly unusual among Southern Populists, in that he "was not anti-Semitic, anti-Negro, or, in the true sense, anti-Southern." Throughout his life he argued in favor of black suffrage and free elections, often in opposition to his own party. A good overview of the man known as the "Evangel" for his oratory and fervor.

D347. Romero, Sidney James, Jr. "The Political Career of Murphy James Foster, Governor of Louisiana, 1892-1900." *Louisiana Historical Quarterly* 28 (October 1945): 1129-1243. Foster's gubernatorial career spanned the rise and fall of Louisiana Populism. In his lengthy article, Romero notes the "peculiarities" that cropped up regarding black voting during these years, particularly during the gubernatorial election of 1896, which pitted the Populists, Republicans, and sugar planters against the machine Democrats. In St. Landry Parish, Republicans and Populists "went through the form of registering negroes" when the sheriff failed to appear because of threats on his life.

D348. Roscigno, Vincent J., and M. Keith Kimble. "Elite Power, Race, and the Persistence of Low Unionization in the South." *Work and Occupations* 22 (August 1995): 271-300. In this study of unionization in North Carolina, the authors note that the landed elite were instrumental in promoting race fear and hatred, which subsequently undermined any chance of effective biracial worker mobilization and class-based politics. However, such manipulation has also resulted in increased insurgency and political activity by poor blacks who see ultimate favorable outcomes. Particularly in North Carolina, the influence of black population concentration on unionization was shown to be positive and strongest in regions where a landed elite continues to dominate the economy.

D349. Rosengarten, Theodore. "'I Stand Where My Boyhood Put Me': Reconsidering Woodward's Tom Watson." *Georgia Historical Quarterly* 72 (winter 1988): 684-97. Woodward's *Tom Watson* is still widely read, although Rosengarten suggests curiosity will gradually shift from Watson to Woodward himself. Woodward predicted that the Southern theme of one race holding domination over another would die, and Watson's career demonstrates that.

D350. Rusk, Jerrold G. "The Effect of the Australian Ballot Reform on Split Ticket Voting: 1876-1908." *American Political Science Review* 64 (December 1970): 1220-38. Rusk examines the effect of the Australian Ballot on split-ticket voting, with comparative charts for pure party versus all party strips. The article doesn't specifically touch on Populism, but the Australian Ballot had a significant variable in Deep South voting patterns.

D351. Russell, Phillips. "The Plowboy from Edgefield." *Virginia Quarterly Review* 8 (October 1932): 514-29. A reconsideration of Ben Tillman, whose political career "rested on a recognition of the concealed warfare between town and country. . . ." Historians have passed over Tillman's participation in the disfranchisement movement in South Carolina, but he bragged about using violence and intimidation to remove blacks from the political arena.

D352. Saloutos, Theodore. "The Agricultural Problem and Nineteenth Century Industrialism." *Agricultural History* 22 (July 1948): 156-74. Although he does not mention racial factors, Saloutos is an excellent summation of why late 19th century farmers' movements failed. A series of organizations, from the Grange to the Populist Party, failed to evolve a cohesive agricultural policy to cope with the growing farm problem. Each organization emphasized a different formula with which it became identified, which suggested to critics that the farmers lacked an understanding of the broader issues.

D353. _____. "The Agricultural Wheel in Arkansas." *Arkansas Historical Quarterly* 2 (June 1943): 127-40. Although preceded by the Grange (1872), the Wheel gained state prominence amongst Populist movements rapidly. Traditional distinctions between farmer and labor were absent within the organization, although blacks were initially barred from membership. The constitution and by-laws of the Wheel after its merger with the Brothers of Freedom, however, permitted the organization of "colored farmers" into separate Wheels.

D354. _____. "The Grange in the South, 1870-1877." *Journal of Southern History* 19 (November 1953): 473-87. Before the Farmers' Alliance, there was the Grange, which saw state chapters emerge in 1872 and spread quickly throughout the South. Sentiment over black participation in the movement was divided into two schools of thought, a Northern view which admitted blacks presumably on an equal basis with whites, and the Southern view which called for a separate black farmers' organization. The national organization's by-laws and constitution did not deny membership to anyone on the basis of race, and blacks joined the Grange in Louisiana and throughout the country on the local level. The Council of Laborers was simultaneously formed as the black arm of the Grange to assuage Southerners and constructed a pattern for the development of later agrarian organizations.

D355. Saunders, Robert M. "The Southern Populists and the Negro in 1892." *University of Virginia Essays in History* 12 (1966-1967): 7-25. General overview of the relationship between black and white Southern Populists just prior to the movement's heyday. Populist leaders sought issues which would induce blacks to the polls, with mixed success.

D356. _____. "Southern Populists and the Negro, 1893-1895." *Journal of Negro History* 54 (July 1969): 240-61. General overview of the relationship between black and white Southern Populists during the movement's heyday. Saunders notes that only Virginia made any serious effort to bring blacks into the party at the local level, but even that state party quickly abandoned its efforts. Populist leaders often urged "strong inducements" which would bring out black voters, including anti-lynching, convict lease reform, and election reform platforms, but implementation of these efforts varied throughout the region. One of the great failings of the Populists was their inability to come to grips with election fraud, which regularly lead to Democratic victories and subsequent anti-black legislation. Additionally, the white Populists drew a line between social and legal equality with their fellow black Populists, supporting the latter while recognizing that the former would be political suicide.

D357. _____. "The Transformation of Tom Watson, 1894-1895." *Georgia Historical Quarterly* 54 (fall 1970): 339-56. Saunders argues that successive defeats for political office "accentuated a feeling of being an outsider" in Tom Watson and drove him to gain the support of those people who rejected his reform programs. Watson wanted acceptance by his fellow Southerners more than he desired to preserve the Populist ideology. Turning rather quickly against other reformers, Watson also denied his earlier support of black rights. By 1894, he advocated separate schools, denied that he favored jury service for blacks, and supported Jim Crow transportation legislation. After his defeat in that year's election, he increased his attacks on black leaders, although he continued to be ambivalent on the rights of the common black man.

D358. Scarborough, W. S. "The Race Problem." *Arena* 11 (October 1890): 560-67. Blacks are "quietly disposed and inclined to accept" any solution to what whites call "the race problem" in the interest of the common good. In response to Hampton (**D181**) and others, Scarborough argues that decolonization is not the answer, as it would mean certain death for the black colonists. It is better, he continues, for blacks to migrate West.

D359. Schott, Matthew J. "Progressives against Democracy: Electoral Reform in Louisiana, 1894-1921." *Louisiana History* 22 (summer 1979): 247-60. Schott argues that antimachine progressive reformers did not benefit from the white primary and Democratic party solidarity. The move toward disfranchisement came in part from the Populist fusion campaign of 1896 and well-intentioned electoral reform by Governor John Parker.

D360. Schwartz, Michael. "An Estimate of the Size of the Southern Farmers' Alliance, 1884-1890." *Agricultural History* 51 (October 1977): 759-69. One of the central questions revolving around agrarian organizations of this period is the actual membership size. Schwartz point out that there are no accurate reports of Alliance membership, and the same can be said of the Colored Farmers' Alliance. Simply defining "membership" in any organization is problematic, as even dues collection could be haphazard at all levels. Record-keeping was imprecise and unaligned, with local and state groups reporting figures at various times. Schwartz' methodology would be interesting as applied to the CFA, to counteract "guesstimates" of black participation.

D361. _____, Naomi Rosenthal, and Laura Schwartz. "Leader-Member Conflict in Protest Organizations: the Case of the Southern Farmers' Alliance." *Social Problems* 29 (October 1981): 22-36. As Robert Michels predicted, an inevitable oligarchy arose in the Southern Farmers' Alliance, for such is the nature of political organizations. However, rather than simply an internally-generated clique, the SFA leaders were primarily from the planter class, with a history of office-holding and political ambition. The forced exclusion of black members from the SFA and the formation of the CFA underscores a flaw in Michel's logic, in that the oligarchy naturally would have followed the lead of the rank and file members and kept membership biracial.

D362. Schweiger, Beth Barton. "Putting Politics Aside: Virginia Democrats and Voter Apathy in the Era of Disfranchisement." In Edward L. Ayers and John C. Willis, ed., *The Edge of the South: Life in Nineteenth-Century Virginia.* Charlottesville, VA: University Press of Virginia, 1991. A factor unmentioned in most articles on the elections of the period is voter apathy, which was particularly strong in Virginia during the brief Populist era. Democrats pointed to political corruption and universal manhood suffrage as the culprits and quickly made the black voter the scapegoat. The Kent Bill controversy of 1892, rather than serving as a rallying point for Populists, only fueled voter cynicism of party politics.

D363. Scott, Rebecca J. "'Stubborn and Disposed to Stand Their Ground': Black Militia, Sugar Workers and the Dynamics of Collective Action in the Louisiana Sugar Bowl, 1863-87." *Slavery and Abolition* 20 (April 1999): 103-26. One interesting early example of Deep South biracial collectivist action was the fall 1887 unification of black, mulatto, and white sugar workers in St. Mary, Terrebonne, and Lafourche Parishes under the guidance of the Knights of Labor to insist on their right to bargain with their employers. Although the subsequent strike came to a bloody conclusion, the episode proved that black workers in particular were not willing to passively accept their economic fate.

D364. Scott, Roy V. "Milton George and the Farmers' Alliance Movement." *Mississippi Valley Historical Review* 45 (June 1958): 90-109. George was the founder of the National Farmers' Alliance, which was ultimately absorbed by the People's party in the 1890s. As editor of the *Western Rural and American Stockman*, one of the largest of the agrarian papers, George urged the primacy of the farming class and the necessity for a more equitable distribution of wealth. His National Farmers' Alliance was a leader in the organization of rural blacks, having chartered a separate alliance in Prairie County, Arkansas in 1882.

D365.   Shaffer, A. W. "A Southern Republican on the Lodge Bill." *North American Review* 151 (November 1890): 601-609. Shaffer served as Chief Federal Supervisor of Elections in North Carolina. Federal legislation to oversee Southern elections (the "Force Bill") is "sickly-sentimental" and "half-hearted." The primary cause of its lack of adaptation in the South is the difficulty of obtaining efficient supervisors to attend the registration and election. Under existing legislation, enormous frauds take place regularly, primarily because local officials realize that they strongly outnumber any federally-appointed overseers. An interesting article by someone who was regularly on the "front lines" of the election battles.

D366.   Shannon, Fred A. "C. W. Macune and the Farmers' Alliance." *Current History* 28 (June 1955): 330-35. Passing reference to the CFA: "From the beginning Negroes organized in their own Colored Alliances. The race line being stronger than class interest, white men could not work with Negroes in the same organization."

D367.   Shapiro, Herbert. "The Populists and the Negro: A Reconsideration." In August Meier and Elliott Rudwick, ed. *The Making of Black America: Essays in Negro Life and History, Volume 2*. New York: Atheneum, 1969. Although some modern scholars view black participation in the Populist movement as a genuine expression of feelings of interracial solidarity, Shapiro argues that the white Populists' interest in the black vote was rather based on political expediency.   "The Populists may well be hailed for seeking to subdue racial hates to achieve an alliance of common interests . . . ."

D368.   Sharp, James A. "The Entrance of the Farmers' Alliance into Tennessee Politics." *East Tennessee Historical Society Publications* No. 9 (1937): 77-92. A useful overview article which covers much the same territory as Robison's "Tennessee Politics" (**D334**), with a further examination of the influence of the new 1889-90 state election laws on black participation. The new laws required voters to mark their own ballots secretly, present registration certificates to election officials, and pay a poll tax—measures it was believed would prevent hundreds of black Republicans from voting. The Alliance succeeded in dominating the Democratic Party and elected Buchanan to the governorship.

D369.   _____. "The Farmers' Alliance and the People's Party in Tennessee." *East Tennessee Historical Society Publications* No. 10 (1938): 91-113. Plans for a continuation of the governorship of John P. Buchanan were stymied by the appearance of the People's party in the state in 1891. At first, state Alliance leaders opposed the formation of the third party, but ultimately the People's party gained strong Alliance support. After a campaign filled with accusations of bribery and treachery with the Republican-Populist fusion ticket camp, the Democrats regained control of the state and the People's party declined rapidly.

D370. Shook, Robert W. "The Texas 'Election Outrage' of 1886." *East Texas Historical Journal* 10 (spring 1972): 20-30. Washington County, Texas was roughly fifty percent black at the time of the 1886 elections. Although the dominant Republicans ran a full slate, the People's party took all seats save that of county tax assessor. The U.S. Senate undertook an investigation of the election, where election irregularities, voter intimidation, and murder were all ultimately revealed. Although both federal and state election reform laws were proposed as a result, interest waned, and the subsequent disfranchisement of Texas blacks can only suggest that Populism represented the termination of reform rather than a contribution to Progressivism.

D371. Shugg, Roger Wallace. "The New Orleans General Strike of 1892." *Louisiana Historical Quarterly* 21 (April 1938): 547-60. The New Orleans General Strike of 1892 was the first in U.S. history to enlist both skilled and unskilled labor, black and white. Although this peaceful strike finally failed, it proved that a biracial coalition could be effective in the South. Shugg suggests that a successful strike would have "raised up urban allies for the rural Louisiana Populists."

D372. Simkins, Francis Butler. "Ben Tillman's View of the Negro." *Journal of Southern History* 3 (May 1937): 161-74. Simkins argues that Tillman, a powerful speaker popular with Southern and Northern mass audiences alike, contributed significantly to reactionary Depression Era attitudes towards blacks. Tillman believed that the "Northern millions" invested in Southern black schools created racial antagonism, and that education ultimately lead to crime and discontent among blacks. He was instrumental in disfranchising South Carolina blacks through the "understanding clause" of 1895, an act he described as great statesmanship and more consistent with civil morality than the violence of earlier days.

D373. Simms, L. Moody, Jr. "A Note on Sidney Lanier's Attitude Toward the Negro and Toward Populism." *Georgia Historical Quarterly* 52 (September 1968): 305-07. Popular Southern writer Sidney Lanier's essay "The New South" (1880) **(D241)** suggests the sort of agrarian alliance between black and white farmers which should make the Populist movement a Southern success.

D374. Simms-Brown, R. Jean. "Populism and Black Americans: Constructive or Destructive?" *Journal of Negro History* 65 (autumn 1980): 349-60. After a lengthy historiography on blacks and populism, Simms-Brown posits that the constructiveness of the black-Populist coalition was derived from the black leaders' awareness of the political picture, their active involvement towards increasing the fears of whites, and the long-range effects of the movement. Self-interest, in particular, played a major role in black party loyalty, as voters moved from Republican to Populist and occasionally into Democratic camps, dependent upon local white support (or lack of). Blacks understood the Populists better than the Populists understood them and played on that strength.

D375. Singal, Daniel J. "Beyond Consensus: Richard Hofstadter and American Historiography." *American Historical Review* 89 (October 1984): 976-1004. Good overview of the man who cast a more jaundiced eye on the Populists than did Woodward. Hofstadter's Populists were men "who looked primarily backwards," seeing themselves as mythical yeoman while simultaneously trying to advance in the modern world. Consequently, they were doomed to repeated failures, which in turn lead them down the paths of bigotry and xenophobia. The key question, Singal asks, is why Hostadter could not grant the hungry rural classes their symbolic comforts?

D376. Sisk, Glenn N. "Social Life in the Alabama Black Belt, 1875-1917." *Alabama Review* 8 (April 1955): 83-103. Sisk notes the presence of both the Grange and Farmers' Alliance as fraternal organizations for blacks in 1880s-1890s Alabama. "The Grange and Farmers' Alliance held all day meetings as well as agricultural fairs at which farm products were displayed, and concerts, tournaments, and baby shows held."

D377. Smalls, Robert. "Election Methods in the South." *North American Review* 151 (November 1890): 593-600. Smalls at the time of this writing was a former U.S. representative from South Carolina. In South Carolina, "there is neither a free ballot nor an honest count." Notes numerous examples of fraud and the futility of protest, and that "the election of the ticket headed by Tillman mean a perpetuation of all of the evil meantioned in this article, and more."

D378. Smith, Charles H. "Have American Negroes Too Much Liberty?" *The Forum* 16 (September 1893): 176-83. Although Smith acknowledges the success of black Southern businesses and even small towns, "some radical change will have to be made in the laws if crime and outrage continues. The negro will have to be disfranchised and a separate code enacted, that will fit him."

D379. Smith, Hoke. "The Disastrous Effects of a Force Bill." *The Forum* 13 (August 1892): 686-92. The future governor offers his opinions on the Force Bill. Passage of the bill would be a calamity for Southern blacks; their hope of development rests on the current "kind feeling" between the races. Smith notes the efforts of Governor Northen to improve the condition of Georgia blacks.

D380. _____. "The Resources and Development of the South." *North American Review* 159 (August 1894): 129-36. Populist Hoke Smith was U.S. Secretary of the Interior when he wrote this article. Slavery kept the South from becoming the greatest manufacturing, agricultural, and mining section of the Union. Notes in passing the potential influx of Chinese laborers and the necessity of using black laborers to stop their spread.

D381. Smith, R. Drew. "African American Protestants, Political Activism, and 'Liberal' Redemptive Hopes." *Theology Today* 53 (July 1996): 191-98. From the colonial era to the present, African American Protestant preachers have resisted efforts to exclude their congregations from the economic mainstream. Underlying the concessionary spirit of these leaders was their belief that aligning with core American values would work towards achieving fundamental political objectives. An economic path-to-progress theory flowed through the messages of Martin Luther King, Jr., Adam Clayton Powell, Leon Sullivan, and other minister-activists; these messages occasionally took the form of consumer boycotts at the local level. However, a divergent critical stream found fault in church-led civil rights campaigns as not focusing on economic issues.

D382. Smith, Ralph A. "The Farmers' Alliance in Texas, 1875-1900: a Revolt Against Bourbon and Bourgeois Democracy." *Southwestern Historical Quarterly* 48 (October 1948): 346-69. General but detailed history of the Farmers' Alliance in Texas, notes the participation of Humphrey in the 1888 Fort Worth convention of July 2 and the first Union Labor Convention in Texas on July 5. The CFA is given only a passing reference.

D383. Smith, Robert L. "An Effort to Improve the Negro Farmers in Texas." *Annual Report of the Hampton Negro Conference.* Hampton, VA: Press of the Hampton Normal and Industrial Institute, 1902. Report on the Farmers' Improvement Society, founded by Smith in 1890 in Colorado County, Texas as a black-owned and -operated agricultural association.

D384. _____. "An Uplifting Negro Cooperative Society: The Farmers' Improvement Society for Texas which is Substituting Among the Negroes Order and Prosperity for Shiftlessness and Poverty." *The World's Work* 16 (July 1908): 10462-66. General overview of the work of Smith's Farmers' Improvement Society of Colorado County, Texas.

D385. Smith, Willard H. "William Jennings Bryan and Racism." *Journal of Negro History* 54 (April 1969): 127-49. "Let the people rule" was Bryan's slogan through much of his political career, starting in the 1890s. Smith notes that Bryan was not a "consistent racist," although his attitude toward blacks would be acceptable to a segregationist. Although supported by the Populists, Bryan had mixed feelings concerning black rights. As citizens, they had the same constitutional rights as whites. However, the qualifications of the franchise were important in the South as 'absolutely essential to the welfare' of that region. Blacks were not to be placed on the same social setting as whites, and Bryan roundly condemned President Theodore Roosevelt for inviting Booker T. Washington to a White House dinner. There is no one explanation for the Great Commoner's views on race, which are the weakest points in his armor.

D386. Somers, Dale A. "Black and White in New Orleans: a Study in Urban Race Relations, 1865-1900." *Journal of Southern History* 40 (February 1974): 19-42. New Orleans has always been perhaps the most un-Southern of all Southern cities, particularly in the area of race relations. Somers notes that, prior to the early 1890s, black and white New Orleaneans forged a less than rigid color line on matters political, social, and economic. However, with the growing realization among Southerners that the federal government had all but abandoned oversight of race matters, New Orleans slowly followed the rest of the Deep South in imposing restrictions and other discriminatory measures.

D387. Soule, Sarah A. "Populism and Black Lynching in Georgia, 1890-1900." *Social Forces* 71 (December 1992): 431-49. Soule addresses the recurrent question of the relationship between Populism and lynching by studying county-level variations in 1890s Georgia. Black counties and counties with a higher degree of farm tenancy were more likely to support Populist candidates, and manufacturing counties were less likely. Lynching rates increased when economic competition increased, but counties that voted Populist did not have significant increases in black lynching rates.

D388. Spindler, Frank MacD. "Concerning Hempstead and Waller County." *Southwestern Historical Quarterly* 59 (April 1956): 455-72. Waller County, Texas had a predominently black population in the late nineteenth century and was a hotbed of radical politics. Spindler notes the appearance of black candidate J. E. Freeman on the "people's ticket" in 1886. The People's party also effected a complete party organization, with six precinct chairmen and at least seventy individuals in the local convention.

D389. Spriggs, William Edward. "The Virginia Colored Farmers' Alliance: a Case Study of Race and Class Identity." *Journal of Negro History* 64 (summer 1979): 191-204. The CFA in Virginia collapsed from internal weakness and the failure of its economic program. Party members primary identity was with their race, rather than class, and unity with poor white farmers never materialized. Spriggs also notes that the white leadership of the CFA controlled the organization's communications, thus cutting off the rank-and-file from any controversial movements by the black leaders, particularly William H. Warwick, state lecturer, and determining public image statewide. Additionally, disagreement over the running of the exchanges, especially the black exchange becoming part of the greater district organization, seriously impacted cooperation.

D390. Stahl, John M. "Are the Farmers Populists?" *North American Review* 163 (September 1896): 266-76. As secretary of the Farmers' National Congress of the United States, Stahl was in a perfect position to answer this basic question at the penultimate moment of the agrarian movement. Basing his argument primarily on monetary issues, Stahl claims that the farmer barely tolerated Populism, and that the Populist party was successful primarily in urban areas. One must also not believe that farmers are hostile to city people, as "tens of thousands of farmers' daughters are in the cities," and nearly all of them have savings accounts. One of the few articles surveyed which pointedly describes Populism as an urban rather than rural movement.

D391. Steelman, Joseph Flake. "Republican Party Strategists and the Issue of Fusion with Populists in North Carolina, 1893-1894." *North Carolina Historical Review* 47 (July 1970): 244-69. Following the election of 1892, Republican strategists sought to prevent any fusion with the Populist ticket, arguing that such a merger would be devious and illogical. They pointed out that Populists had supported division of school funds on the basis of taxes paid for each race, while fusionists pointed to disfranchisement of black Republicans in 1889 and polling place fraud. It was also assumed that Democrats would attempt to purchase or influence black votes. Steelman cites numerous North Carolina black leaders on both sides of the fusion issue—R. H. W. Leak, Jim Young, R. B. Russell, and Samuel H. Vick, to name a few--which makes this an especially rich article for locate studies.

D392. _____. "Vicissitudes of Republican Party Politics: The Campaign of 1892 in North Carolina." *North Carolina Historical Review* 33 (autumn 1966): 430-42. The 1892 election saw Republican leaders in a quandary over whether to focus on local or national campaigns. Party leaders advised against campaigning at the state level because of the fear of black aspirations for local office. Blacks, on the other hand, argued strongly for local focus. They also realized that the party divisions caused by the growth of the Populist party would give black voters the balance of electoral power. Party leaders meeting in executive session noted the deep cleavages along racial lines, with black leaders supporting the faction lead by state chairman Eaves. Good examination of the role of race in a single election at local/state levels.

D393. Steelman, Lala Carr. "Leonidas LaFayette Polk, North Carolina Allianceman, and Some Conflicts of Agrarian Leadership, 1887-1892." In Joseph F. Steelman, ed., *Of Tar Heel Towns, Shipbuilders, Reconstructionists and Alliancemen: Papers in North Carolina History (East Carolina University Publications in History, Volume 5)*. Greenville, NC: East Carolina University Publications, 1981. Steelman explores the conflicts between Polk and other North Carolina Alliance leaders, including Carr, Alexander, and Butler. Notes Polk's warning that the state could not risk "Negro supremacy."

D394. Stein, Judith. "'Of Mr. Booker T. Washington and Others': the Political Economy of Racism in the United States." *Science and Society* 38 (winter 1974-75): 422-63. In attempting to understand the relationship between blacks and the Populist movement, Stein argues from a Marxist perspective that to understand the behavior of various white groups towards blacks, and vice versa, one must understand the larger forces at work and the structures of power in the society. "By reifying and isolating race consciousness and racism, these relationships are ignored, with the result that the function of racism in maintaining the power of the bourgeoisie is distorted, and we are led to believe that men make history according to their racial likes and dislikes."

D395. Stone, James H. "A Note on Voter Registration Under the Mississippi Understanding Clause, 1892." *Journal of Southern History* 38 (May 1972): 293-96. The 1890 Mississippi constitution was designed to disenfranchise state blacks. After voter registration was completed for the 1892 presidential election, less than 9000 remained on the rolls. Many of the disenfranchised were victims of the literacy clause, which gave local registrars the legal right to bar illiterate blacks but enroll illiterate whites, as long as the officials decided that the potential voter could understand a portion of the state constitution as read to him, or give a reasonable interpretation of it. Contrary to popular belief, however, when the statistics are examined, illiterates (white or black) had a better chance of becoming voters in Mississippi's white counties than in the black belt. Stone provides county breakdowns to demonstrate the surprising fairness of administration of the understanding clause.

D396. Straton, John Roach. "Will Education Solve the Race Problem?" *North American Review* 170 (June 1900): 785-801. Mercer University's Professor J. R. Straton addresses one of the major platforms of the black self-help movement of the era as posed by both Washington and Du Bois—the effect of education on the race problem. Education appears to have increased criminality among blacks, although Washington's program of industrial education should be supported on a limited term basis. The basic problem arises from the physical proximity of the races; conditions must be established wherein blacks willingly (and without much governmental financial support) move to distant lands apart from whites, to fulfill their evolutionary development and ultimately reach the level of the Aryans. See also Washington's reply (**D421**).

D397. Summers, Mary. "Putting Populism Back In: Rethinking Agricultural Politics and Policy." *Agricultural History* 70 (spring 1996): 395-414. We can best understand twentieth century farm policy if we look to the nineteenth century, especially as examined in Goodwyn's *Democratic Promise* (**C129**). Goodwyn focused on the very best aspects of the movement, noting that the enemies of Populism's economic program would not have been able to play the race card in the South if Southern farmers had not already been so deeply divided on racial, social, and other political questions.

D398. Summersell, Charles G. "The Alabama Governor's Race of 1892." *Alabama Review* 8 (January 1955): 5-35. Charges of scandal and corruption made this one of the most controversial gubernatorial races in Alabama history. The race pitted Governor Thomas G. Jones against former agriculture commissioner Reuben Kolb, who had the backing of many prominent Alliance leaders. The black vote was a major point of contention. The Black Belt counties which formerly had supported Kolb were now in Jones' camp, particularly in areas with predominantly black populations. Jones pushed the issue in his convention acceptance speech, which called for harmony between the races. Kolb, in turn, received the support of the People's party, black Republicans, and the Alliance. Ultimately, black support tended towards Jones, although this demonstration of voting power in part lead to the suffrage provision in the 1901 state constitution that sought to circumvent the Fifteenth Amendment.

D399. _____. "Kolb and the Populist Revolt as Viewed by Newspapers." *Alabama Historical Quarterly* 19 (fall and winter 1957): 375-95. Following a biography of Kolb's early years, Summersell discusses in detail Kolb's failed attempt to win the Alabama governorship in 1890. Summersell cites numerous newspaper articles attacking Kolb as the representative of the Alliance gone astray into the political field. As the campaign developed, the candidate "learned the pose of the martyr which he was to wear in succeeding campaigns."

D400. Taylor, Joe Gray. "The Democratic Idea and the Deep South: An Historical Survey." *Mississippi Quarterly* 18 (fall 1965): 76-83. To regard Southern Populism as a class movement in the Marxist sense is mistaken; it is, rather, "agricultural interest politics." The Populists sought black support because they needed their votes, but they did not do so cynically. They realized that black farmers were also agrarians, and that measures that helped white farmers would also benefit blacks. The Populists failed in part because their appeal for black support was "of little avail."

D401. Taylor, Joseph H. "Populism and Disfranchisement in Alabama." *Journal of Negro History* 34 (October 1949): 410-27. Taylor posits that the Alabama Constitution of 1901 was the direct result of the threats of Populism in the 1892 and 1894 gubernatorial elections, and that the cry of "Negro domination" both prior to and during the Convention was a red herring designed deliberately to obscure the real motive of the Democratic leadership. It was claimed in the 1890s that because of their sheer numbers, Colored Farmers' Alliance members could outvote their white counterparts in the Supreme Council of the Affiliated Alliance and orders and could force a program of government allotment of the lands of white farmers to blacks. Following the tumultuous Kolb-Oates gubernatorial campaign of 1894, a movement arose to strengthen state suffrage laws. Voting records demonstrate, however, a lack of enthusiasm for the subsequent constitutional election, with "white" counties tending to vote against suffrage restrictions.

D402. Terrell, Mary Church. "Lynching from a Negro's Point of View." *North American Review* 178 (June 1904): 853-68. Written in response to Thomas Nelson Page's earlier NAR essay on lynching (**D304**), Terrell argues that one of the main reasons lynching persists is that Northerners do not know the extent to which lynchings occur and too often despair of eradicating them. As Honorary President of the National Assocation of Colored Women, Terrell was in a position to influence her predominantly white audience. The greatest obstacle to eliminating lynching is changing the public's attitude toward this crime.

D403. Thompson, Alan. "Populism in Shreveport: Cal Hicks Versus Newton C. Blanchard." *North Louisiana Historical Association Journal* 17 (1986): 17-27. Shreveport, in North Louisiana, was not known as a hotbed of Populist activity, although it was the home of Cal Hicks, editor of the independent-minded newspaper The Progress. Hicks initially ran for congress as a Democrat in the Jeffersonian-Jacksonian mold, but after little support from that party reluctantly accepted the nomination as the Populist candidate. Although he polled well in some areas, he lost the election, claiming that Democratic ballot-stuffing using blacks, minors, and non-residents did him in. For the 1896 gubernatorial race, Hicks supported Democrat Murphy J. Foster, as he "could not stomach" the Populist fusion with the Louisiana Republicans and their candidate J. N. Pharr, who supported black rights.

D404. Thornbrough, Emma Lou. "The National Afro-American League: 1887-1908." *Journal of Southern History* 27 (November 1961): 494-512. Almost completely forgotten now, T. Thomas Fortune's National Afro-American League was one of the most important—although unsuccessful—organizations designed to fight racial discrimination during the heyday of Populism. As opposed to the Colored Farmers' Alliance, the League looked to black leadership and met in convention in 1890 and 1891, before disbanding for lack of funds in 1893. A reconstituted organization formed in 1898, with Booker T. Washington joining forces with Fortune, which in turn lead black intellectuals to criticize both men. The group regularly addressed the disfranchisement issue.

D405. Tindall, George B. "The Campaign for Disfranchisement of Negroes in South Carolina." *Journal of Southern History* 15 (May 1949): 212-34. Even after the exit of federal troops from the state, blacks continued to vote in significant numbers, with a number of black legislators holding state office both as Republicans and Democrats. The rise of the Reform or "Tillman" Movement reversed the trend, as Democrat Party leader "Pitchfork" Ben Tillman pushed through constitutional measures aimed at disfranchisement. The Democratic state convention of 1894, dominated by Tillman forces, secured a resolution which supported the Populist Ocala platform of 1890. Tillman's disfranchisement plan, which combined an educational qualification with a property alternative and understanding clause, passed the convention by a wide margin.

D406. _____. "The People's Party." In Arthur M. Schlesinger, Jr., *History of U.S. Political Parties, Volume II, 1860-1910: The Gilded Age of Politics*. New York: R. R. Bowker, 1973: 1700-1807. Excellent single source for basic documents of the Populist movement, including the Cleburne and St. Louis Demands, the Ocala and St. Louis Platforms, Weaver's *A Call to Action* (**C298**), Marion Butler's keynote address and the People's Party Platform of 1896 (**F6**), Watson's "The Negro Question in the South" (**D425**), and Lloyd's "The Populists at St. Louis" (**D251**). Tindall also provides a general overview of the movement, with some attention paid to the role and effects of blacks upon the party.

D407. _____. "The Question of Race in the South Carolina Constitutional Convention of 1895." *Journal of Negro History* 37 (July 1952): 277-303. The 1895 South Carolina Constitutional Convention marked the end of voting and other rights for blacks in that state. The convention was dominated by Tillmanites and Conservative Democrats, although six black Republican delegates took part. After the introduction of suffrage amendments, all six Republicans addressed the assembly in speeches praised by delegates and the press. In addition, articles concerning miscegenation and lynching were also proposed. Tindall speculates on the possibility of Tillman joining forces with the Populists against the Conservatives.

D408. Tomaskovic-Devey, D., and Vincent J. Roscigno. "Racial Economic Subordination and White Gain in the U.S. South." *American Sociological Review* 61 (August 1996): 565-89. The authors argue that no one theory completely explains racial inequality, with competition theory and the class exploitation perspective both valid for particular elements. Competition theory suggests that racial inequality varies spatially and historically, and that group competition is driven in part by group size. However, competition theory often does not take into account the political economy of localities. Exploitation theory, on the other hand, suggests that "racial inequality both shapes and is the result of local class dynamics," yet it is also limited by a monolithic approach to the power of elites. These theories should be viewed as poles on a continuum—all politics is local. The authors note the rise of the Populist movement and the role of power elites in the Southern class struggle.

D409. Tracy, Frank Basil. "Rise and Doom of the Populist Party." *The Forum* 16 (September 1893): 240-50. It was inevitable, given the tides of change, that a nation's thought should be often misguided and led into fanaticism, economic blunders and financial fallacies—the combined result of which is the People's party. The American people have discovered that the Populists are little more than socialists, lead by "scores of these stump electricians" who have had lifelong careers as "mountebanks."

D410. Trelease, Allen W. "The Fusion Legislatures of 1895 and 1897: A Roll-Call Analysis of the North Carolina House of Representatives." *North Carolina*

Historical Review 57 (summer 1980): 280-309. The 1895 and 1897 legislative sessions were the only two not controlled by state Democrats. Trelease examines in detail the voting patterns of members to try and establish party coalitions and the success or failure of fusion. Of particular interest is the comparison of black House Republicans with Populists on various issues.

D411. Turner, James. "Understanding the Populists." *Journal of American History* 67 (September 1980): 354-73. Turner attempts to answer one of the basic questions in this area: who, exactly, were the Populists? Noting changes in farm tenancy rates and other variables particularly in Texas counties, he concludes that one common theme weaving through the Populist world is "relative isolation from the society surrounding them." Isolation, in turn, bred a political culture at odd with mainstream political habits and attitudes. Turner suggests that historians should try to understand Populism not only as an economic phenomena but as a "manifestation of one of the most central and venerable characteristics of the American political system."

D412. Uzee, Philip D. "The Republican Party in the Louisiana Election of 1896." *Louisiana History* 2 (summer 1961): 332-44. The state Republican Party was in a shambles after the withdrawal of Federal troops in 1877, steadily losing power as legislators were defeated and replaced by Democrats. The 1896 election, however, attracted former Democrats, particularly sugar growers, to the Republican fold after the McKinley Tariff of 1890; these expatriates formed the National Republican Party of Louisiana in 1894. The Nationals entered into a fusion ticket with the Populists in January, 1896 with a "lilywhite" ticket which mixed white supremacists, free silverites, and prohibitionists. The resulting election had all parties clamoring for black votes, with state troops called in to maintain the peace. The 1896 election brought the issue of black vote buying to a head and culminated in the suffrage clauses of the Constitution of 1898.

D413. Van De Graaff, A. S. "The Unaided Solution of the Southern Race Problem." *The Forum* 21 (March 1896): 332-45. Van De Graaff examines the race problem from a statistical standpoint. According to Census figures for 1890, the South has three distinct "black regions," all of which are underproductive and violent. The simple solution to the problem is to encourage black migration from the rural South to Northern cities and mining areas, where blacks can also enjoy the benefits of full citizenship.

D414. Van Deusen, John G. "The Exodus of 1879." *Journal of Negro History* 21 (April 1936): 111-29. Van Deusen argues that three primary factors influenced the mass exodus of blacks from the Deep South in 1879: a sense of personal insecurity following the Democratic return to power and fear of disfranchisement; economic discontent over low cotton prices and the debt-servitude system; attractive propaganda. Interesting in particular for its charts on black population gains in Kansas, an area of intense black Populist activity.

D415. Wakelyn, Jon L. "Southern Protestant Clergy and the Disfranchisement of Blacks." In M. L. Bradbury and James B. Gilbert, ed., *Transforming Faith: The Sacred and Secular in Modern American History*. Westport, CT: Greenwood Press, 1989. Most Southern ministers of the Populist era either actively worked towards black disfranchisement or retreated from activism into individual spiritual healing. Although Populism is not named per se, Wakelyn discusses some of the legislative efforts of the period in states with significant Populist activity.

D416. Walden, Daniel. "The Contemporary Opposition to the Political and Educational Ideas of Booker T. Washington." *Journal of Negro History* 45 (April 1960): 103-15. Washington's political philosophy, as delivered in the famous Atlanta Exposition speech of 1895, focused on the belief that only through moral and economic advancement would blacks attain their constitutional rights. Although most people, including the white press, applauded Washington's sentiments, a small but vocal group of intellectuals, led by Du Bois and Monroe Trotter, argued against the politics of appeasement, noting that conciliation had only resulted throughout the South in disfranchisement and suffering.

D417. Wallace, D. D. "The South Carolina Constitutional Convention of 1895." *Sewanee Review* 4 (May 1896): 348-60. Study of the machinations behind complete disfranchisement of South Carolina's black population. Conservative and Reform Democrats, the latter led by Tillman, were in contention for control of the state, with some Conservatives in the early 1890s contemplating the pursuit of black voter support to defeat the Tillman machine. However, the concensus was to completely remove blacks from the electoral picture before the 1896 elections, a move which led to the Constitutional Convention of 1895, "which was more the outcome of sociological questions than of purely political ones." The new suffrage laws will hopefully "put negro control of the State beyond possibility and still preserve the suffrage for the illiterate whites of the present generation."

D418. Walsh, Julia Mary. "'Horny-handed Sons of Toil': Mill Workers, Populists, and the Press in Augusta, 1886-1894." *Georgia Historical Quarterly* 81 (summer 1997): 311-44. The Tenth Congressional District of Georgia included a contingent of black Populists. As the 1892 elections approached, the campaign grew increasingly ugly. A black Populist, Isaiah Horton, was killed, and a policeman wounded. The Democratic press portrayed Populists as un-American or as young black "henchmen." Tom Watson and other Populist candidates lost, with party members complaining about black voter fraud. Walsh suggests the need for further research on Augusta's black voting behavior.

D419. Walters, Pamela Barnhouse, David R. James, and Holly J. McCammon. "Citizenship and Public Schools: Accounting for Racial Inequality in Education in the Pre- and Post-Disfranchisement South." *American Sociological Review* 62 (February 1997): 34-52. Following the Populist defeat and the rise of the Democratic Party in the South, local governments began to distribute educational funds inequitably to black and white children, which produced greater racial inequalities in school enrollments. Racial inequalities were greatest in counties with relatively large black populations, with relatively strong tax bases, and where the Democratic Party was least challenged. The Democratic Party was largely controlled by the planter class, which sought to maintain separation of the races and classes. One of the greatest barriers to local control by poor whites and blacks was the lack of formal organizations—unions, ethnic organizations, challenger political parties, large powerful churches—to see to their interests.

D420. Ward, Judson C., Jr. "The Republican Party in Bourbon Georgia, 1872-1890." *Journal of Southern History* 9 (May 1943): 196-209. Republicans had very little power in Georgia following the Civil War, save in select regions and especially black-dominated counties. An Independent movement arose, and some Republicans occasionally tried to help it, which lead to factional bickering within the party. Ward notes that election analysis shows that Republicans had even lost control of the black vote to the Democrats by 1882, with Democrats in firm control by 1884. In 1890, what Republican strength was left gave way to Populism.

D421. Washington, Booker T. "Education Will Solve the Race Problem: a Reply." *North American Review* 171 (August 1900): 221-32. Washington's response to the earlier article by Professor John Roach Straton (**D396**) focuses on the need for education for everyone, not just Southern blacks. Given the obstacles he has had to overcome, the black man should be given large credit for reaching as far as he has, especially in the South. Industrial education is strongly supported by almost all blacks, and entry into industrial labor will lead to greater morality. Washington mentions lynching but seems oblivious to the loss of black political rights.

D422. Wasserman, Ira M. "Southern Violence and the Political Process." *American Sociological Review* 42 (April 1977): 359-62. Comments on the basic substantive premise of Inverarity's article (**D217**) on the relationship between lynching in Louisiana and Populism. Data from other Deep South states, however, does not support the causal link between these two forces. Wasserman also argues that a "collective violence" model developed by Snyder and Tilly in 1972 is more apt for this study than Inverarity's "boundary crisis" model. See also Baggozi (**D19**) and Pope and Ragin (**D317**) for additional critiques.

D423. Watson, Richard L., Jr. "From Populism Through the New Deal: Southern Political History." In John B. Boles and Evelyn Thomas Nolen, ed., *Interpreting Southern History: Historiographical Essays in Honor of Sanford*

W. Higginbotham. Baton Rouge, LA: Louisiana State University Press, 1987. Lengthy historiographical essay in part covers the Populist era in the South. Useful in particular for its amplification of many of the studies of Populist which fall outside of the scope of the present work.

D424. _____. "Furnifold M. Simmons and the Politics of White Supremacy." In Jeffrey J. Crow, Paul D. Escott, and Charles L. Flynn, Jr., ed., *Race, Class, and Politics in Southern History: Essays in Honor of Robert F. Durden*. Baton Rouge, LA: Louisiana State University Press, 1989. After the resounding success of North Carolina Populists in the 1896 elections, state Democrats turned to Furnifold M. Simmons to restore the party to power. Simmons launched a vicious white-supremacy campaign which culminated in the Wilmington Riots, in which white Democrats overthrew the elected city officials and slaughtered an unknown number of blacks.

D425. Watson, Tom. "The Negro Question in the South." *Arena* 6 (October 1892): 540-50. A seminal document by one of the most problematic Populist thinkers. Watson claims that the great problem of the South is the party split: whites joining the Democrats and blacks joining the Republicans. To solve "the Negro Question," the two races must demonstrate each to the other a desire to permanently leave old party affiliations and join a new one, the People's party, based upon the conviction that, acting together, both races are seeking new laws which will be mutually beneficial. The People's party will settle the race question by enacting the Australian ballot system, by offering both races a rallying point of freedom from former discords, presenting a platform beneficial to the interest of both races, and making it to the interest of blacks to have the same patriotic Southern zeal as whites. However, Watson differentiates between political and social equality—"each citizen regulates his own visiting list." See also **C220, C231, C283, C311.**

D426. _____. "Why I Am Still a Populist." *American Review of Reviews* 34 (September 1908): 303-06. One of the most famous articles in the entire Populist canon, although also one of the last hurrahs. Watson briefly outlines the history of the Farmers' Alliance and People's party struggles against Corporate America. At varying times, both the Republican and Democratic parties adopted planks from the Populist platform, and by 1904 both major party platforms were virtually indistinguishable. The Populist party is necessary in 1908 because, if there were no party "eternally preaching the gospel which we proclaim, there would soon be no opposition party at all." Watson makes no mention of race in his article, although he notes that in 1896 there were roughly 1800 Populist newspapers in the United States.

D427. Webb, Samuel L. "From Independents to Populists to Progressive Republicans: The Case of Chilton County, Alabama, 1880-1920." *Journal of Southern History* 59 (November 1993): 707-36. Chilton County serves as a model for other regions of the Deep South, in that its people show a continuous "reform" streak from populism and progressivism, although that element of reform could often take strange and divergent turns. Webb takes to particular task Sheldon Hackney (**C142**) for painting a broad picture of Populism based on the evidence of a few movement leaders. When conservative Democrats discovered that blacks voted not only for Populist candidates in the 1890s but also in 1900, and that a potential combination of blacks and upcountry whites could threaten their power structure, they moved toward disfranchisement.

D428. _____. "A Jacksonian Democrat in Postbellum Alabama: The Ideology and Influence of Journalist Robert McKee, 1869-1896." *Journal of Southern History* 62 (May 1996): 239-74. Robert McKee, editor of the Selma, Alabama *Argus* from 1869 to 1878, has been called the "most renowned commentator on public questions" in postbellum Alabama. His editorials against both Republican and Democratic officeholders were reprinted statewide. In 1873, the *Argus* became the voice of the Alabama Grange, urging white farmers to join the movement. After serving as the governor's private secretary, McKee eventually moved to north Alabama and supported the Farmers' Alliance and Kolb's gubernatorial campaign of 1890. Most importantly, McKee focused on the economic issues of the period and made sure that the discourse "transcended race."

D429. Weeks, Stephen B. "The History of Negro Suffrage in the South." *Political Science Quarterly* 9 (December 1894): 671-703. Weeks, an official with the federal Bureau of Education, presented this overview of black voting rights in the South before the World's Congress Auxiliary on Government in August, 1893. The author outlines the earliest legislation forbidding the ballot to blacks, through the Civil War and Reconstruction eras, in a straightforward fashion, noting that the lack of education and political experience of Southern blacks resulted in them becoming the tools of massive fraud. Election reforms measures in each state are examined and on the whole praised. Disfranchisement is a good thing for the white and black populations and often, as in Mississippi, eliminated the "Negro Problem" by forcing blacks to learn to read and write in order to vote. Weeks also notes that many northern states either enacted or sought to enact literacy legislation, and even Grant in 1875 proposed that all voters who could not read or write after 1890 should be disfranchised.

D430. Welch, Richard E. "The Federal Elections Bill of 1890: Postscripts and Preludes." *Journal of American History* 52 (December 1965): 511-26. Welch argues that the debates surrounding the Federal Elections Bill of 1890—the so-called "Force Bill"--must be reinterpreted in light of mid-Sixties realities and perspectives. The papers of Senator George Frisbie Hoar, floor leader for the bill in the Senate, suggest that the bill offered little coercion and was as much inspired by a wish to validate the principles of the Fifteenth Amendment as it was to undermine the power of the Bourbon control of Southern politicians.

D431. Wellborn, Fred. "The Influence of the Silver-Republican Senators, 1889-1891." *Mississippi Valley Historical Review* 14 (March 1928): 462-80. The Silver Republicans, that group of Western Senators who demanded free coinage of silver and gold or favorable terms for silver, were an influential voting bloc in the Fifty-first Congress, particularly in relation to the Force Bill. Although initially not seriously opposed to an election reform bill, by 1891 this group voted en masse in concert with the Democrats, which killed the legislation and hope for federal intervention in local elections.

D432. Werner, Randolph D. "The New South Creed and the Limits of Radicalism: Augusta, Georgia, before the 1890s." *Journal of Southern History* 67 (August 2001): 573-600. Werner takes to task Paul Gaston (**C124**) for not directly confronting the question of why radical agrarians did not embrace the New South creed and questions to what extent Populist and New South advocates shared commonsense assumptions about their world. He takes as his sample Augusta, Georgia, a somewhat atypical Southern city, and argues that the rise of the Alliance and later Tom Watson in the region would do little to stymie the growth of the industrial state.

D433. Wetherington, Mark V. "The Savannah Negro Laborers' Strike of 1891." In Merl E. Reed, Leslie S. Hough, and Gary M. Fink, ed., *Southern Workers and Their Unions, 1880-1975. Selected Papers, The Second Southern Labor History Conference, 1978*. Westport, CT: Greenwood Press, 1981. Account of the strike called by Savannah's black wharf workers against the Central Railroad in 1891 for a wage increase. Almost all of the workers belonged to the Labor Union and Protective Association, a black general union that included all types of workers and their supporters. Wetherington notes that the strike was an "unexpected example of the possibilities of cohesion and unity in the face of overwhelming social and economic adversity."

D434. White, Melvin Johnson. "Populism in Louisiana During the Nineties." *Mississippi Valley Historical Review* 5 (June 1918): 3-19. The local organization of the People's party began during the 1890 congressional campaign, in Winn Parish, Louisiana, building on groundwork laid by farmers in other northern Louisiana parishes. The party sought in part to reform the convention system for nominating candidates for state offices, a process which counted a black vote that was never actually cast. Another reform aimed at the appointive power of the governor, which worked to the detriment of white parishes. During the 1892 campaign, Republican and People's party committees forged a fusion ticket, which lasted through the "free silver" campaign of 1896. Both sides played the race card and sought black votes, with ex-governor McEnery noting that "the negro today is the dominant power in this state." After the poor showing of the People's party at the polls, power brokers were able to insert into the Louisiana constitution of 1898 the nation's first "grandfather clause," which disfranchised blacks without interfering with white voters.

D435. Wickett, Murray R. "The Fear of 'Negro Domination': The Rise of Seg-regation and Disfranchisement in Oklahoma." *Chronicle of Oklahoma* 78 (spring 2000): 44-65. While the Deep South was engaged in disfranchising its black citizens, African Americans in the Oklahoma Territory of the 1890s en-joyed a remarkable degree of freedom, including attending integrated schools and political power. As emigration increased from the South, however, more and more restrictions were put into place by white powerholders who feared a black majority. By 1910, however, new Democratic suffrage laws effectively eliminated blacks' right to vote, with Oklahoma Socialists as one of the few voices against the new laws.

D436. Wickliffe, Jno. C. "Negro Suffrage a Failure: Shall We Abolish It?" *The Forum* 14 (February 1893): 797-804. The Fourteenth and Fifteenth Amendments were major mistakes, in that they removed from the states the right to deny blacks the electoral process. "The Northern idea of Negro political equality must be abandoned; the Southern advantage of additional political rep-resentation must be surrendered." After disfranchisement, blacks would be free from molestation and consider the change as affecting them solely from a politi-cal point of view.

D437. Wilhoit, Francis M. "An Interpretation of Populism's Impact on the Georgia Negro." *Journal of Negro History* 52 (April 1967): 116-27. Few social forces more critically influenced Southern blacks than Populism, possibly mo-reso in Georgia than the other Southern states. Wilhoit concentrates on the Georgia congressional campaign of 1892, which he considers the high tide of Southern Populism. Widespread violence by anti-Populist forces against black voters and Populist speakers and candidates resulted in Democratic victories throughout the state, and Populist candidate Tom Watson's relatively liberal views towards his black constituents rapidly soured, until he became a strong proponent of black disfranchisement. The final blame, however, for the decline of the Georgia black voting rights lies more with poor whites and demagogues than the plutocratic Bourbons. Populism must be finally considered as having a pernicious effect on Georgia blacks.

D438. Williams, Frank B. "The Poll Tax as a Suffrage Requirement in the South." *Journal of Southern History* 18 (November 1952): 469-96. The poll tax was effectively adopted by most Southern states in the 1890s and 1900s as a means of disfranchising not only blacks but poor whites. During the debates of the late 1880s, the poll tax was supported by members of the Farmers' Alliance in some states and editorially by its newspapers as a means of providing school funds. In Mississippi, Farmers' Alliance legislators voted for the new state constitution that included a poll tax designed for disfranchisement. Alabama Populists agreed with state Republicans and Democrats that blacks must be dis-franchised, although the race issue did not arise among Kentucky's Alliance.

D439. Winton, Ruth M. "Negro Participation in Southern Expositions, 1881-1915." *Journal of Negro Education* 16 (Winter 1947): 34-43. The history of black participation in Southern agricultural and trade expositions mirrors the problems of the agrarian crusade of the period. Wishing to highlight black achievement, Booker T. Washington and other black leaders won funding from Congress to house separate black exhibition halls at the Atlanta Cotton States and International Exposition of 1895 (site of Washington's famous "Atlanta Exposition" speech) and other settings. However, other black leaders and intellectuals either opposed or were leery of the separatist facilities. Overall, the exhibits were successful in demonstrating black progress over the centuries.

D440. Wish, Harvey. "Negro Education and the Progressive Movement." *Journal of Negro History* 49 (July 1964): 184-200. This article's title can be a little misleading, as Wish devote most of his energies to summarizing the ongoing Du Bois-Washington debates over industrial vs liberal education and the rise of racist policies designed to undercut funding for black schools in the South.

D441. Woodman, Harold D. "Economic Reconstruction and the Rise of the New South, 1865-1900." In John B. Boles and Evelyn Thomas Nolen, ed., *Interpreting Southern History: Historiographical Essays in Honor of Sanford W. Higginbotham*. Baton Rouge, LA: Louisiana State University Press, 1987. Useful for its broad coverage of recent scholarship on the economic effects of Reconstruction and the rise of the New South. Woodman addresses both black and Populist issues.

D442. _____. "The Political Economy of the New South: Retrospects and Prospects." *Journal of Southern History* 67 (November 2001): 789-810. In a fiftieth anniversary critique of Woodward's Origins, Woodman argues that in the gradual transformation from slaver to bourgeois society, the South has lost its significant economic distinctiveness from the North. Woodward's compassion for the Populists does not lead him into a full analysis and appreciation of the extent to which yeoman transformed into tenant farmers.

D443. _____. "Post-Civil War Southern Agriculture and the Law." *Agricultural History* 53 (January 1979): 319-37. Rpt. in Donald G. Nieman, ed., *Black Southerners and the Law, 1865-1900*. New York: Garland, 1994. Southern agriculture, particularly for black farmers, developed in part in response to the need as seen by the Federal government and radical legislatures to protect the rights of the freedmen. The new written contract labor system designed to protect these rights quickly became vague and oral, protecting only the employers. Croppers lost power in farm management and learned that their duties to their employers often extended beyond "work hours." An interesting overview of the developing system which lead to calls for reform.

D444. Woods, Randall B. "C. H. J. Taylor and the Movement for Black Political Independence, 1882-1896." *Journal of Negro History* 67 (summer 1982): 122-35. Rejecting the accomodationist line of Booker T. Washington and the "back to Africa" stance of Bishop Henry McNeal Turner, former slave Charles H. J. Taylor sought a third route, similar to that of some Populist leaders—through purely political means achieve a biracial coalition of interest groups to gain black Americans the same rights as those held by their white brethren. After being admitted to the Indiana state bar, Taylor moved to Kansas and eventually switched his political affiliation to the Democratic Party. Returning to the U.S. after a stint as ambassador to Liberia, Taylor settled in Atlanta and began his campaign for black political independence from the Republican Party. A coalition with northern Democrats would more likely benefit the race. Back in Kansas, he was nominated in 1890 for a seat in the state legislature on the Democratic-Populist ticket; although he lost, the coalition won control of the House of Representatives. Although Taylor failed in his ultimate quest of black power through coalition building, his personal successes were many.

D445. _____. "Integration, Exclusion, or Segregation? The 'Color Line' in Kansas, 1878-1900." *Western Historical Quarterly* 14 (April 1983): 181-98. Useful article for understanding the background of the popularity of Populism for black Kansans. Statistically, in 1880 one out of every six persons in greater Topeka was black, and although they comprised only six percent of the state's population, they cast 15-20 percent of the votes. Populist Governor Leedy actively courted the black vote.

D446. Woodson, Carter G. "The Cuney Family." *Negro History Bulletin* 11 (March 1948): 123-25, 143. A brief article on the Cuney Family of Texas by one of our leading African American historians. Norris Wright Cuney distinguished himself in Texas Republican politics, often combating John Rayner and other third party black leaders. Woodson notes that his success was due largely in that he was a man of honor and unquestioned loyalty to what he considered to be right. Article includes photos of Cuney and his family.

D447. Woodward, C. Vann. "Bourbonism in Georgia." *North Carolina Historical Review* 16 (January 1939): 23-35. Woodward examines the "Bourbon" culture in Georgia, noting that "the political philosophy of the new order in Georgia" included "the reconciliation of the farmers and laborers to the continuation of the business man's regime, in the name of 'White Supremacy'" and the reconciliation of "the Negro race to the domination of the white race." In contrast stood the Populists, who sought reconciliation "between Negro farmer and white farmer, between Negro worker and white worker, on a basis of equal political rights for both races and support by both of the Populist platform."

D448. _____. "The Populist Heritage and the Intellectual." *The American Scholar* 29 (winter 1959-60): 55-72 (reprinted in his *The Burden of Southern*

History, 1960). Woodward seeks to understand why Populism in the late 1950s was suddenly identified with "radical right" movements and the implied rejection of the Populist tradition. Populism was neither "class politics" nor "status politics," but rather "agricultural interest politics." Despite Southern prejudices, Southern Populist leaders were determined to create among their white followers a spirit of tolerance in which the two races could work together towards a common goal.

D449. _____. "*Strange Career* Critics: Long May They Persevere." *Journal of American History* 75 (December 1988): 857-68. *The Strange Career of Jim Crow*, like *Origins of the New South*, has received more than its share of critical attention over the years. Woodward accepts the blame for stressing the question of when over where and how in his work, but he also notes that recent critics, including Cell, Kousser, and especially Rabinowitz, have found his basic thesis to hold. Historic revisionism will be neverending as long as consequences of events and developments under study remain unresolved.

D450. _____. "Tom Watson and the Negro in Agrarian Politics." *Journal of Southern History* 4 (February 1938): 14-33. After his break with the Democrats and election to the 10th Congressional District in 1890 on the Populist ticket, Tom Watson was poised to construct a political alliance between white and black Georgians, particularly those multitudes who joined the Colored Farmers' Alliance. Watson's planned to recruit party members from both races and all classes, believing that interracial cooperation was a lost cause in either the Republican or Democratic parties. Blacks flocked to the new party and strongly supported Watson's efforts, even in the face of violence and death. Embittered by political and financial losses in the mid-1890s, Watson joined forces with his old enemy Hoke Smith after the turn of the century and came to view blacks as holding back the Populist dream. Woodward contends that Watson was still thinking in the capitalist-agrarian conflict pattern of the nineties in an era when that dichotomy no longer applied.

D451. Worthman, Paul B. "Black Workers and Labor Unions in Birmingham, Alabama, 1897-1904." *Labor History* 10 (summer 1969): 375-407; rpt in Donald G. Nieman, ed., *African Americans and Non-Agricultural Labor in the South, 1865-1900*. New York: Garland, 1994: 353-85. Wortham posits that despite the spread of racial antagonism at the start of the twentieth century, "the heritage of interracial cooperation in the Knights of Labor and in Populist campaigns lingered among many white and black workingmen." Although local black leaders, supported in part by Booker T. Washington, denounced interracial cooperation between workers, the American Federation of Labor, United Mine Workers, and other national organizations sought to make inroads.

D452 Wright, Gavin. "Comment on Papers by Reid, Ransom and Sutch, and Higgs." *Journal of Economic History* 33 (March 1973): 170-76. Commentary on Reid (**D331**), Ransom and Sutch (**D325**), and Higgs (**D193**). Wright raises a number of valid questions concerning the authors' theses: the viability of examining average farm size and discrimination; the significance of the "indirect effects" addressed by Higgs; the lack of strong evidence to bolster Reid's argument. All the papers also overlook the landlord's ability to push his tenants in the "right" direction by limiting the size of the plots.

D453. Wyatt-Brown, Bertram. "Tom Watson Revisited." *Journal of Southern History* 68 (February 2002): 3-30. Woodward's Tom Watson: Agrarian Rebel has received less critical attention than Origins, although others brought up the difficulties inherent in the Jekyll and Hyde personality of the Georgia Populist. Wyatt-Brown in turn focuses on Watson's mental state--chronic manic-depression and madness, with a desire for honor--in an attempt to explain Watson's "inability to stay the course with one theme and his easy switch of loyalties from one side to another." Not much attention to the 1890s, but an interesting theory which could explain his ideological swings.

D454. Wynes, Charles E. "Charles T. O'Ferrall and the Virginia Gubernatorial Election of 1893." *Virginia Magazine of History and Biography* 64 (October 1956): 437-53. O'Ferrall won the Virginia governor's chair in 1893 by the largest majority ever, in an election that saw the last hurrah of Populism in the state. Blacks played a considerable role in the election, although the state Populists were afraid of their support. No black attended the state Populist convention, and the common belief was that to vote against O'Farrall and the Democrats was to vote for Republican candidate William Malone and the Republicans. One state paper estimated that two-thirds of eligible black voters stayed away from the polls and that one-fifth of those voting favored the Democrats.

D455. _____. "Lewis Harvie Blair, Virginia Reformer: The Uplift of the Negro and Southern Prosperity." *Virginia Magazine of History and Biography* 72 (January 1964): 3-18. Blair's *The Prosperity of the South Dependent Upon the Elevation of the Negro* (**C27**) denied the existence of a prosperous New South just when regional leaders were presenting quite a different picture to the country. Using census reports and other official statistics, Blair argues that the only way for the South to prosper is to obliterate race and color prejudice. His work received much favorable attention throughout the United States and can be read as an early attack by a Southerner on the growth of segregation as an economic pitfall.

D456. Zabawa, Robert E., and Sarah T. Warren. "From Company to Community: Agricultural Community Development in Macon County, Alabama, 1881 to the New Deal." *Agricultural History* 72 (spring 1998): 459-86. Booker T. Washington was instrumental in formulating a program of uplift and self-sufficiency for black Southern farmers at the time of the first Farmers' Conference at Tuskegee in 1892. The conference was significant in that it launched state conferences organized by black educational institutions from Virginia to Texas. A plan for a black "Co-operative Land Association" with members owning stock in the organization was proposed at the third conference in 1899.

D457. Zimmerman, Jane. "The Penal Reform Movement in the South During the Progressive Era, 1890-1917." *Journal of Southern History* 17 (November 1951): 462-92. One of the major concerns of the Populist movement was penal reform, or more specifically the abolition of the convict lease system. The move toward the reform of the lease system coincided with the rise of agrarian interests who required improved systems built primarily with convict labor. Populists were in some part responsible for some reforms, many of which did not take effect until the collapse of the People's party in the South. Zimmerman notes that one major reform was the development of racially segregated reform schools for boys in most Southern states.

E. THESES AND DISSERTATIONS

E1. Abernathy, John H. "The Knights of Labor in Alabama." Master's thesis, University of Alabama, 1960.

E2. Abramowitz, Jack. "Accommodation and Militancy in Negro Life, 1876-1916." Ph.D. diss., Columbia University, 1950. Along with Hicks' monograph (C154), this dissertation is probably the most essential document in this bibliography for the study and understanding of blacks and Populism. The chapter headings alone give readers the best idea of the significance of this work: "Colored Alliance Co-operatives," "Tom Watson and Negro Populism," and "Populism and the Negro Question" are excellent examples. In relating the black Populist movement to other militant and conservative ideologies of the period (the leadership role of some blacks in the 1891 Prohibitionist campaign is particularly fascinating), Abramowitz not only re-evaluates the nature of the agrarian revolution but also the merit of Rayner, Washington, Du Bois, and Cuney.

E3. Adams, Olin Burton. "The Negro and the Agrarian Movement in Georgia, 1874-1908." Ph.D. diss., Florida State University, 1973. Adams explores each step in the reform movement at length, from black participation in early agrarian discontent and the Farmers' Alliance through the rise and fall of Populism. Although representatives of the Georgia CFA participated in white Populist conventions, many took issue with the formation of the People's party.

E4. Anders, James M. "The History of Marengo County, Alabama, 1890 to 1900." Master's thesis, University of Alabama, 1940.

E5. Arnesen, Eric. "Waterfront Workers of New Orleans: Race, Class and Politics, 1863-1923." Ph.D. diss., Yale University, 1986. Excellent study of the successful biracial dockworkers movement during Populism's heyday.

E6. Asbury, Doris T. "Negro Participation in the Primary and General Elections in Texas." Master's thesis, Boston University, 1951. The 1902 Texas constitution and subsequent poll tax and primary system considerably reduced the participation of blacks in Texas politics. Asbury should be read in conjunction with Cantrell and Barton (**D73**) on biracial politics and Kousser (**C173**) on Southern politics for other views on the poll tax and primary system in Texas.

E7. Bacote, Clarence A. "The Negro in Georgia Politics, 1880-1908." Ph.D. diss., University of Chicago, 1956. Bacote provides much detail about blacks in the Georgia Populist movement. His dissertation should be supplemented with the several studies published from his efforts.

E8. Barnes, Brooks Miles. "Triumph of the New South: Independent Movements in Post-Reconstruction Politics." Ph.D. diss., University of Virginia, 1991. Barnes examines Southern independent political movements, including the Readjusters and Populists, with their less successful counterparts in the region. Section Two describes President Chester Arthur's Southern Policy and explores the origins of Southern Independentism (DAI).

E9. Bates, Joel Leontz. "Politics in Bullock County from 1890-1900." Master's thesis, University of Alabama, 1942.

E10. Beck, John Jacob. "Development in the Piedmont South: Rowan County, North Carolina, 1850-1900." Ph.D. diss., University of North Carolina at Chapel Hill, 1984. Examining in detail Rowan County, which is fairly typical of the Piedmont region in that it was neither dominated by plantations prior to nor overly industrialized after the Civil War, Beck focuses on the debate between Woodward, who claimed Southern development came from a rising middle class, and Barrington Moore, Jr., who believed development was directed by a ruling elite. Rowan County's upper class survived the War relatively intact and launched the industrialization campaign, defeated both Populism and labor unions, and removed the threat of Black Republicanism.

E11. Beckel, Deborah. "Roots of Reform: The Origins of Populism and Progressivism as Manifest in Relationships Among Reformers in Raleigh, North Carolina, 1850-1905." Ph.D. diss., Emory University, 1998. Beckel examines the lives of four major North Carolina reformers influential in the Populist and Progressive movements. All hold interest for the study of biracial coalitions in this period, with black artisan Harris involved in 1880s reform coalitions, Nichols leading the Knights of Labor and Republican-Populist coalition of 1894-96, Polk taking national control of the party, and Heck developing interracial initiatives in the 1890s. Although they often worked at cross-purposes to each other, these four leaders left a legacy of reform.

E12. Beeby, James Matthew. "Populism in North Carolina: A Response to the Socio-Political Hegemony of the Bourbon Democratic Elites." Master's thesis, Bowling Green State University, 1995. North Carolina's black and white agrarians had considerable success uniting under the fusion Populist-Republican banner to fight against the Democratic Party ruling elite. As the power shift continued, however, Democrats fought back with a white supremacy campaign.

E13. Beeby, James Matthew. "Revolt of the Tar Heelers: A Socio-Political History of the North Carolina Populist Party, 1892-1901." Ph.D. diss., Bowling Green State University, 1999. Beeby narrates the history of North Carolina's Populist revolt, which was enormously successful in the 1894 campaign against the entrenched Democratic machine, from a grassroots viewpoint rather than focusing on the party's leadership. The author examines the racial attitudes of the white Populist leaders and analyzes the reform legislation passed by the new legislature. By the 1898 campaign, however, Democrats had re-organized and used the threat of black power and the danger to Southern Womanhood to woo voters back into their camp. Back in office, the Democrats pushed through disfranchisement legislation that removed blacks and poor whites from the rolls.

E14. Blackburn, Helen M. "The Populist Party in the South, 1890-1898." Master's thesis, Howard University, 1941. Although somewhat dated, this thesis provides a good overview of the Populist movement, focusing more on the active states such as Georgia.

E15. Bland, Gayle K. "Populism in Kentucky, 1887-1896." Ph.D. diss., University of Kentucky, 1979. The People's party had mixed success in Kentucky, yet made one last effort at capturing the state in 1895. The Kentucky party nominated Thomas Pettit for governor, a former pro-Confederate newspaperman and House clerk who was able to draw the support of some state blacks, including the black Louisville New South newspaper, to his unsuccessful campaign. However, most blacks remained loyal to the state Republican Party, while former white Populists often turned to the Democrats.

E16. Blosser, Robert H. "A History of Major Agricultural Organization Movements in the U.S. Before 1920." Master's thesis, Ohio State University, 1937.

E17. Bode, Frederick A. "Southern White Protestantism and the Crisis of the New South: North Carolina, 1894-1903." Ph.D. diss., Yale University, 1969. Bode analyzes the role of North Carolina's white Protestant churches as they faced the Populist challenge of the 1890s. When the state's Methodist and Baptist leaders attacked public support for the University of North Carolina, the Populists used the opportunity to develop a critique of the traditional way in which religion, like racism, had made Southern society resistant to change (DAI).

E18. Bonner, James Calvin. "The Gubernatorial Career of W. J. Northen."
Master's thesis, University of Georgia, 1936.

E19. Boras, Mary A. "A Case Study of the Speeches of the Birmingham, Alabama Populist Party Convention, September 15-16, 1892." Master's thesis, University of Alabama, 1952.

E20. Boyette, Robert Sidney, Jr. "The North Carolina Alliance Legislature of
1891: Harvest Time for the Farmer."   Master's thesis, East Carolina University,
1984.

E21. Bratton, O. M. "Elmore County Politics, 1890-1900."   Master's thesis,
University of Alabama, 1938.

E22. Brier, Stephen Burnett. "'The Most Persistent Unionists': Class Formation and Class Conflict in the Coal Fields and the Emergence of Interracial and
Interethnic Unionism, 1880-1904." Ph.D. diss., University of California at Los
Angeles, 1992. Part Two of Brier's study, in which he examines biracial unionism in West Virginia's coalfields between 1885 and 1897, is of most interest
here.   Black Southern miners repeatedly showed their interest in uniting with
white miners to form local interracial unions against the mine managers.

E23. Brittain, Joseph Matt. "Negro Suffrage and Politics in Alabama Since
1870." Ph.D. diss., Indiana University, 1958. Before the combination of violence and legislative maneuvering led to the wholesale disfranchisement of Alabama blacks, there arose a series of third party movements supported in varying
degrees by the race. Kolb ran for governor with the backing of the Alliance,
which in turn set the Democrats to arguing that a Kolb victory would return the
state to black domination. Brittain quotes extensively from the Montgomery
Advertiser on campaign tactics, including "counting out" black ballots. The role
of Bill Stevens in keeping blacks within the Republican camp is noted (DAI).

E24. Broadway, Lilibel Hurshel Henry. "Frank Burkitt: Man In the Wool Hat."
Master's thesis, Mississippi State University, 1948. Biography of Frank Burkitt,
Mississippi Populist leader and newspaper editor. Extremely useful as one of
the few lengthy works on the agrarian movement in the state.

E25. Bromberg, Alan B. "'Pure Democracy and White Supremacy': the Redeemer Period in North Carolina, 1876-1894." Ph.D. diss., University of Virginia, 1977. North Carolina Democrats during the Redeemer period repeatedly
returned to the race issue and appealed to white voters to set aside issues that
would split their vote and put Republicans and blacks into office. When the
Farmers' Alliance appeared on the scene, the Democratic strategy broke down,
as Alliancemen were more interested in economic issues than white supremacist
rhetoric (DAI).

E26. Brown, Marsha G. "The People's Party Paper: a Consideration in the Light of Recent Controversy." Master's thesis, Emory University, 1968.

E27. Bryant, Girard T. "The Populist Movement and the Negro." Master's thesis, Atlanta University, 1937. Focuses primarily on Georgia.

E28. Buckelew, Richard Allan. "Racial Violence in Arkansas: Lynchings and Mob Rule, 1860-1930." Ph.D. diss., University of Arkansas, 1999. During the period 1860-1930 in Arkansas history, lynchings and mob violence not only increased in number and severity but also took on an unprecedented racial flavor. The 1880s saw a particular rise in lynchings which did not abate into the 1890s with the rise of Populism. Buckelew argues that, despite the uniqueness of Arkansas' pattern of violence, there is no single explanation as to 'why.' Lynching occurred relative to time, place, and local conditions.

E29. Budd, Harrell. "The Negro in Politics in Texas, 1867-1898." Master's thesis, University of Texas, 1925. Although dated, Budd provides a good overview of the Texas movement. When examined in conjunction with Roscoe Martin's book (C189) prepared during the same era, the reader receives a generally balanced picture of the period.

E30. Byrd, Ruth E. "The History of the Force Bill of 1890 and Its Effect Upon State Constitutions." Master's thesis, University of North Carolina, 1932.

E31. Cammack, Ruth Stodghill. "Reuben Francis Kolb: His Influence on Agriculture in Alabama." Master's thesis, Alabama Polytechnic Institute, 1941. Although concerned primarily with the details of Kolb's career as Alabama's leading agriculturalist, especially his "Alabama on Wheels" program of immigration, Cammack devotes a chapter to the general history of populism and the People's party in the state. The information here is readily found elsewhere in the literature, although Cammack includes a portrait of Kolb in her thesis.

E32. Cannon, Charles A. "The Ideology of Texas Populism, 1886–1894." Master's thesis, Rice University, 1968.

E33. Carageorge, Ted. "An Evaluation of Hoke Smith and Thomas E. Watson as Georgia Reformers." Ph.D. diss., University of Georgia, 1963. Carageorge investigates how the reforms of Smith and Watson succeeded or failed as a result of the hold their tradition had on them. Watson's vision especially was to overthrow state leaders who had sided with Northern industrialists and financiers to the detriment of the agrarian community. He was also the first prominent Georgian to treat seriously the black voters' desire for political equality. Watson was repudiated in turn by the voters of Georgia for his support of black electoral rights, and he subsequently gained power using white support (DAI).

E34. Carawan, James Terry. "Populism and the Poll Tax: The Politics and Propaganda of Suffrage Restriction in North Texas, 1892-1904." Master's thesis, University of North Texas, 1997. Using precinct-level returns, Carawan argues that voters from predominantly Populist areas in North Texas did not support the poll tax amendment passed in 1902, but it also had a significant effect in reducing the numbers of the electorate in the area (DAI).

E35. Carlson, Andrew James. "White Man's Revolution: North Carolina and the American Way of Race Politics, 1896-1901." Ph.D. diss., Brown University, 1993. More dramatically than any other state, North Carolina defined the American way of race politics in the 1890s. A combination of a large black electorate, strong mountain Republican Party, and the rise of the Populist party lead to a government guided by a fusion of Republicans and Populists. Democrats fought back with a white supremacy campaign which culminated in the Wilmington Massacre of 1898 and ultimately the re-establishment of Democratic control of the state government (DAI).

E36. Carroll, Robert. "Robert L. Smith and the Farmer's Improvement Society." Master's thesis, Baylor University, 1974.

E37. Cartwright, Joseph Howard. "The Negro in Tennessee Politics, 1880-1891." Master's thesis, Vanderbilt University, 1968.

E38. Chafe, William H. "The Negro in Kansas Populism." Master's thesis, Columbia University, 1966. A thesis prepared by one of the recognized scholars of the Populist movement, this effort is much more valuable as an appendage to Chafe's many subsequent contributions to the literature. Kansas represents a different political environment for Black Populism than the Deep South states and caution should be exercised in extending conclusions here to those states.

E39. Church, Joseph. "The Farmers' Alliance and the Populist Movement in South Carolina, 1887-1896." Master's thesis, University of South Carolina, 1953.

E40. Cole, Houston. "Populism in Tuscaloosa County." Master's thesis, University of Alabama, 1927.

E41. Conrad, Frederick Allen. "Agrarian Movements in the United States Since the Civil War: A Study in Class Conflict." Ph.D. diss., Stanford University, 1933.

E42. Corlew, Robert E. "The Negro in Tennessee, 1870-1900." Ph.D. diss., University of Alabama, 1954. Corlew argues that the situation for blacks in that state slowly improved during the Populist era, despite the efforts of "well meaning outsiders."

E43. Cowden, Frances Kay. "H. S. P. Ashby: a Voice for Reform, 1886-1914." Ph.D. diss., University of Oklahoma, 1996. H.S.P. "Stump" Ashby was one of the leading lights of Texas's Populist movement during the 1880s and 1890s. Cowden traces his political development from his early movement activities in agrarian politics through his role as spokesperson for the People's party in Texas and finally his terms in the Oklahoma state legislature from 1907-1914.

E44. Creech, Joseph Whitfield, Jr. "Righteous Indignation: Religion and Populism in North Carolina, 1886-1906." Ph.D. diss., University of Notre Dame, 2000. In this massive study of the religious roots of North Carolina Populism, Creech notes that although the movement tended to attract reformers from a variety of causes and backgrounds, Populists in North Carolina tended to be white Democrats or black Republicans who aimed to restore Jeffersonian principles to a state and nation moving toward centralization and plutocracy. White detractors recognized the danger to white supremacy and party fealty, and also forced a reconfiguration of the way evangelicals situated themselves in society. Includes county/precinct election returns, 1880-1900.

E45. Crofts, Daniel Wallace. "The Blair Bill and the Elections Bill: the Congressional Aftermath to Reconstruction." Ph.D. diss., Yale University, 1968. One of the first complete studies of both the Blair and "Force" Bills of the 1890s. The actions of the 51st Congress showed that the North and more particularly the Republican Party had abandoned Southern blacks and given white Southerners the continuation of home rule without minimal federal interference in elections and education (DAI).

E46. Cunningham, George E. "Constitutional Disfranchisement of the Negro in Louisiana, 1898." Master's thesis, University of Wisconsin-Madison, 1953.

E47. Daniel, Michael Jackson. "Red Hills and Piney Woods: A Political History of Butler County, Alabama, in the Nineteenth Century." Ph.D. diss., University of Alabama, 1985. Daniel analyzes the political history of Butler County, Alabama from its foundation in 1819 to the rise of the Populist movement in 1892. County farmers always had an independent political streak, and in nearly every election independent Democrats challenged the party slate. Both Populists and Democrats eagerly battled for the black vote, and white supremacy was threatened. The solution was disfranchisement in 1901 (DAI).

E48. Demme, Genevieve Pyle, "Owen Pinkney Pyle: Champion of the Farmer." Master's thesis, Rice Institute, 1958. Pyle was a leading Populist editor and reformer in Texas during the 1890s. The most interesting comment, however, comes from Judge Ewing Boyd, interviewed by Demme in 1957, on why Populism failed: "Populism was for the underdogs and the Negroes were 'under the underdogs'." The judge also stated that the party in northeast Texas was "entirely too full of Negroes."

E49. Dethloff, Henry C. "Populism and Reform in Louisiana." Ph.D. diss., University of Missouri, 1964. The reform movement in Louisiana had many faces in the 1890s, including the Farmers' Alliance, the People's party, and the Anti-Lottery League. A mass exodus of sugar planters from the Democratic into the Republican Party menaced Democratic power, as did the fusion of Populists and Republicans, who in turn gained support from the reformist New Orleans Citizens' League. After their loss in the 1896 elections, Populists returned to the Democratic fold, and that party forced disfranchisement measures into the state's constitution. Political power thus shifted from the alluvial parishes to the upland white parishes and city of New Orleans (DAI).

E50. Dew, Lee A. "Populist Fusion Movements as an Instrument of Political Reform, 1890-1900." Master's thesis, Kansas State Teachers College, 1957.

E51. Dudley, Harold M. "The Populist Movement." Ph.D. diss., American University, 1928.

E52. Edwards, Martin Leon. "The Farmers' Movement in Delta County." Master's thesis, East Texas State Teachers College, 1964.

E53. Ellis, Mary Louise. "'Rain Down Fire': the Lynching of Sam Hose." Ph.D. diss., Florida State University, 1992. Ellis examines the lynching of Sam Hose, a black man accused of rape and murder in central Georgia in the late 1890s. Hose's lynching was widely publicized in both the national and international press, and Ellis argues that his death was the inevitable result of regional distrust and hatred. Underlying conditions, including politcs, are discussed (DAI).

E54. Fain, James Harris. "The Political Disfranchisement of the Negro in Arkansas." Master's thesis, University of Arkansas, 1961.

E55. Feins, Daniel M. "Labor's Role in the Populist Movement, 1890-96." Master's thesis, Columbia University, 1939.

E56. Fergeson, James Alan. "Power Politics and Populism: Jackson County, Georgia, as a Case Study." Master's thesis, University of Georgia, 1975.

E57. Ferguson, James S. "Agrarianism in Mississippi, 1871-1900: a Study in Nonconformity." Ph.D. diss., University of North Carolina, 1952.

E58. Fine, Bernice R. "Agrarian Reform and the Texas Negro Farmers, 1886-1896." Master's thesis, North Texas State University, 1971. Texas black farmers had various support groups to give them a voice. Also, the severe weather, hard fines, and depressed prices prompted the initiation of several organizations to support black farmers.

E59. Foley, Neil Francis. "The New South in the Southwest: Anglos, Blacks, and Mexicans in Central Texas, 1880-1930." Ph.D. diss., University of Michigan, 1990. Foley studies the triangular relationship between rural white landowners and black and Hispanic sharecroppers and migrant workers in central Texas during the rise and fall of the agrarian revolt. He also examines the nature of rural proletarianization that accompanied the growth of large-scale agriculture, which transformed semi-independent farmers into wage laborers, as in other parts of the Deep South. Foley assesses the role of the region's white Socialists, who preached class unity but resisted the efforts of black farmers to form their own locals of renters' unions.

E60. Fox, Elbert Leonard. "A History of Populism in Tennessee." Master's thesis, George Peabody College for Teachers, 1950. Fox presents an overview of the Populist movement in Tennessee, but it is a generalist approach and should be supplemented with Roger Hart, et al. work on the same state.

E61. Gaither, Gerald H. "The Negro in the Ideology of Southern Populism, 1889-1896." Master's thesis, University of Tennessee, 1967. Gaither's thesis, doctoral dissertation and subsequent book on the topic provide substantial statistical data on Southern elections as well as cartoons from primary sources of the period.

E62. Gallashaw, Woodrow Wilson. "The Negro and the Populist Movement in South Carolina." Master's thesis, Atlanta University, 1946.

E63. George, John Palmer, Jr. "'With Friends Like That....': the Role of the White Upper Class in the Etiology of Southern Racism, 1790-1975." Ph.D. diss., Mississippi State University, 1990. The Southern white upper class understood that, in order to maintain economic control over the region, they needed a stable, docile, and cheap labor force for cotton production. As cotton prices fell and production arose simultaneously with the rise of the Populist movement, the white upper class institutionalized racism through any means necessary to oppose threats to their power.

E64. Gerteis, Joseph Howard. "Class and the Color Line: the Sources and Limits of Interracial Class Coalition, 1880-1896." Ph.D. diss., University of North Carolina at Chapel Hill, 1999. Gerteis examines the "simultaneous negotiation of class and race boundaries" in the Knights of Labor, Farmers' Alliance, and the People's party, with attention paid to how these organizations construct and articulate their identities. He more specifically studies "how each movement's success in interracial organizing was shaped by the structure and process of interactions at the local level." Gerteis pays special attention to the race in the agrarian movements in Virginia and Georgia.

E65. Ginn, Duane E. "Radical Violence in Texas, 1884-1900." Master's thesis, University of Houston, 1974.

E66. Gnatz, William. "The Negro and the Populist Movement in the South." Master's thesis, University of Chicago, 1961. Examines the Colored Farmers' Alliance in Georgia. Ali notes that Gnatz is "an excellent source for the detailed events that preceded the Colored Farmers' Alliance and the dynamics of the organization in that particular state."

E67. Goodman, Wallis M. "Populism's Silver Lining: the Election of 1896 and the Decline of the People's Party in Erath County, Texas." Master's thesis, University of Texas at Austin, 1997.

E68. Graham, Donald Ralph. "Red, White, and Black: an Interpretation of Ethnic and Racial Attitudes of Agrarian Radicals in Texas and Oklahoma, 1890-1920." Master's thesis, University of Saskatchewan, Regina Campus, 1973. Davidson (C84) notes that Graham's thesis "documents in detail" "Texas and Oklahoma radicals' attitudes toward blacks." Graham notes: "There was no typical Populist. . . . the response to local conditions could overcome verbal support for the State Platform."

E69. Graham, Glennon. "From Slavery to Serfdom: Rural Black Agriculturalists in South Carolina, 1865-1900." Ph.D. diss., Northwestern University, 1982. While black populations in other Southern states witnessed some degree of success, both economically and politically, South Carolina's rural blacks barely rose out of slavery. Graham places much of the blame on the class consciousness of black politicians who helped destroy the Republican Party's power base in 1877 and committed internecine warfare rather than unite against the growing white Democrat power elite. By the onset of Populism, white supremacy had taken hold and state blacks were practically re-enslaved.

E70. Gray, Sarah Lois. "Thomas E. Watson: Leader of Georgia Populism." Master's thesis, Emory University, 1933. Gray offers a general overview of Watson's career and should be supplemented with Woodward's biography, published during the same era, and subsequent articles on Watson.

E71. Gregg, William B. "The Agrarian Movement in Grenada County." Master's thesis, Mississippi State University, 1953.

E72. Gross, Jimmie Frank. "Alabama Politics and the Negro, 1874-1901." Ph.D. diss., University of Georgia, 1969. A substantial number of black and white Republicans held legislative seats after the 1874 election and were especially strong in the Black Belt. Soon afterwards, however, Democrats gained control of the Black Belt and dominated the largest block of black voters in the state. The greatest threat to their power came with the rise of Populism, and after the agrarian revolt subsided, the Democrats were split on electoral reform issues. Although they initially promised to only disfranchise blacks, in reality they also removed many poor whites from the rolls with the poll tax (DAI).

E73. Hanchett, Thomas Walter. "Sorting Out the New South City: Charlotte and Its Neighborhoods." Ph.D. diss., University of North Carolina at Chapel Hill, 1993. Hanchett's is the first scholarly urban study of the largest city in the Carolinas. For most of the city's history, black and white lived and worked side-by-side in a 'salt and pepper' land use pattern. However, with the rise of Populism, the races started to coalesce into separatist neighborhoods, a process which parallels the postbellum segregation patterns of Northern cities. Once separatist neighborhoods took root in Charlotte, black and white leaders pushed the parallel businesses, Main Streets, and even suburbs to keep the races apart.

E74. Harris, David Alan. "The Political Career of Milford W. Howard, Populist Congressman from Alabama." Master's thesis, Auburn University, 1957.

E75. Hearn, Thomas K. "The Populist Movement in Marshall County Alabama." Master's thesis, University of Alabama, 1935.

E76. Hennington, Randy. "Upland Farmers and Agrarian Protest: Northwest Arkansas and the Brothers of Freedom." Master's thesis, University of Arkansas, Fayetteville, 1973.

E77. Herrin, Michael Gary. "The Populist Party in North Georgia." Master's thesis, Vanderbilt University, 1990.

E78. Hershman, James Howard, Jr. "The North Carolina Republican Party: The Years of Revitalization, 1888-1892." Master's thesis, Wake Forest University, 1971.

E79. Hild, Matthew. "The Knights of Labor in Georgia." Master's thesis, University of Tennessee at Knoxville, 1996.

E80. Hill, Harry Max, "Populism and the Failed Realignment: Texas Populism in the 1890s." Master's thesis, University of Texas at Arlington, 1985.

E81. Hines, Mary Elizabeth. "Death at the Hands of Persons Unknown: the Geography of Lynching in the Deep South, 1882 to 1910." Ph.D. diss., Louisiana State University, 1992. Explores the county-level lynching rate in four Deep South states--Alabama, Georgia, Louisiana, and Mississippi--to discover its relationship to the economic and social climate of the times. Hines' research methods determine the possible causes within counties where lynching was endemic and if and when legal execution was used as a substitute for lynching (DAI).

E82. Hinton, Robert. "Cotton Culture on the Tar River: The Politics of Agricultural Labor in the Coastal Plain of North Carolina, 1862-1902." Ph.D. diss., Yale University, 1993. Hinton examines the cotton plantations along the Tar River in eastern North Carolina from the Civil War through the exclusion of state blacks from the Republican Party in 1902. Focusing on agricultural labor and how it interacted with race and politics, Hinton argues that the "Redemption" of North Carolina in the 1870s was motivated primarily by the traditional white elites attempt to gain more control over 'free' labor. As the century progressed, elites gained more political control as a means of increasing their economic control.

E83. Hinze, Virginia Neal. "Norris Wright Cuney." Master's thesis, Rice University, 1965. With so little written about Cuney in relation to his significance to black Texas Republican politics, Hinze's thesis is almost essential reading, particularly for her use of original sources throughout. With the state Republican Party in turmoil over the conflicting demands of blacks and "lily-whites" resentful of black control, the time was ripe for fusion with the Populists, who were at their peak. The Populists, however, were in "complete disagreement with Cuney and Republican principles. . . . " Governor Hogg also sought the black vote, although the Populists, lead by Rayner, made major inroads.

E84. Horton, Paul. "Lawrence County Alabama in the Nineteenth Century: A Study in the 'Other South'." Master's thesis, University of Texas at Austin, 1985.

E85. Howard, James E. "Populism in Arkansas." Master's thesis, George Peabody College, 1931.

E86. Hucles, Michael Edward. "Postbellum Urban Black Economic Development: the Case of Norfolk, Virginia, 1860-1890." Ph.D. diss., Purdue University, 1990. As in other large Southern cities, postbellum Norfolk, Virginia saw the rise of an urban black middle class which took advantage of federal legislation designed to protect their voting and other legal rights. As this class grew in power, it interacted with the city's white community, although with restrictions and limitations. However, with the increasing power of the black community came the inevitable white power backlash which would culminate in the early 1890s with the advent of Populism.

E87. Huggins, Carolyn R. "Bourbonism and Radicalism in Alabama: The Gubernatorial Administration of Thomas Goode Jones, 1890-1894." Master's thesis, Auburn University, 1968.

E88. Hunt, James Logan. "Marion Butler and the Populist Ideal, 1863-1938." Ph.D. diss., University of Wisconsin-Madison, 1990. As president of the National Farmers' Alliance, U.S. Senator from North Carolina, and national chair of the Populist Party, Butler was in the center of agrarian reform activities throughout the 1890s. Hunt's dissertation is primarily a detailed factual account of Butler's life and directly challenges many of the early assessments of Butler, particularly those of Woodward and Goodwyn (DAI).

E89. Jenkins, William H. "Independent Political Movements in Alabama Since 1880." Master's thesis, Emory University, 1931.

E90. Johnson, Cecil. "The Agrarian Crusade, with Special Reference to Mississippi." Master's thesis, University of Virginia, 1924.

E91. Jones, Allen Woodrow. "History of the Direct Primary in Alabama, 1840-1903." Ph.D. diss., University of Alabama at Tuscaloosa, 1964. During the Populist eras, Alabama Democrats posed as champions of white supremacy and barred blacks from the parties' primaries and conventions. The Populists and Jeffersonians became champions of black voting rights while the Democrats manipulated black votes to defeat the reformers and maintain white supremacy. After 1896, Populism declined and the reformers returned to the Democratic ranks (DAI).

E92. Jones, Theron Paul. "The Gubernatorial Election of 1892 in North Carolina." Master's thesis, University of North Carolina, 1949. The 1892 election represented the launching of Populism in the Tarheel state and was a period in which the movement was establishing allies and methods of political activity which would be used in subsequent gubernatorial campaigns.

E93. Kantor, Shawn Everett. "Property Rights and the Dynamics of Institutional Change: The Closing of the Georgia Open Range, 1870-1900." Ph.D. diss., California Institute of Technology, 1991. One of the recurring motifs in the rise of Populism is the "open range" or "fence law" question, which most historians have portrayed as a class conflict. Kantor argues instead that the "fence law" debate centers on the materialistic goals of individuals concerned with the benefits of separating crops and livestock. The author states that the struggles over the "fence law" do not correlate closely with the rise of Populism.

E94. Kantrowitz, Stephen David. "Reconstruction of White Supremacy: Reaction and Reform in Ben Tillman's World, 1847-1918." Ph.D. diss., Princeton University, 1995. Benjamin Tillman essentially was the political boss of the state of South Carolina from the birth of Populism to the end of World War I. Although the Farmers' Alliance gave him a degree of support, Tillman never considered himself a Populist. He viewed the combined forces of blacks, money interests, and the federal government as a conspiracy to destroy white control of the state, and he often addressed white farmers with the need to band together as a race with other elements of the white "producer class" to fight what he saw as their common foe.

E95. Kimmel, Bruce Ira. "The Political Sociology of Third Parties in the United States: a Comparative Study of the People's Party in North Carolina, Georgia and Minnesota." Ph.D. diss., Columbia University, 1981. Kimmel evaluates three theoretical approaches to the study of third parties in the U.S.: the functional, political conflict and Marxist perspectives. Using each approach, the author analyzes the state organizations of the People's party, with attention paid to class structure and reform movements. The research indicates that the tendency to generalize at the national level obscures significant facts at the state level (DAI).

E96. King, Keith Lynn. "Religious Dimensions of the Agrarian Protest in Texas, 1870-1908." Ph.D. diss., University of Illinois at Urbana-Champaign, 1985. King's chapter on "Populist Challenge to the Southern Subcultural Consensus" discusses the the need for Southern Populists to challenge both white supremacy and Southern Evangelical Protestantism to achieve political victory. Notes especially the conservative sentiments of Texas Baptists, Methodists, Presbyterians, and Disciples of Christ and their efforts to keep blacks separate and out of the political process.

E97. Kirven, Lamar L. "A Century of Warfare: Black Texans." Ph.D. diss., Indiana University, 1974. Includes section on blacks and the Populist movement as part of a chapter on post-Reconstruction state politics. Notes election of Henry J. Jennings and R. H. Hayes to the state executive committee and that "the Negro boss controlled the votes of a particular county." Brief account of the role of Populism, but well worth examining for its localized perspective.

E98. Kochan, Millie L. "The Jaybird-Woodpecker Feud: a Study in Social Conflict." Master's thesis, University of Texas, 1929.

E99. Lester, Connie L. "Grassroots Reform in the Age of New South Agriculture and Bourbon Democracy: The Agricultural Wheel, The Farmers' Alliance, and the People's Party in Tennessee, 1884-1892." Ph.D. diss., University of Tennessee, 1998. The agrarian revolt in Tennessee took on a special dimension, as that state, with the aid of Alliance legislators, became one of the first to disfranchise black voters. Populist fusion with Republicans also opened the door to charges by white supremacists. Lester includes a number of charts to illustrate farm tenancy and voting strength in the state.

E100. Letwin, Daniel Lazar. "Race, Class, and Industrialization in the New South: Black and White Coal Miners in the Birmingham District of Alabama, 1878-1897." Ph.D. diss., Yale University, 1991. Letwin explores the interaction between black and white coal miners from the introduction of large-scale production in the region to the labor battles of the 1890s. Successive organizations, including the Greenback-Labor Party, the Knights of Labor, and the United Mine Workers, tested race relations in an attempt to united black and white workers into a biracial coalition. Letwin posits that the workers forged their identities and dealt with each other in more subtle ways than can be suggested simply by class or race politics (DAI).

E101. Lever, Webbie Jackson. "The Agrarian Movement in Noxubee County." Master's thesis, Mississippi State University, 1952.

E102. Lewis, Robert David. "The Negro in Agrarian Uprisings, 1865-1900." Master's thesis, State University of Iowa, 1938. Lewis presents an overview of the role of blacks in the various agrarian movements which erupted between the end of the Civil War and the turn of the century. A sense of continuity is present during the thirty-five year period under consideration.

E103. Mabry, William Alexander. "The Disfranchisement of the Negro in the South." Ph.D. diss., Duke University, 1933. Reprinted as a series of articles in various historical journals (D256-59).

E104. Martin, Henry Pelham. "A History of Politics in Clay County During the Period of Populism from 1888-1896." Master's thesis, University of Alabama, 1936.

E105. Matthews, John Michael. "Studies in Race Relations in Georgia, 1890-1930." Ph.D. diss., Duke University, 1970. The short-lived Republican regime during Reconstruction was not popular with black voters and was easily overthrown by state Democrats in 1872. Tom Watson and the Populists challenged the ruling elite and sought black support, but except for the state election of 1894, they rejected the movement. After the failure of Populism, there was no immediate move toward black disfranchisement, but Hoke Smith seized on the issue in his 1906 gubernatorial campaign (DAI).

E106. McCain, William D. "The Populist Party in Mississippi." Master's thesis, University of Mississippi, 1931. A good overview of a state that has not received the amount of scholarly attention conveyed to other Deep South states.

E107. McGuire, Mary Jennie. "Getting Their Hands on the Land: the Revolution in St. Helena Parish, 1861-1900." Ph.D. diss., University of South Carolina, 1985. During federal occupation of the state following the Civil War, Louisiana's St. Helena Parish blacks purchased at least 3,000 acres of land with their own earnings in an effort to attain self-sufficiency. A thriving community developed, and many area blacks were able to purchase their own homes. The presence of a literate majoritarian black population induced fusion politics up through 1900.

E108. McMath, Robert C., Jr. "The Farmers' Alliance in the South: The Career of an Agrarian Institution." Ph.D. diss., University of North Carolina at

Chapel Hill, 1972. Only three years after its birth in Texas, the Alliance was larger than even the Methodist Church in the South. McMath traces the rise and fall of the Alliance, including its relationship to the CFA (DAI).

E109. Mead, James Andrew. "The Populist Party in Florida." Master's thesis, Florida Atlantic University, 1971.

E110. Miller, Clark Leonard. "'Let Us Die To Make Men Free': Political Terrorism in Post-Reconstruction Mississippi, 1877-1896." Ph.D. diss., University of Minnesota, 1983. The threat to Bourbon Democrat rule in Mississippi was especially threatened in the post-Reconstruction years when Republicans formed alliances with independent and third party groups. Bourbons used intimidation, beatings, whippings, political assassinations, and mass murder to stem the tide. State Populists were ineffective, and Republicans did little to stop the passage of a disfranchisement amendment to the state constitution (DAI).

E111. Miller, Worth Robert. "The Populist Return to the Democratic Party and Their Influence on the Progressive Era in Texas, 1896-1906." Master's thesis, Trinity University, 1977.

E112. Moore, John Hammond. "The Life of James Gavin Field, Virginia Populist." Master's thesis, University of Virginia, 1953.

E113. Muller, Philip Roy. "New South Populism: North Carolina, 1884-1900." Ph.D. diss., University of North Carolina at Chapel Hill, 1971. Muller examines the relationship between the North Carolina People's party and the rise of agrarian discontent, the tensions of biracial coexistence, and the yearnings of the elite ruling class for stability. The state's Populist leaders often could not control the activities of the rank and file, while Democrats, faced with discipline problems from top to bottom, resorted to a combination of institutionalization and mass appeal to form the state's first true modern political party (DAI).

E114. Neal, Diane. "Benjamin Ryan Tillman: the South Carolina Years, 1847-1894." Ph.D. diss., Kent State University, 1976. Political biography of Ben Tillman, who squashed the incipient People's party and disfranchised the state's blacks long before other state movements started.

E115. Nelson, Richard Wayne. "Two Machiavellian Moments in Twentieth Century Political Culture." Ph.D. diss., University of Minnesota, 1986. Nelson examines, among others, the political career of Tom Watson as representative of a Southerner who could not balance the contradictory principles of virtu and virtue into a Pocockian "Machiavellian moment." One consequence of the study is its provision of a cultural context for understanding fears associated with race shared by the turn-of-the-century South and U.S. culture in the 1980s.

E116. Norman, Paul. "The Upheaval of 1894: the Effect of Populism on State and Congressional Elections." Master's thesis, Catholic University, 1961.

E117. Paoli, Donna Jeanne. "Marion Butler's View of the Negro, 1889-1901." Master's thesis, University of North Carolina at Chapel Hill, 1969.

E118. Patridge, Jeffrey Don. "Attempts at Reform: the Agrarian Movement in Grundy County, Missouri, 1870-96." Master's thesis, Southern Illinois University at Carbondale, 1991.

E119. Paul, Brad Alan. "Rebels of the New South: the Socialist Party in Dixie, 1892-1920." Ph.D. diss., University of Massachusetts—Amherst, 1999. The Socialist Party of America's activities in the Deep South paralleled those of the People's party, Farmers' Alliance, Greenback Party, and Union-Labor Party, enjoying popularity in those same areas where the Populists found strength. Although Paul's study focuses primarily on the period immediately after the collapse of the People's party, he underlines the radical continuum in both the industrial and agrarian South, with attention paid to the race issue.

E120. Pavlovsky, Arnold Marc. "'We Busted Because We Failed': Florida Politics, 1880-1908." Ph.D. diss., Princeton University, 1974. Little has been written concerning the People's party in Florida, so Pavlovsky's dissertation is worth examining. In 1884 a coalition of blacks, white Republicans, and disgruntled Democrats, known as the Independents, unsuccessfully challenged the Florida Democratic Party for control. By 1889, a complicated process of electoral reforms disfranchised blacks just as the Farmers' Alliance arose. The Florida People's Party formed in 1892 but failed to attract much support from state blacks, and Florida Populism ceased to exist after 1896 (DAI).

E121. Penny, James Sterling. "The People's Party Press During the Louisiana Political Upheaval of the Eighteen-Nineties." Master's thesis, Louisiana State University, 1942.

E122. Perry, Douglass Geraldyne. "Black Populism: The Negro in the People's Party in Texas." Master's thesis, Prairie View University, 1945. Oft-cited thesis seeks to demonstrate that Texas blacks were motivated to participate in the People's party and other Populist movements during the period 1891-96 for personal rather than class gains. Most Texas blacks remained loyal to the Republican Party, however, despite the dislike some of them had for state Republican leader Norris Wright Cuney. Some of the aftermath of the movement include the growth of black bloc voting, more repressive measures to deter black voter participation, and the collapse of the state Republican Party. Only the final third of the thesis focuses on black Populism, but excerpts from interviews with black Republican leader William Madison "Gooseneck Bill" McDonald are scattered throughout.

E123. Perry, Geraldine Jiggitts. "The Negro as a Political Factor in Georgia, 1896-1912." Master's thesis, Atlanta University, 1947.

E124. Pfeifer, Michael James. "Lynching and Criminal Justice in Regional Context: Iowa, Wyoming, and Louisiana, 1878-1946." Ph.D. diss., University of Iowa, 1998. Pfeifer examines the phenomenon with reference to African-Americans and the legal system in each state. In Southern Louisiana, most lynchings were committed by small, secretive, well-organized mobs, as opposed to the large spontaneous lynchings in northern Louisiana. However, "not a single lynching can be tied to retribution against supporters of the Populist Party."

E125. Porterfield, Charles Ellington. "A Rhetorical-Historical Analysis of the Third Party Movement in Alabama, 1890-1894." Ph.D. diss., Louisiana State University, 1965. Porterfield evaluates the rhetoric of the third party gubernatorial campaigns of 1890-1894, using the works of Kolb, Manning, and others of the period. Kolb and others rarely attempted to analyze the fundamental issues of the times before popular audiences, instead focusing on local issues such as election fraud, the convict lease system, and "the Negro problem." Although all speakers used ethical proof to enhance their own characters, much of the rhetoric centered around the ethos of Kolb, who portrayed himself as a martyr (DAI).

E126. Pruitt, Paul McWhorter, Jr. "Joseph C. Manning, Alabama Populist: A Rebel Against the Solid South." Ph.D. diss., College of William and Mary, 1980. Biography of one of the most racially liberal of all the Southern Populists. Manning founded the People's party in Alabama in 1892 and fought to preserve its independence. After Populism's collapse, Manning joined the Republican Party and continued to write on civil rights and other issues (DAI).

E127. Purington, Frances B. "The Texas Gubernatorial Campaign of 1896." Master's thesis, University of Texas, 1955.

E128. Quillian, Bascom Osborne, Jr. "The Populist Challenge in Georgia in the Year 1894." Master's thesis, University of Georgia, 1948.

E129. Reddick, Jamie Lawson. "The Negro and the Populist Movement in Georgia." Master's thesis, Atlanta University, 1937. One of the better, and oft quoted, early theses on the Populist movement in Georgia. Reddick is worth reviewing but only in consultation with more recent and extended studies.

E130. Redding, Kent Thomas. "Making Power: Elites in the Constitution of Disfranchisement in North Carolina, 1880-1900." Ph.D. diss., University of North Carolina at Chapel Hill, 1995. Redding focuses on the disfranchisement movement in North Carolina during the height of Populism, arguing that formal disfranchisement came about in the 1890s rather than the 1870s because of the breakdown in the Democrats' localist strengths. The rise of the Populists and Farmers' Alliance wrested power from the longtime ruling party, but the Democrats were able to remobilize their forces and wage a virtual white supremacy campaign. Ultimately, the organizational and political bases of the new movements were destroyed by disfranchisement.

E131. Reid, Debra Ann. "Reaping a Greater Harvest: African Americans, Agrarian Reform, and the Texas Agricultural Extension Service." Ph.D. diss., Texas A&M University, 2000. After the collapse of the Populist movement, Texas black farmers organized a racially separatist organization, the Farmers' Improvement Society. As this new group remained relatively apolitical, Texas white progressives found they could support it. The FIS gave forth a positive self-image for its small membership coterie, but most rural blacks in the state were outside its reach. Despite the work of FIS and the black arm of the Texas Agricultural Extension Service, which followed some years later, rural blacks remained politically powerless.

E132. Reid, George W. "A Biography of George Henry White, 1852-1918." Ph.D. diss., Howard University, 1974. The only lengthy biography of the Second District (North Carolina) black congressman. Reid argues that White's postcongressional career was more significant than his earlier years.

E133. Reinhart, Cornel Justin. "Populism and the Black: A Study in Ideology and Social Strains." Ph.D. diss., University of Oklahoma, 1972. Reinhart attempts to isolate the critical points of interpretive difference on the relationship of blacks to the Populist movement in the hope of forging a new synthesis about the Populist revolt. He examines in detail the several facets of the Populist mind, with considerable attention to the Populist conception of society and the individual's role in society. Reinhart then traces the Populists' treatment of black voters and their racial attitudes and perceptions of blacks (DAI).

E134. Riney, James Edward. "The Farmers' Alliance in Wise County, Texas, 1880-1897." Master's thesis, North Texas State University, 1979.

E135. Roberts, William P. "The Public Career of William Harrell Felton." Ph.D. diss., University of North Carolina, 1953. Study of the political career of Georgia congressman William H. Felton, who served in the Georgia state legislature until 1890 as a Democrat and then switched his allegiance to the Independents.

E136. Rodabaugh, Karl. "The Turbulent Nineties: The Agrarian Revolt and the Alabama Politics." Ph.D. diss., University of North Carolina at Chapel Hill, 1981. Excellent overview of the Populist movement in Alabama of the 1890s. Small white farmers moved into the Populist ranks despite Bourbon Democrat appeals to white supremacy. Kolb's political campaigns were characterized by what Goodwyn calls "shadow movement"--focusing on short-term political goals to the detriment of the agrarian ideology (DAI).

E137. Rodriquez, Alicia Esther. "Urban Populism: Challenges to Democratic Party Control in Dallas, Texas: 1887-1900." Ph.D. diss., University of California, Santa Barbara, 1998. In late nineteenth-century Dallas, two major groups contended for the political power held by the Democrats—an independent faction of business-oriented leaders and urban laborers, and a People's party comprised also primarily of urban workers. Rodriquez examines the tactics used by the Democrats to undermine the strength of the Populists in addition to providing a general history of the urban movement's growth and development.

E138. Ross, John Raymond. "Andrew Jackson Spradley, 'A Texas Sheriff.'" Master's thesis, Stephen F. Austin State University, 1973. Biography of the famed East Texas Populist sheriff whose evenhanded treatment of whites and blacks earned him widespread respect.

E139. Saunders, Robert M. "The Ideology of Southern Populists, 1892-1895." Ph.D. diss., University of Virginia, 1967. Saunders examines the thesis that Southern Populism represented a broad-based coalition of farmers, laborers, and blacks. Economically, the interests of Populists and blacks coincided much more fully than those of Populists and labor, but the Populists failed to give blacks any meaningful voice in their party. After 1892, the Populists dropped any Marxist-like rhetoric of class conflict and grew increasingly conservative, as can be witnessed by the transformation of Tom Watson and their failure to champion either labor or the civil rights of blacks (DAI).

E140. Shahan, Joseph Michael. "The Limits of Agrarian Protest: The Tennessee Alliance Movement, 1888-92." Master's thesis, Vanderbilt University, 1973. Of only minor interest, compared to works by Hart, et al.

E141. Sharp, J. A. "The Farmers' Alliance and Tennessee Politics, 1890-1892." Master's thesis, University of Tennessee, 1931. Sharp's thesis is helpful for understandling Bob Taylor's role in Tennessee politics. This document should be read in consort with his 1937 article on the same subject (D368).

E142. Silveus, Marian. "The Antecedents of the Campaign of 1896." Ph.D. diss., University of Wisconsin, 1932.

E143. Sipress, Joel M. "The Revolt of the Smallholders: Origins of Populism in Grant Parish, Louisiana, 1860-1892." Master's thesis, University of North Carolina at Chapel Hill, 1989.

E144. _____. "The Triumph of Reaction: Political Struggle in a New South Community, 1865-1898." Ph.D. diss., University of North Carolina at Chapel

Hill, 1993. Sipress explores race relations in the political climate of Grant Parish, Louisiana during the agrarian revolt. For years, black laborers and white yeoman competed for power but were finally overcome by the parish elite, who used violence to achieve control. Occasionally, circumstances forced the laborers and yeoman to come together in common cause, but normally black and white opponents of conservative rules stood apart (DAI).

E145. Smith, Florence E. "The Populist Movement and Its Influence in North Carolina." Ph.D. diss., University of Chicago, 1928.

E146. South, Oron Percy. "Agricultural Organizations in Alabama from 1872-1907." Master's thesis, Alabama Polytechnic Institute, 1940.

E147. Sparkman, John. "The Kolb-Oates Campaign of 1894." Master's thesis, University of Alabama, 1924. Essential for understanding the machinations behind Kolb's defeat in the Alabama gubernatorial race of 1894 by General William Oates.

E148. St. Clair, Grady Stafford. "The Hogg-Clark Campaign." Master's thesis, University of Texas at Austin, 1927. One of the greaetest barriers to Populist success with black Texans was the progressive racial stance of Governor James Stephen Hogg. Detailed account of the campaign between 1892 gubernatorial campaign between Hogg, Nugent, and George Clark includes vote tallies by county and contemporary cartoons and newspaper accounts of the race.

E149. Steelman, Joseph Flake. "The Progressive Era in North Carolina, 1884-1917." Ph.D. diss., University of North Carolina, 1955.

E150. Steely, Leathis. "Populism in Birmingham and Jefferson County." Master's thesis, University of Alabama, 1927.

E151. Stone, Olive M. "Agrarian Conflict in Alabama." Ph.D. diss., University of North Carolina at Chapel Hill, 1939.

E152. Straw, Richard Alan. "'This is not a Strike, It is simply a Revolution': Birmingham Miners Struggle for Power, 1894-1908." Ph.D. diss., University of Missouri-Columbia, 1980. Focuses on the 1908 coal miners' strike, which united black and white workers against the companies. Straw examines the elements that lead up to the strike, including the struggles to unite the races. Most useful for its parallels to the Populist movement in the region (DAI).

E153. Summersell, Charles G. "A Life of Reuben F. Kolb." Master's thesis, University of Alabama, 1930. One of the only lengthy treatments of the life and career of the Alabama Populist leader. Traces Kolb's career as commissioner of agriculture, his experiment with the "Alabama on Wheels' immigration plan, and his gubernatorial candidacies of the 1890s.

E154.   Taylor, Jon Edward. "Thomas Lewis Nugent: Portrait of a Populist Leader." Master's thesis, Baylor University, 1992.

E155.   Terry, Robert Lewis. "The North Carolina Populists: A Study of Attitudes in the Light of Historiographic Issues." Master's thesis, University of Utah, 1967.

E156.   Terry, Ronald Ray. "A Historical and Critical Analysis of the Texas Populist Lecture Bureau, 1895-1896." Master's thesis, Louisiana State University, 1973.

E157.   Thurtell, Craig Martin. "The Fusion Insurgency in North Carolina: Origins to Ascendancy, 1876-1896." Ph.D. diss., Columbia University, 1998. After the "redemption" of North Carolina from Republican control in 1876, the Democrats forged a political economy designed to promote the authority of the Black Belt planter class. Republicans and Independents fought back, and the rise of the Farmers' Alliance and Populist Party brought a new fusion politics to the state. The resultant growth of black political power in the east proved worrisome, and a violent white supremacy campaign in 1898 reversed fusion reforms and lead to the ratifiication of a disfranchisement amendment to the state constitution in 1900.

E158.   Upchurch, Thomas Adams. "The Billion Dollar Congress and Black America: Debating the Race Problem on the Eve of Jim Crow, 1889-1891." Ph.D. diss., Mississippi State University, 2001. The "Billion Dollar Congress,"so named for its propensity for dealing with economic legislation, also was faced with crucial postbellum racial issues which affected North and South alike. Despite the presence of Populist and other "reformist" congressmen, the general agreement amongst the legislators assembled was to accept that the "race problem" was part of the American Way. As a result, the Fifty-first Congress failed to pass legislation designed to improve the lot of Southern blacks and left an anti-civil rights legacy that would remain until the 1960s.

E159.   Vegas, Lena Marie. "The Populist Party in Louisiana." Master's thesis, Tulane University, 1942.

E160.   Walsh, Julia Mary. "'Horny-handed Sons of Toil': Workers, Politics, and Religion in Augusta, Georgia, 1880-1910." Ph.D. diss., University of Illinois at Urbana-Champaign, 1999. Focusing on one Southern city—Augusta, Georgia—during the turbulent period 1880-1910, Walsh notes how significant religion was to all aspects of urban life, including the political. With an influx of rural workers into the city, Populism rose and took on an urban flavor, uniting farmers and city workers. Religion served as the cultural link between the two classes, and Walsh argues that the two groups found common ground in the movement. However, as elsewhere in the South, Populism collapsed under the weight of voter fraud, a rise in white supremacy, and race baiting.

E161. Warren, Millard J. "A Study of Racial Views, Attitudes, and Relations in Louisiana, 1877-1902." Master's thesis, Louisiana State University, 1965.

E162. Watts, Trent Alan. "Imagining a White South: narratives of (b)order and community." Ph.D. diss., University of Chicago, 2000. Watts studies the turn-of-the-century South in terms of its public culture--education, literature, politics, public space--in an effort to explain the making of its racial culture. By the 1890s, Southern writing, including the multivolume Library of Southern Litera-ture, portrayed the South as bound by 'Southern Culture,' with a stable white elite. The narratives disregarded the varying class structure of whites, however, preferring to present the region as homogenous and united. An interesting study for understanding the Southern racial mindset during the height of Populism.

E163. Weaver, Garrett. "The Development of the Black Durham Community, 1880-1915." Ph.D. diss., University of North Carolina at Chapel Hill, 1987. Durham, North Carolina saw the rise of a black middle class which coalesced into racially separatist neighborhoods in the 1890s. Weaver discusses Durham's policy of "positive discrimination," which controlled access and power relations and led to a relatively peaceful entente between the races. Blacks were able, however, to participate actively in the Populist and fusionist politics of the pe-riod, which Weaver further argues led to a "strong black leadership based on ethnic consciousness, economics, and an ideology of community-building." Rather than stress political power, however, the leaders chose the economic route to success.

E164. Weaver, Philip Johnson. "The Gubernatorial Election of 1896 in North Carolina." Master's thesis, University of North Carolina, 1937.

E165. Webb, Allie Bayne Windham. "A History of Negro Voting in Louisiana, 1877-1906." Ph.D. diss., Louisiana State University, 1962. During the first decade after Reconstruction, Bourbon Democrats controlled black voters through a variety of means, including fraud and purchase. Later, poor white Populists and rich white Bourbons attempted to exploit black votes, a move which culminated in the fierce gubernatorial election of 1896. Afterwards, the Populists demanded disfranchisement of black voters, and the Bourbons acqui-esced (DAI).

E166. Westphal, Corinne. "The Farmers' Alliance in Tennessee." Master's the-sis, Vanderbilt University, 1929. Westphal should be read in consort with Sharp, Hart, and Dan Robinson's biography of the colorful Bob Taylor. These publications in combination provide a good overview and introduction to the Tennessee Alliance and politics.

E167. Wheeler, John McDaniel. "The People's Party in Arkansas, 1891-1896." Ph.D. diss., Tulane University, 1975. Arkansas Populists entered full slates of candidates in the state elections of 1892 and 1894, garnering roughly nineteen percent of the vote. The strongest Populist showing was in predominantly white counties, since the race issue tended to predominate in predominantly or heavily black counties. Township returns indicate that the greater proportion of Populist votes came from rural, white precincts, although it is also apparent that black voting swelled the Populist totals (DAI).

E168. Wingo, Horace Calvin. "Race Relations in Georgia, 1872-1908." Ph.D. diss., University of Georgia at Athens, 1969. Race relations in Georgia seriously deteriorated following Reconstruction. Following the Independent movement from 1878 to 1882, a period of one-party rule was established until the Populists entered the picture. Blacks once again became politically powerful during the Populist era, but calls for white supremacy and disfranchisement were also awakened (DAI).

E169. Witherspoon, William Orville. "Populism in Jack County, Texas." M.A. thesis, University of North Texas, 1973.

E170. Wooley, Robert H. "Race and Politics: The Evolution of the White Supremacy Campaign of 1898 in North Carolina." Ph.D. diss., University of North Carolina at Chapel Hill, 1977. Wooley argues that North Carolina's position was open to an interracial rather than biracial option, with benign white Bourbons seeing no reason to push the race issue and black leaders well aware of the ambiguous yet open-ended nature of the relationship. The Populist movement changed all that. A feeling arose within the black community that race relations were improving, which resulted in a growing political assertiveness, but this in turn disquieted whites who regarded equal citizenship as too revolutionary (DAI).

E171. Yelderman, Pauline. "The Jaybird Democratic Association of Fort Bend County." Master's thesis, University of Texas, 1938. The Jaybird Democratic Association was formed around 1889 to keep local blacks out of politics. Membership was limited to whites, and anyone was considered a member if his name appeared on the official list of county voters. The Association held a "pre-primary" primary in May of each election year to endorse a slate of candidates for the Democratic nomination.

F. WEBSITES

F1. Ali, Omar. "Preliminary Research for writing a history of the Colored Farmers Alliance in the Populist Movement, 1886-1896."   Available at http://www.geocities.com/SoHo/Workshop/4275/.   Accessed 9/21/01.   Brief essays explores the key secondary and some of the primary literature of the Colored Farmers' Alliance and its role in the Populist movement. Notes the scholarly neglect of this topic and the total absence of any mention of African-American women in any of the formal political organizations.

F2. Burson, George. "United States 1890s: Populism." Available at http://www.jmu.edu/madison/teach/burson/1890.htm. Accessed 9/21/01. Discusses generally the history and issues of the Populist movement at the end of the century. Addresses race issues after Reconstruction, with special attention to the Populists, noting that the Conservative Democrats were able to turn the black vote to themselves, through intimidation and fraud.

F3. Dickson, Patrick. "A Brief History of the Colored Farmers' Alliance through 1891." Kalamu Magazine: the Pen of African History. Available at http://kalamumagazine.com/black_populism_2.htm. Accessed 8/9/01. Dickson argues that the CFA cannot be solely defined by its relationship to the Southern Alliance. Despite the problems it faced, the influence of the CFA can be seen in later groups, including the Sharecroppers Union.

F4. Donnelly, Ignatius. "Populist Platform 1892 (The Omaha Platform)." Available at http://www.pinzler.com/ushistory/popparplatsupp.html. Accessed 8/9/01. Extended excerpt from the preamble to the Populist Platform, adopted by the People's Party at its first national convention in Omaha on July 4, 1892.

F5. Edwards, Rebecca. "SHGAPE Bibliographical Essays: Recent Literature on American Populism." Available at http://www2.h-net.msu.edu/~shgape/bibs/populism.html. Accessed 8/9/01. Brief essay highlights nineteen books and dissertations written 1951-1995. No specific mention of black involvement in the movement, but presents a useful outline of relatively recent scholarship as pertains to Populism throughout the United States, particularly in the West and Midwest.

F6. Miller, Worth Robert. "Populism." Available at http://history.smsu.edu/wrmiller/Populism/. Accessed 12/20/01. Good collection of primary documents and contemporary cartoons, in addition to reprints of some of his articles.

"The Platform of the Populist Party." Available at http://www.iath. virginia.edu/seminar/unit8/popplat.htm. Accessed 10/8/01. The "St. Louis Platform" of July 24th, 1896 features eight "principles" of the party, including safe national money, free silver, and a graduated income tax, all designed to help the lower classes regain economic stability. Black farmers would have been most interested, however, in "General Proposition Eight," in which the People's party condemns "the wholesale system of disfranchisement adopted in some of the States as unrepublican and undemocratic," and further calls for state legislatures to take action "as will secure a full, free, and fair ballot and honest count."

F7. "Populism in Alabama." Alabama Moments in American History, Alabama Department of Archives and History. Available at http://www. alabamamoments.alalinc.net/sec33qs.html and /sec33det.html. Accessed 8/9/01. A few pages devoted to Populism in Alabama, with mention of the Colored Farmers' Alliance. Notes the successes of the party (one-third of the state legislature was Populist) and the potential for biracial coalition politics in the state.

F8. Stephens, Randall. "Populism and the South: a Review of the Historiography." Available at http://web.clas.ufl.edu/users/brundage/ history5405/populism_intro.htm. Accessed 7/16/01. Seven-page review of the historiography of the South and populism notes the "cacophony" of the many and diverse planks of the movement: free silver, land ownership restriction, anti-monopolism, etc. Notes especially the contrasting views of Hofstadter, who felt the Populists were racist, and Woodward, who underscored the biracial elements. Stephens suggests examining the relationship between religion or gender roles and Populism, two areas which would also be ripe for examination with a racial twist.

APPENDIX: SELECT BLACK POPULISTS

Austin, Edward. Appomattox (VA) delegate to the CFA August 1891 meeting

Banks, R. P. Paola, KS minister

Beasely, D. C. Farmer/landowner VCFA delegate

Brooks, W. B. Kansas City, KS supporter

Browder, J. W. Kansas campaigner

Cabel, E. C. Kansas delegate to the 1892 Alliance convention

Carothers, Andrew J. Leader in the National Colored Alliance

Carrington, Morris. Grimes County (TX) school principal and Populist leader

Carter, J. W. Georgia State Lecturer for the Colored Farmers' Alliance

Cassdall, H. D. Missouri delegate to the 1892 Alliance convention.

Crawford, Lectured. Member of the Georgia Assembly from McIntosh County

Cromwell, Oliver. Leader of the Leflore County (MS) uprising of 1889

Currin, Green I. Most prominent black Populist in Oklahoma

Deveaux, John H. Savannah Tribune editor who supported the Populists

Doyle, Rev. H. Sebastian ("Seb"). Georgia preacher and speechmaker for Tom Watson c.1892

Ferguson, C. M. Member of the Populist campaign committee, 1896; from Houston, TX

Foster, Benjamin F. First prominent black Kansan to support the FA; nominated for state auditor in 1890

Foster, Rev. Turner. Olanthe, KS minister

Gavins, Gordon Blaine. Leading black sociologist and economic self-help writer

Gillam, Isaac. Little Rock (AR) Greenback Party candidate

Glopsy, I. Attended Arkansas state convention in 1892 and introduced a resolution on race relations

Gordon, A. A. Editor of the Atlanta Reporter who supported the Populists

Grant, W. A. President of the South Carolina Colored Farmers' Alliance

Grant, William L. Topeka minister and Populist leader

Graves, Anton. Georgia speaker on Watson's behalf; former secretary of the state Republican Party

Green, Harry C. Businessman/farmer member of the VCFA board of directors

Gwaltney, George A. Isle of Wight County (VA) delegate to VCFA convention

Hayes, R. H. Texas Colored Alliance member and Populist executive committee member, from Fort Worth, TX

Haynes, Jack. Grimes County (TX) Populist leader (murdered)

Ish, J. G. Prominent Little Rock physician and supported of the Bull Moose ticket

Ivy, Frank B. VCFA board of directors member

Jackson, J. S. Attended Ocala convention, signed "Communication from the Colored Farmers Alliance"

Jeltz, Fred. Editor of the Topeka Kansas State Ledger

Jennings, Henry J. Texas Colored Alliance state committeeman, from McKinney, TX

Jones, Col. A. A. "Most active and effective campaigner" in Kansas

Jones, Rev. M. F. Secretary of the Virginia CFA from Lynchburg

Langley, I. P. Union Labor Party nominee for Arkansas state representative, Second Congressional District, 1890

Kennard, Jim. Grimes County (TX) Populist leader.**

Langhorne, Rev. B. Presided over the second day of the Virginia CFA convention in August 1890

Langley, Reverend I. P. Ran for Congress on the Populist ticket in Arkansas in 1890

Laurent, L. D. Louisiana delegate to the 1892 Alliance convention; Attended Ocala convention, signed "Communication from the Colored Farmers Alliance"

Lytle, Lutie. Assistant enrolling clerk for the Populists in Topeka, later the second black female lawyer in the U.S

McDonald, William M. "Gooseneck Bill". Texas black anti-Populist leader

McGhee, Frederick L. St. Paul, MN lawyer recommended as Kansas speaker

McManaway, L. W. Alabama Populist leader

Moore, J. L. Superintendent of the Putnam County (Florida) CFA, delegate to the 1892 Alliance convention

Murray, George Washington. Elected to Congress as a Republican after serving as a CFA lecturer in South Carolina. Also an inventor!

Nevils, J. P. Topeka, KS supporter

Nichols, J. H. Attended Ocala convention, signed "Communication from the Colored Farmers Alliance"

Norris, John D. Attended Ocala convention, signed "Communication from the Colored Farmers Alliance"

North, Nick. Kansas deputy commissioner of elections and Populist, 1894

Pattillo, Rev. Walter A. North Carolina delegate to the 1892 Alliance convention; attended Ocala convention, signed "Communication from the Colored Farmers Alliance"

Patterson, Ben. Memphis organizer of the Arkansas Cotton Pickers Strike of 1891

Rayner, John B. Texas black Populist leader

Rector, Elias. Nominee for Pulaski County (AR) Circuit Clerk, 1890

Richardson, Edward S. Georgia state president of the Colored Farmers' Alliance, schoolteacher by trade, "polite and well liked" by whites

Roxborough, C. A. People's Party nominee for Louisiana state treasurer, 1892

Ross, Rev. T. Jeff. Oswego, KS pastor recommended to the state committee

Sanders, James C. Attended Ocala convention, signed "Communication from the Colored Farmers Alliance"

Shuffer, J. J. First president of the Colored Farmers' Alliance (Texas native)

Smith, H. L. Established the Farmers' Improvement Society in TX

Spellman, J. J. Fusion (Greenback-Republican) candidate for Mississippi secretary of state, 1881

Spencer, H. J. Secretary of the Colored Farmers' Alliance (Texas native); attended Ocala convention, signed "Communication from the Colored Farmers Alliance"

Stevens, William J. "Black and Tan" party leader in 1890s Alabama

Stith, George. Member of STFU executive council, VP of National Agricultural Workers Union, AFL

Sublett, L. M. Texas black Populist leader

Tandy, C. H. Independent Republican C. H. Tandy supported by Populists for an Oklahoma house seat, 1894

Taylor, C. H. J. Editor of the Kansas American Citizen, Populist candidate for the state legislature, 1892

Thompson, C. W. Leader of the Richmond, VA Tobacco Laborers' Union and member of Greenback Labor Party

Thompson, Green. Little Rock (AR) Greenback Party candidate and state legislator

Thompson, P. M. E. Arkansas delegate to the national Populist convention in 1888

Venerable, W. D. Kansas City, KS supporter

Wade, Melvin. Dallas Populist leader

Walker, T. L. Douglas County, KS canvasser

Warwick, William H. Virginia state superintendent of the Colored Farmers' Alliance, following Rogers; served as assistant secretary to the St. Louis convention

Williams, Miles. Edgecombe County, North Carolina legislative candidate, 1892

Wilson, Anthony. Shared the platform with Tom Watson on several occasions

Wright, John. Black Populist in Topeka.

INDEX

Numbers refer to the accession numbers of each item found in the text.

About the Authors

ANTHONY J. ADAM is Assistant Director of John B. Coleman Library at Prairie View A&M University.

GERALD H. GAITHER is Director of the Office of Institutional Effectiveness, Research, and Analysis at Prairie View A&M University.